"Moua explores the fusion—and sometimes collision—of cultural and family dynamics. As in a good novel, the characters shine through her narrative. Her mother, *Niam*—smart, opinionated, hard-working, demanding, and the epitome of tough love—is simply unforgettable."

—JIM HEYNEN, author of *The Boys' House: New and Selected Stories*

"A tradition is a living work of art. A great tradition should pass the test of time, being scrutinized, analyzed, modernized. In her groundbreaking and fearless memoir, *The Bride Price*, Mai Neng Moua shows us the meaning and practice of the Hmong tradition of paying the bride price, in the past, the present, and as it might be in the future."

—SOUL VANG, author of *To Live Here*

"The *Bride Price* is both a literary achievement and a cry for change in the Hmong community. Bold, witty, and unapologetic, Mai Neng Moua deconstructs and challenges patriarchal traditions and cultural expectations in an attempt to redefine herself as a Hmong daughter, wife, and mother."

—BURLEE VANG, founder of the Hmong American Writers' Circle

"Eloquently, with succinct personal experience and insights, Moua has left no stone unturned in considering the philosophical and ideological controversy over traditional Hmong wedding practices. With sensitivity and nuance, she explores the issues and their roots, contemplates the purpose of a Hmong 'bride price,' and illuminates the murky, painful conflict she experienced as she and her mother wrestled over the practice. Mai Neng's daring voice offers the reader a unique and thoroughly Hmong perspective on Hmong culture and wedding practice. Fascinating, insightful, and good reading!"

—POS L. MOUA, author of *Where the Torches Are Burning*

Mayia Hoalk (signature)

The Bride Price

A Hmong Wedding Story

Mai Neng Moua

MINNESOTA
HISTORICAL
SOCIETY PRESS

www.mnhspress.org

The Minnesota Historical Society Press is a member of the Association of American University Presses.

Manufactured in the United States of America

10 9 8 7 6 5 4 3 2 1

♾ The paper used in this publication meets the minimum requirements of the American National Standard for Information Sciences—Permanence for Printed Library Materials, ANSI Z39.48–1984.

Versions of some sections of *The Bride Price* appeared previously in the following journals, books, and anthologies: *Bamboo Among the Oaks: Contemporary Writing by Hmong Americans, Healing By Heart: Clinical and Ethical Case Stories of Hmong Families and Western Providers, How Do I Begin? A Hmong American Literary Anthology, Rehabilitation Counseling Bulletin,* and *We Are the Freedom People: Sharing Our Stories, Creating a Vibrant America.*

May Lee-Yang's "Hmongspeak" appeared in *Bamboo Among the Oaks.*

International Standard Book Number
ISBN: 978-1-68134-036-4 (paper)
ISBN: 978-1-68134-037-1 (e-book)

Library of Congress Cataloging-in-Publication Data available upon request.

This and other Minnesota Historical Society Press books are available from popular e-book vendors.

Contents

For my daughters,

ERICA PACHIA YANG and SAMANTHA SUA YANG,

who taught me to love unconditionally.
May you grow up to be brave women.

AUTHOR'S NOTE: This is a memoir, told from my perspective. Others will have their own versions of what was said or what happened. I have tried my best to recall events and conversations as they happened, but it is impossible to remember them play by play or word for word. The issue of translation adds another layer of complexity to the mix. I believe I have been true to the tone and essence of the conversations.

This book is not an academic or scholarly work on Hmong customs, rituals, and traditions. Because of my own level of knowledge, the literal interpretations of animist rituals and traditions that I provide are at the first stage of translation only. That is, they are at the stage of little kids' talk, rather than the second level of polite, nuanced, flowery language or metaphors (*Hmongspeak*) and the advanced level of practitioners such as shamans or *mej koob* (marriage negotiators).

The Hmong concept of family extends beyond the nuclear family. Out of respect, we even call people *aunt, uncle, grandmother,* or *grandfather* who are not our relatives by blood because they are of that same generation. In this book, for simplicity's sake, when I use these terms, I may be referring to an uncle, aunt, grandmother, or grandfather on my mom's or my dad's side, or to a person who is not considered by Western readers to be a relative.

The notes on Hmong customs at the beginning of each of the book's parts are based on conversations with cultural experts and on the books noted in the "For More Information" section.

The Bride Price

Prologue

"You were like animals that had left their pens, animals vulnerable to tiger attacks. But now you have recognized your masters and you have returned home," said my uncle.

That was how the *noj rooj tshoob,* or meal, started.

This was the Hmong American version of the prodigal son whose parents threw him a party after he had returned home. Only I wasn't a son, and this wasn't a celebration.

It was 2012, nine years after the church wedding that my family did not attend, and nine years after the *rooj tshoob*, the traditional Hmong marriage ceremony, that my husband, Blong, and I did not attend. *Niam*— Mother—and my uncles have decided to finish the *noj rooj tshoob*, the final part of the *rooj tshoob*.

This meal is the public piece of the *rooj tshoob* that permits both families to acknowledge the marriage. When it is done, *Niam* will finally feel that we recognize her as our mother. Blong will earn his titles of *Vauv* or Son-in-Law and *Yawm Yij* or Brother-in-Law. I will get my dowry from my family, which will include the Hmong clothes that *Niam* has saved up since I was a little girl. With my Hmong clothes, I will finally feel Hmong and loved.

The *noj rooj tshoob* gives my male relatives the opportunity to introduce themselves to my husband. They do this by drinking rice wine, beer, or other alcoholic beverages, in a kind of hazing for the groom. The more male relatives I have, the more Blong will drink. It is a show of strength that says, "Don't mess with our daughter/sister/niece/cousin or you will answer to us."

3

For most Hmong couples, the *noj rooj tshoob* is an automatic part of the *rooj tshoob*. It usually takes place immediately after the marriage negotiations. Blong and I, however, had to earn our *mov rooj tshoob*. Or, at least, that was what it felt like. It took us nine years. While other couples have married and divorced during the nine years since Blong and I were legally married, we have only now earned our Hmong anniversary. Finally, in the eyes of the Hmong community, we are officially married.

PART I

Poob Plig (Soul-Loss)

I do not see how it is possible that creatures in such different positions and
with such different powers as human individuals are, should have exactly
the same functions and the same duties. No two of us have identical
difficulties, nor should we be expected to work out identical solutions.
Each, from his [or her] peculiar angle of observation, takes in a certain
sphere of fact and trouble, which each must deal with in a unique manner.

—WILLIAM JAMES, *The Varieties of Religious Experience*

when we speak we are afraid
our words will not be heard
nor welcomed
but when we are silent
we are still afraid

So it is better to speak

—AUDRE LORDE, "A Litany for Survival," from *The Black Unicorn*

The animist Hmong world is a spiritualized one that is still enchanted.
That is, things in the natural world, from trees to animals, have spirits
associated with them. Even certain activities such as herbal medicine,
blacksmithing, and hunting have spirits associated with them. Some of
these spirits are tame or friendly, while others are wild.

   Animist Hmong also believe that each of us has multiple souls. When
these souls get lost or become traumatized, they leave or run away from
home—the body. They call this *poob plig* or soul-loss. Oftentimes, the
frightened soul is left at the spot of trauma, permanently stuck in place.
That is when you get sick or become depressed.

The Trouble with Me

"Niam, if I got married, would you want to collect a bride price?" I asked my mother.

"Of course. What parent does not collect a bride price?" she said, her face glued to the TV screen.

It was 2003, and we were at the Margaret Street house on the east side of St. Paul, our first home. I'd bought the house when I started my first salaried job in 2000. I was so proud of my family, finally living one piece of the American dream.

"There have been parents who have not collected a bride price," I insisted.

One cultural expert told me that, in Laos, leaders such as General Vang Pao, Touby Lyfoung, and Dr. Yang Dao did not collect bride prices for their daughters. Even one of my maternal uncles, a major in General Vang Pao's army, had done this. Here in the United States, other Hmong parents who did not collect bride prices were often Christians whose daughters married other Christians.

My family had converted from animism to Christianity when we came to the United States in 1981. My boyfriend's family had been Catholics since the early 1970s in Laos. *Niam* had met Blong when he came over to our house for Thanksgiving dinner in 2002. She never asked if I was planning to marry him. Whom and when you were marrying were things you did not discuss until they happened. Hmong parents did not want to give the impression that they had consented to the couple's courtship in case things did not work out.

"You are a daughter, and so we must ask for a bride price," she stated calmly.

"Niam, I'm not a bag of grapes."

"Even a bag of grapes, you have to have money to get it," said *Niam* with a gleam in her eyes.

She often had this gleam in her eyes when she was trying to be sneaky or funny about something, but this was no laughing matter. I did not know if she was trying to lighten the mood or if she was happy that her twenty-eight-year-old daughter was finally asking about marriage. I thought she would feel differently about the bride price given her own history with it, but she was even more insistent. Not wanting to start an argument, I did not push her further.

"Do you think *Niam* will want a bride price when I get married?" I asked my older brother, Kai.

As he had always done since we were kids, he was up early watching Saturday morning cartoons. I stood to the side of the TV, making sure I was not blocking his view. It was a lame question since I knew the answer already, but I needed an opening. If I could not get through to *Niam*, maybe Kai could. Maybe if I had his support, the two of us could more easily persuade her to change her mind.

Although I was younger, Kai consulted with me in making decisions that affected the family—buying *Niam*'s vans, buying the Margaret Street house. We were good partners when it came to dealing with *Niam*. Since our father died when we were young, we took turns handling her.

"I think so," said Kai. "Anyway, it's not up to you to decide."

"Why isn't it up to me? It's my wedding."

"That's not how it works, Mai. Usually it's the parents who decide whether or not to collect the bride price."

What he meant was, I didn't get a say in this.

"Well, I don't want one. I don't want to feel like I'm bought and paid for."

"It's not like that, Maaai," said Kai, turning off the TV. He called me Mai with a long "ai," as if trying to placate me. "You just don't understand what it is. That's why you say that."

LATER, I WOULD LEARN from my elders that the bride price is known as *nqi mis nqi hno*, which translates as the "price for milk and care." It is the debt owed to the parents for the milk and care used to raise a good daughter. It thanks them and says, "We are marrying your daughter." It compensates the bride's family for their future economic loss because the bride will leave her family. Anything she makes from this point on will belong to her husband and his family.

The elders say the bride price is a promise that the groom and his family will love and care for the bride and will not abandon or abuse her. Since they have invested good money in the bride, she is valuable, and they will take good care of her. If the groom's family pays the requested bride price, it means they want the bride in their family.

ALTHOUGH I DIDN'T fully understand it, I said, "I understand what it is. I just don't want it."

"Stop talking like that, Mai. It's not up to you. *Niam* will decide that."

"Can you talk to *Niam* and ask her not to collect a bride price?"

Kai looked at me as if to say, *Did you not hear anything I said?*

"After all she's done for us, don't you think she deserves something?" he asked.

He meant, after my father died in Laos in 1975, *Niam* took care of my two brothers and me on her own. Kai was five or six years old. I was two or three, and my younger brother, Yia, could barely sit by himself. *Niam* was in her mid-twenties. She could have remarried and left us to our paternal grandparents, as other young widows have done, but she did not. When I asked her why she stayed, she said, "Even when I was there, they'd hit you. I can't even imagine what would've happened to you if I'd left. You can't let your kids become their slaves or get punished by them. If you have your kids, then you can be a family."

He meant, in 1976, a year after the "Secret War" ended, we fled our mountain villages and hid in the jungles of Laos. On her back, *Niam* carried a bag of rice, a blanket, a parachute, and my little brother. With one hand, she held my hand. With the other, she carried live chickens so we would have food to eat. Kai carried a small pot of cooked rice and walked alongside her. In the jungle, men who had guns hunted monkeys, squirrels, and birds. *Niam* caught fish in the streams and looked for crabs among the rocks. She scrounged for palm hearts, potatoes, and other edibles. *Niam* worked hard so her three children, all under the age of eight, would not die of starvation or malnutrition as so many others did. After two years, we successfully made it across the Mekong River to the other side. The Mekong was the barrier between death or re-education camps in Laos and safety in refugee camps in Thailand.

He meant, during the two years in Ban Vinai refugee camp, *Niam* protected us from physical harm and disease, which killed a lot of people. He meant, when we finally made it to Pittsburgh, Pennsylvania, in 1981, *Niam*, who did not read, write, or speak English, navigated the social service system so that we had a roof over our heads, clothes on our backs, and food in our stomachs. He meant, *Niam* brought us to St. Paul, Minnesota, in 1987 to live with our uncles. She worked hard to make sure we stayed out of trouble. He meant, although *Niam* was poorly educated, she made sure we went to school on time, did our homework, and graduated from high school or college.

Yes, after all that *Niam* had done for me, she deserved the money and respect of other Hmong parents—parents who believed that by getting a bride price, they were good parents of good daughters worthy of someone wanting them.

"Of course *Niam* deserves something," I said. "Look, you guys can do all the Hmong culture and rituals you want as long as you don't ask for a bride price."

"Did Blong put you up to this?"

"No."

It had not occurred to me that Kai would think Blong had suggested it.

"Every Hmong man has to pay a bride price: why shouldn't he?"

"No, Blong didn't put me up to this. It's me. I don't want the bride price."

I could see that I was getting nowhere with Kai. I was getting angry, and he was starting to speak faster.

"You're still Hmong, aren't you?" asked Kai.

"Of course I am."

"Then this is how Hmong people get married."

"I'm not saying I'm against Hmong marriages. I just don't want a price on my head."

"That's part of Hmong marriages."

"I know, but . . ."

"Look, don't you want to make *Niam* happy?"

"Of course I do. But what about what I want?"

"You have to choose if it's more important to make yourself happy or to make *Niam* happy."

"Why can't I have both?"

"Because you can't. What you want is not what *Niam* wants."

"But can't we try to compromise?"

"There is no compromise."

"Just talk to *Niam* for me. Tell her I don't want a bride price."

Kai stood up. He was talking louder.

"Look, *Niam* is already unstable. This is going to make things worse. You can survive not being happy for a day. *Niam* can't."

Kai was probably right. *Niam* suffered from post-traumatic stress disorder, PTSD.

One time when I came home from college, *Niam* told me about the pills she was taking. Pills she had gotten after talking to a doctor.

"Did the doctor take your blood pressure and temperature?" I asked. "Did he look at your mouth or eyes?"

Niam shook her head from side to side.

"Did he listen to your heart or lungs?"

"No, I just talk to him."

I went with *Niam* to her appointment on the east side of St. Paul. While she was talking to her doctor, I walked up to the receptionist.

"Excuse me, what kind of doctor is he? And what is my mother being treated for?"

"He's a psychiatrist. Your mother has PTSD."

The psychiatrist had diagnosed *Niam* with PTSD while I was at St. Olaf College and Kai was at St. Mary's University and later St. Cloud State University.

Niam often could not sleep, waking up at three or four in the morning. She had recurring nightmares of family members who had passed away in Laos during the Secret War. Among them were her husband, three brothers, her brother-in-law, and countless other male relatives. I often heard about my maternal grandparents, who died while trying to escape the Pathet Lao and North Vietnamese Communist soldiers along the way to the Mekong River. In *Niam*'s dreams, we were always crossing the Mekong, never making it to the other side. Sometimes, when she did not think anyone would hear, I heard her crying softly and whispering to herself.

As if PTSD was not enough, *Niam* was going through menopause, too. I did not know the Hmong word for menopause, but *Niam*'s symptoms included mood swings and irritability. Sometimes when she came home, *Niam* was a tornado, blowing us to bits and pieces. She yelled at us for no apparent reason. We scattered to different corners of the house, far away from the flying debris.

Niam was hard on us, demanding total obedience. She was emotional and easily irritated. When she asked you to do something, if you did not do it yesterday, she got mad at you or she left without you. I remember once she asked my brothers and me to go to the garden with her. We were too slow for her. By the time we made it out the door, her car was nowhere in sight.

Niam always had to be doing something. She was constantly in motion, a blur, cooking, cleaning, and sewing. She was the queen of multitasking. She often said, "While you're watching TV, your hands could be doing something else like snapping the ends off of green beans." *Niam* could not relax. When we rested, she made us feel as though we were lazy.

When Kai and I left for college in 1991, *Niam* slept in the living room. It was not that she did not have her own bed or her own room. She has had the same lumpy queen-size bed for as long as I can remember. She just preferred to sleep in the living room, where she was not isolated in some corner of the house. She liked being central to whatever might happen in the house—such as my younger brother, Yia, sneaking in and out late at night. *Niam* often curled up on the sofa with a pillow and blanket and watched TV until she fell asleep.

Like many Americans who survived the Depression, *Niam* saved everything—pots and pans whose bottoms were scratched up, clothes she did not wear anymore, plastic flowers brown with dust. As if preparing for another Secret War, *Niam* had a garden where she harvested green beans, sugar snap peas, and bitter melons. She blanched and stored these vegetables in Ziploc bags, filling two chest freezers. Also in the freezers were squirrel, fish, and venison that Kai caught or killed, and fresh pork and chicken from Long Cheng, a slaughterhouse in South St. Paul, or JD Meats, the farm in Lonsdale, Minnesota, where *Niam* had her garden. There was plenty for a family of four.

This was *Niam*. She was normal to us kids.

I FELT LIKE KAI AND I were giving up without even trying. If he had asked *Niam* and she had said "No," it might have been easier for me to "let go" of the issue. Yes, on the face of it, I could survive not being happy at the *rooj tshoob*. *Niam* probably could not. But I had heard the stories of *Niam*'s bride price. Could I live with the consequences of my bride price?

Niam's Bride Price

Since I was a little girl, *Niam* has told me about the bride price of four silver bars that my father's family paid for her. I assumed four silver bars was a lot of money for a woman back then given the reaction from my grandfather and uncles. What I remembered most from *Niam*'s stories was that the four silver bars became an anchor weight around her neck, threatening to sink her to the bottom of the ocean. It gave Grandfather and my uncles the excuse they needed to hate her.

"Why didn't we throw the four silver bars over the cliff to see what kind of noise they made?" remarked an uncle who did not want to pay the bride price.

"How many sows could we have gotten with four silver bars?" asked another uncle.

Though they never said it, it seemed when *Niam* did something wrong, my father's family wondered if she was worth the four silver bars.

Growing up in the long shadows of the four silver bars, I vowed that when I got married, if I married a Hmong man, there would be no bride price. If I married a non-Hmong, there definitely would not be a bride price. Never would I let a man and his family determine my worth. I would not let anyone tie that bride price around my neck, a noose ready to strangle me. Never would I let anyone wonder if I was worth the price they paid for me. I would not let them threaten to send me back home if I did not work my ass off like an indentured servant or slave. I would not be bought and paid for like I was a piece of meat or furniture, or a bag of grapes. I know this is not the intention of the bride price, but that is how it makes me feel.

I know, too, that many Hmong women, including my cousins and friends, have gone through the *rooj tshoob* and their in-laws have paid bride prices for them. These women are happy their parents got bride prices for them because it shows they are valued and treasured. I respect these women's decisions to honor their parents in this way.

In fact, Hmong women have told me that their in-laws treat them differently—worse—when their parents have not collected bride prices for them. Like free goods that are not appreciated, they felt less valuable.

For me, however, when I heard *Niam*'s stories about her bride price, I felt such injustice that I decided I would never have one. I wanted to do this for myself. And for *Niam*.

I learned these details about *Niam*'s *rooj tshoob* from Uncle Naw-Karl Mua, a pastor and one of the sons of our late clan leader. The man who wanted to marry *Niam* was her first cousin, the son of an aunt. He was already married with two wives and children, but he wanted *Niam* as a third wife.

Back then in Laos, it was normal for a man to have multiple wives as long as he could afford to pay the bride prices. For Hmong people, it is okay to marry your first cousin, as long as both parties have different last names. We believe the closer you are, the better. When problems arise between the couple, the families, who already know and love each other, can resolve the problems more easily. Both sides are invested in keeping the couple together.

When my father heard that another man had come to *Niam*'s house to ask for her hand in marriage, my father consulted with our clan leader, who encouraged him to go and get *Niam*.

Another uncle told me that when my father showed up at *Niam*'s house, the *rooj tshoob* had already started. *Niam*'s first cousin had come to the *Tasseng*'s house. Being a *tasseng* meant that my grandfather was in charge of ten to twenty Hmong villages. I could only imagine all the important men my grandfather had summoned to sit at the table at *Niam*'s *rooj tshoob*. By all accounts, it was inevitable. My grandfather was going to marry *Niam* off to her first cousin, to be his third wife. There was nothing *Niam* could say or do about it. That was what everyone understood.

But *Niam* did something about it. She ran off with my father while her father, uncles, and brothers were in the middle of negotiating the *rooj tshoob*. After *Niam* ran off with my father, they hid out in the jungles. They did not go to my grandfather's house as was the custom.

I do not know how long they had to hide out or what they ate or where they slept. I had never heard this story from *Niam*. I did not even know about it until my uncles told me, and I wanted to know more. A Hmong woman defying Hmong culture, rebelling against her father, uncles, and brothers. A Hmong woman making her own decisions about her life. That was *Niam*.

My guess was that my clan leader told my father to go get *Niam* because he wanted to improve our clan's social status. My grandfather was a *tasseng*, and my uncles were high-ranking military officials in General Vang Pao's army. Most Hmong elders consider the late general, who worked with the Central Intelligence Agency to fight the Pathet Lao during the Secret War, to be their leader. They credit him with bringing the Hmong to America so that we might have a better life. I remembered *Niam*'s stories of how her family had to house the Japanese and later the French who came through their village. Hmong people from near and far came to *Niam*'s house to have the *Tasseng* and, later, my uncles settle disputes.

By Hmong standards, they were royalty. *Niam* once told interviewers, "Before, in our own country, we were at the top. We controlled our own lives. . . . There were always people who came to work for us. There were always people who came to ask us for food."

My father was one of the few men who could read and write in his village. He worked for our clan leader as his scribe. After he married *Niam*, he also worked as the scribe for one of my maternal uncles. Before my father died, an uncle had a dream that my father's old boss, who had already passed away, came back for him. In the dream, my dead maternal uncle said, "Chee, I need you. I need you to write for me." Being connected to *Niam*'s family made my father a wanted man in life and death.

Did my father marry *Niam* because he loved her? Did he marry her because he, too, wanted the social capital of being connected to her family? I wanted to know what my father said to *Niam* to convince her to run off with him in the middle of her own *rooj tshoob*. Did she believe she could take matters into her own hands? She must have known her father, uncles, and brothers would be livid with her for causing them to lose face. She must have known they could have disowned her. What was *Niam*'s relationship with her parents and brothers like afterward? How long did it take her to rebuild those relationships? How many years did it take them to forgive her?

And, oh, how the whole village would have talked.

"Did you hear about the *Tasseng*'s daughter?"

"Who does she think she is?"

"Have you seen her? Is she pretty?"

And, oh, how word would have spread like wildfire to other villages.

"The *Tasseng*'s daughter ran off in the middle of the *rooj tshoob*."

"The groom's family was fined one silver bar."

And, oh, how the juicy gossip would have filled the mouths of the people like rice, expanding when it is cooked, making them full for weeks.

Although *Niam* and I have never talked about her *rooj tshoob*, I imagined she had two choices—be a third wife or be the only wife. Be the object of hate of two wives whose eyes shoot daggers at you or be the object of affection of one man. Be bossed around by three women (including the mother-in-law) or be bossed around by one mother-in-law. Love was not a consideration. What could she live with? She had to think quickly. It was now or never. *Niam* must have known that the symbol for war is two women under one roof. In *Niam's* case, it would have been four women under one roof, and she must have realized that. And so, *Niam* took matters into her own hands. She chose to be the only wife despite the consequences.

My father and *Niam* paid heavily for this act of rebellion. He had to right the wrong of "stealing" another man's wife by paying a fine to *Niam's* first cousin, who claimed *Niam* was his. *Niam* spent the rest of her life trying to prove that the *Tasseng's* youngest daughter was worth her bride price.

Unanswered Questions

In Hmong, "to marry" is *yuav poj niam* and *yuav txiv*. Literally, *yuav poj niam* means "buy a wife" or "get a wife" and *yuav txiv* means "buy a husband" or "get a husband." I realize that these literal translations sound barbaric. I am afraid that by supplying this literal definition I will get myself in trouble with Hmong readers. With Minneapolis and St. Paul, Minnesota, having one of the biggest concentrations of Hmong in the world, I am bound to offend some Hmong people. These Hmong people will claim that I don't have any business writing about things I don't know. They have a point. I am not a Hmong elder or a *mej koob*, a marriage negotiator. I don't know a lot about Hmong marriages. Heck, I didn't even go through the *rooj tshoob*, the traditional Hmong marriage ceremony, in the proper way. I don't speak for the Hmong community. I don't speak for Hmong women.

Some Hmong may ask why I am making such a big fuss about the bride price since it is only a small part of the *rooj tshoob*. Even the term itself is disputed. One Hmong cultural expert stated that the "bride price" is not a correct translation of *nqi mi nqi hno*. "'Bride price' makes it sound like we are selling someone," he said. Some suggested that I call it "bride wealth" or a "nurturing fee" instead. *Niam* said it was the equivalent of the price for daycare. These Hmong will argue I am unfairly imposing Western values on the bride price.

Some Hmong may say I am purposely focusing on the most controversial part of the *rooj tshoob* to rile up the emotions of Hmong feminists, who can't wait for any excuse to emasculate Hmong men. These feminists may be loud, these people say, but Hmong men don't respect them. They are the teachers in the Charlie Brown specials who, when they speak, make no sense.

I will get myself in trouble with non-Hmong readers because I will not be able to give them a robust explanation of the full cultural context of Hmong marriages. Even if they are open-minded, they may see the bride price as "selling" Hmong girls. These non-Hmong readers come from a history where people fought for women's social, economic, educational, and political rights. Fed up with the subjugation of women in law and religion, they pushed for women's suffrage in 1920 and the Equal Rights Amendment in America.

And yet, these same well-intentioned progressives have asked me, "Isn't it an oxymoron to be a Hmong feminist?" Because the Hmong are patriarchal, patrilineal, and patrilocal, then I, the Hmong woman, must be powerless. Moreover, if I did not feel like a victim, then there was something wrong with me. They did not see their own hypocrisy. Until recently, American women "married for money." Their marriages involved a sort of sale of the bride, her virginity and fertility, in exchange for being financially stable. They forget about spending an average of $20,000 to $30,000 (not including the honeymoon) for their white weddings. Plus thousands of dollars more for bachelor and bachelorette parties, rings, gifts, rehearsal dinners, tuxedoes, and wedding dresses.

I am calling *nqi mi nqi hno* the "bride price" because money exchanges hands. I read up on the topic, and what I found was hard to believe. Patricia Symonds, who wrote about a Hmong village in northern Thailand, says that the bride price "ties a woman to her husband and his lineage, giving them rights to her labor, sexuality and reproduction." That is, the bride price buys a woman's labor and children.

I know I am taking the bride price out of its cultural context. And this is why there is a problem. The bride price may have worked in Laos and Thailand, but does it still work here in America? Does it work now? Can you have the *rooj tshoob* without the bride price? Can the intent of the *rooj tshoob* be accomplished without the bride price?

The "bride price" is a loaded term for Western women who cannot help but react strongly against it. It takes us (and I include myself in this category of Western women) back to the days when women were treated as chattel/property. It takes us back to America's history with slavery. It conveys the purchase of a commodity (i.e., ownership).

Is it possible for the bride price to convey value without the politics? That is, as a society, don't we want girls and women to be worthy and thus respected? As a friend asked, "What is so wrong with a woman being of value?"

Is it possible to look at the bride price just as an economic exchange?

Is our trouble with the bride price the fact that it is only about the bride? That is, would we be as upset if there was a "groom price"? To be clear, no such thing exists in the Hmong community since the groom does not go live with the in-laws.

In some cultures, a more familiar and accepted term is "dowry." Dowry is money, property, or gifts brought by a bride to her new family to start her marriage. In Hmong culture, the relatives and parents give their daughters dowries at the *rooj tshoob*. The dowry includes Hmong clothes and accessories, pots and pans, dishes and silverware, blankets and pillows, jewelry and money. Oftentimes, the bride's parents also return some or all of the bride price. The dowry often adds up to more than an equal exchange. At one cousin's weddings, her dowry and the money her parents gave her amounted to $20,000.

"What's a bride price of $5,000 compared to $20,000?" asked *Niam*.

The dowry, however, is not the bride price.

The bride price is money that the groom's family gives to the bride's parents (or mother, in my case). Hmong people do not believe the bride price is buying a woman. They say it is a kind of "insurance" so that the groom and his family will love and value the bride. That is, if the husband breaks the promise and divorces his wife without cause, the bride's parents get to keep the bride price. It honors and respects the bride's parents and the bride.

I believe this.

The trouble with me is that I ask questions. I am that annoying kid who asks, "Why?" and keeps asking it until she gets an answer, even if it is something she does not fully understand. When I was younger, I asked *Niam*, "Why is one of Aunt's kids skinny and light while the other's chubby and dark?"

"Shhh! We don't talk about that."

She didn't want to talk about the kids having two different dads.

Another time I asked, "Why are Hmong girls getting married at fourteen or fifteen? They're so young."

"Because they're beautiful."

Thank God I was an ugly duckling and no Hmong man wanted to marry me.

Now that I'm older, my questions are based on economic and cultural comparisons. If the bride price is a symbol of marriage, then can it be a dollar instead of four to six silver bars like it was in Laos, or $5,000 to $10,000 in the United States? I've even heard rumors of a $30,000 bride price.

If the bride price is a token of appreciation, then why not exchange something else of value instead of cash?

Can it be a fixed rate rather than fluctuate with the status of the bride or her family?

Why does a widow or divorcée "cost" less? Are these women "worth" less than a young, never-married woman without a child? Since you pay less for the widow or divorcée, it would seem that they are "used goods" or second best.

If the bride price is a kind of social "insurance" so that the groom and his family will love the bride, what happens when a man cheats on his wife, culturally "marries" a second or third wife, or beats his wife? Don't these acts warrant some type of corrective action from the groom's family? Why are abused Hmong wives told by everyone, including their own families, to go back home, to be more patient, to not talk back to their husbands? What recourse do they have?

If the bride price is supposed to make the groom and the in-laws value the bride more, then why is it used against her?

When I was growing up, *Niam* would yell at me and say, "If you don't learn how to do this, someday your husband and his family won't want to marry you. They'll send you back home. Then what will you do?"

I learned to cook and clean so that I would be a good wife for my husband and a good daughter-in-law, a good *nyab*, for my in-laws. In junior high school, I learned to cross-stitch. Copying *Niam*'s patterns, I cross-stitched simple *paj ntaub* for coin purses. *Niam* sewed in the zipper, and we sold them for five to ten dollars each at different craft fairs in Pittsburgh. I never learned how to do appliqué, reverse appliqué, batik, or anything more complicated, but it was a start. I learned to do these things well so I would be worthy of the bride price my in-laws paid for me.

It might sound like I am purposely poking fun at the bride price. I am not. I really do want to know these things. I want to engage in these kinds of conversations with Hmong elders.

But I come from a people who do not have a history of debate and discourse. Our parents tell us that a good child is one who is quiet and obeys the adults without question. Hmong people do not have a history of valuing the thoughts and opinions of women and children. Even young and single Hmong men are ignored at clan meetings where the older and married men compete to see who is the loudest. I come from a people who do not encourage these groups to speak up or speak out. Why would they, especially if they are part of the group benefiting from the way things are? I come from a people threatened by questions whose answers they may not know, questions that may jeopardize their power. I come from a people who value the group (the family, the clan) more than the individual. A people who value obedience and conformity over conflict. A people who worry about losing face more than doing the right, fair, or moral thing.

I would later learn from an elder that a long time ago, when the Hmong did not have money, they brought a cow as a gift to the parents. Before then, they gave three sticky rice cakes. This elder stated that each area in Laos was able to set its own bride price. In an area where there was a lot of commerce or business, it might have been thirty bars of silver (often reserved for the leaders who could afford it). In poorer parts, it may have been only three to four silver bars. In Minnesota, the nonprofit organization Hmong 18 Council has tried to set a standard for the bride price at $5,000. This move is an attempt to have a uniform bride price across the clans.

When I asked why the bride prices for widows or divorcées are less than that of a single, young, childless woman, many elders told me, "It's like a used car. You don't pay the same amount for it as you do a brand-new car."

In terms of domestic violence, my uncle explained that in Laos and Thailand, there was a way to deal with it. When a woman was abused, her relatives would investigate to find out who was at fault. Was she a "good" woman who fulfilled her duties as a wife and daughter-in-law (obeyed her husband and in-laws, worked hard, did not drink or gamble, did not cheat on her husband)? If she was and her husband still beat her up, then her relatives could force the man to pay a certain amount of money to "fix" the situation (or make the wife and her relatives "whole" again). My uncle admitted that this method of accountability worked in Laos and Thailand but no longer worked here in America. "In America," he said, "you have to go to court."

From what I'd heard about Hmong life in Laos and what I'd seen in the United States, there are three common ways for young Hmong people to start the marriage process. (This does not include parent-arranged and levirate marriages.) The first way is by force. This is when the groom kidnaps a woman and makes her marry him. He may be a man she didn't date, may not know, or would never marry on her own. Although she may not know him, one of his relatives "knows" her and her family. In the village setting in Laos, they may have spotted her at the river, cooking in the mornings, or at the New Year celebration. The groom stalks his future wife. He waits until she is far away from home or alone.

Because she is bound to resist, he enlists the help of friends, cousins, or uncles. A tug-of-war ensues. Being outnumbered, the woman is abducted and brought to the house of the groom's parents, or if he is from out of town, an uncle's house. After she is safely inside the house, the groom's parents send two messengers to the bride's parents to inform them that their daughter is safe and that they intend to marry her. Her family may not personally know the groom, but in the village setting, it is not hard to find out who he is.

Several Hmong elders remind me that sometimes this tug-of-war is a charade. The couple know each other and want to get married. They've agreed that this is the way they will do it. The woman's resistance is a face-saving tactic that protects her. It makes it look like the groom really wants to marry her.

At first in the United States, it took the Hmong a few years to figure out that kidnapping your potential bride is a crime. Parents of underage girls (those under eighteen) called the police on the grooms. The grooms got in trouble with the law. So now, kidnapping your potential bride rarely happens in the United States anymore.

A girl's parents may force a marriage if they catch the couple having sex or in some other compromising position. Sometimes, here in the United States, it could be as innocent as taking the girl out on a date and coming back home "too late." The parents assume you have had sex. To save themselves the embarrassment of their daughter having a child out of wedlock, they impose the marriage. The groom or his parents could resist, but the bride's parents will insist that their daughter's reputation has been ruined and thus no man will want to marry her anymore. Sometimes, in order to restore a woman's reputation or make the family "whole," the groom's parents will pay a certain sum of money to the bride's parents. This is sometimes enough to cancel the marriage.

A woman may also get married by *tuaj nqis tsev hais*. This is when the groom and his family come to the potential bride's house to meet with her family and to ask for her hand in marriage. It is one family asking another family. It is a very public way to give "face" or honor to the bride's parents and the bride. It means the potential groom and his family will do anything in their power to marry the bride. Some women feel flattered by this approach because it means they are good women, deserving of such attention and respect.

The final way to initiate a marriage is for a woman to run off or follow her boyfriend to his parents' house. This is not the romantic idea of eloping. You can't elope if you are Hmong because you can't get married on your own. There is no Hmong Vegas with a wedding chapel. No thirty-minute ceremony.

Sometimes, a woman runs off with her boyfriend to escape her parents forcing her to marry someone else. She decides when and whom she marries. This is the culturally recognized way a woman can have full control of her choice. This is the only part of the *rooj tshoob* where she has a say.

Niam reminds me that running off is not such a bad way to get married. Like marriage by force, the couple know each other and want to get married. They've agreed that they will marry quietly versus the noisy tug-of-war. Sometimes, parents will whisper to their daughters to run off with the boyfriends. This avoids their hand being forced by a stranger who wants to marry their daughters by *tuaj nqis tsev hais*.

However, when people hear that a woman ran off with her boyfriend, the reaction is one of, "Oh, *she* wanted to marry *them*!" as if the groom and his parents did not want her. Or was it that the bride's parents were ashamed that their daughter clearly wanted to marry a man? I guess even if you want to marry a man, you must not be too eager or seem too desperate. I wonder if running off with one's boyfriend puts the bride's parents in a less-favorable negotiating position. That is, since the bride was so eager to marry, her parents could not threaten to disallow the marriage.

Regardless of how you marry, if the bride is Hmong, generally you have to deal with the bride price. It is a part of the *rooj tshoob*. Whenever I talk about the bride price, my non-Hmong friends always ask if it still happens today, as if it is a tradition long past. The answer is yes, it still happens today. This is how most Hmong people get married.

⁓

Growing up, I had always heard that *tuaj nqis tsev hais* was the most respectful way for a woman to marry. When people found out that a woman got married this way, there was a knowing nod of the head. A shared acknowledgment of approval. "Wow. She must really be some girl [for the groom's family to have gone to all that trouble]," people whispered. There was a collective sense of pride for the bride's parents.

The elders told us girls, "If he really wants to marry you, he'll come to *tuaj nqis tsev hais*." In the same breath, they told their sons to do everything possible to escape it. This was true especially if his family was poor. Men want to avoid the negotiation because the bride's parents set the bride price. They may boast of the high value of their daughter, pushing the groom down. Since the negotiations are at the bride's family's house, the groom and his *mej koob* are at their mercy. They cannot leave until the negotiations are done.

I think *tuaj nqis tsev hais* is only the most respectful way to be married if a woman wants to marry her suitor. If she is not interested in marriage yet or if she does not agree to marry her suitor, this is a trap. She is literally trapped in the house, captive to the decision of her father, uncles, and brothers. No woman wants to be in this position. In this situation, it seems *tuaj nqis tsev hais* is good only for the reputation of the bride's parents.

By the time I finished high school here in Minnesota, I knew three Hmong women whose families forced them to marry through *tuaj nqis tsev hais*. One of these women was my cousin. Unlike me—so skinny the wind could blow me away and barely five feet tall, my hair full of split ends—my cousin was tall with silky black hair down to her waist. She had a white face, a shy smile, and a gentle voice. She was beautiful. We talked about going to college before we married and settled down. Even I was in love with her.

When we were juniors in high school, she married a man ten years older than she was. My cousin had never dated this man, but her mother liked him. When he came to *tuaj nqis tsev hais*, my guess is that my cousin did not want to do anything "bad" to tarnish the good reputation of her father, a high-ranking military official in General Vang Pao's army.

A second victim of this method was one of my high school friends. When her first cousin and his *mej koob* came to her house, she refused because she had a serious boyfriend. Nevertheless, after being held captive in her house for a couple days, and having her own grandmother say, "I want to see my great-grandkids before I die," she caved in. Her boyfriend was devastated, but what could he do?

Finally, one of the leaders of my Southern Baptist youth group married a man she had occasionally dated. A college student at the time, she was fluent in both Hmong and English. She was outspoken, standing up to the adults in church and defending the activities of the youth. I, the shy mouse in the corner, wanted to be like her.

None of these women escaped *tuaj nqis tsev hais*. To be fair, I don't know for sure that these women feel like victims. It is only my perspective of what happened to them. Of the three, two are still married to their husbands.

If the suitor was a "good" man—someone who was educated, someone who could take care of the woman, someone from a well-to-do family or a close relative (i.e., first cousin)—it was all over for the woman. Her parents had no plausible objections to refuse the marriage proposal. And because they could not refuse, she could not refuse.

In Laos, a girl facing an unwanted marriage couldn't say "No." Some tried, but very few people respected the "No." Other girls threatened to kill themselves by swallowing opium or some other poison. Some did kill themselves. Whatever they did, however, the decision to marry was not a woman's to make. A man did not need a woman's permission to marry her. He needed her father's. Or he needed to exert enough pressure on his future father-in-law in front of an audience of men who could force the father-in-law to say "Yes."

As a senior in high school, I wondered if Hmong parents could force a woman to do something she did not want to do. *This is not Laos or Thailand; this is America*, I told myself. But a little voice in the back of my head whispered, *Can they?* When my youth leader got married, I realized for the first time that one's parents or uncles could make a woman do something she did not want to do. I mean, if they could coerce my strong, outspoken youth leader to marry someone, what was going to happen to me? I was terrified that my uncles would push me to marry an old Hmong man whom I did not date, did not like, and did not want to marry. I was so scared that I vowed not to date a Hmong man. Or if I was going to, I made sure it was long distance. I promised myself that I would only marry the man I wanted to marry when I was ready. I swore that no one—man or woman—was going to force me to do something I did not want to do. Like some of the women before me, I would rather die.

Who Owns What

If my father were alive, I would not have a choice about the bride price. I would not even be able to question it. Since my father was educated, he would have some status in the community, making me more valuable.

"How much?" would have been the only question the *mej koob* asked.

In Laos, relatives of fatherless children often feared them. *Niam* told me that fatherless children meant extra mouths to feed when you did not have enough for your own. Here in the United States, fatherless children meant uncontrollable kids who would not amount to much. It meant kids who would not finish high school and would thus be jobless. The boys would become gang members. The girls would be promiscuous, getting pregnant and giving birth out of wedlock, after which no decent Hmong men would want to marry them. This was what Hmong people thought about my brothers and me.

My uncles never thought Yia would finish high school. One time, an uncle told *Niam* she should apply for Supplemental Security Income (SSI) or Social Security Disability Insurance (SSDI) for Yia. SSI is a federal program that pays benefits to people who are elderly, blind, or disabled with low income and few resources. Although Yia had no income or resources, he was not elderly or blind. He definitely was not disabled as defined by Social Security: unable to do the work he previously did or to do other work with a medical condition that has lasted or is expected to last at least one year or to result in death.

My aunts did not believe I would amount to anything. When I decided to go to St. Olaf College in Northfield, Minnesota, an aunt had lots of advice.

"Why go to a four-year private college?" she asked. "It'd be a waste of time and money. You'll just get married in the middle of it. You should go to vo-tech. You can get a job afterward."

I was so angry at my aunt. I was in the top 15 percent of my high school graduating class, and St. Olaf had given me almost a full scholarship my first year.

Even *Niam* worried that I wouldn't amount to anything. In high school, she kept saying, "One day, I'll just hear you've had an abortion." I did not understand why she said this. I did not even have a boyfriend until my senior year in high school, and he lived far away. During the two years we dated, I saw him twice.

My first year in college, *Niam* continued to say, "One day, I'll just hear you had an abortion."

I finally blew up at her.

"*Niam*, I never had a boyfriend because of you. If I wanted to do all those bad things, I don't need to go away to college to do it. I can do it right here. I want a good life for myself, too. I'm not going to fuck it up."

Years later, I understood that my aunt was just trying to protect me. Some Hmong girls did get married in the middle of college and never finished. A job was important for taking care of a family. And the abortion comment was *Niam*'s way of telling me her biggest fear. She was not one to say things such as, "I'm worried about you" or "I'm concerned that something will happen and you won't tell me." *Niam*'s way of communicating was to accuse me of doing the exact thing she did not want me to do. This was what the writer May Lee-Yang calls *Hmongspeak*, and I had to decipher it for myself.

Hmongspeak is a way of speaking in which you have to be "discreet and beat around the bush." As Lee-Yang explains, it is so discreet that if you cannot read between the lines, you are screwed. For example,

Coj khaub ncaws, which translates as "wearing cloths," really is menstruation

"We'll see" is "No"
"We are so poor!" is "Give us money" (in Laos and Thailand)
"There was so much work to do!" means "Where the fuck were you?"

Hmongspeak is not all bad. It is purposely veiled to protect the modesty of both the speaker and the person being spoken to.

In general, Hmong parents of *Niam*'s generation are experts at Hmongspeak. It is an art form for them. Like rappers on the mic, the words spill out of the speaker onto the blank canvas. Similar to *kwv txhiaj*, it is composed on the spot with meter and rhyme scheme. Sometimes I'm not even sure if all the words are in Hmong. The receiver takes the ball of words and spins it right back.

Not only do Hmong parents use Hmongspeak on each other, they use it on their kids. They use it on their new daughters-in-law and sons-in-law. The only problem is that Hmong American kids like me, who did not grow up with Hmongspeak, would not know that when the mother-in-law is yelling at her daughters for not sweeping the floors, she is really yelling at the daughter-in-law, the *nyab*.

"You know that anything you have belongs to your family, right?" said Blong.

We were on the road, driving to the University of Wisconsin–La Crosse. In celebration of the Hmong New Year, the students had invited me to speak about the importance of Hmong artists creating their own images of themselves.

"I've been to weddings where the car a woman owns had to be 'given' to her," continued Blong.

Although not all Hmong parents followed this rule, it was the case with his aunt. It was the case with my cousin. At the *rooj tshoob*, there is a designated scribe who writes down all the gifts that family members give to the bride and groom. The scribe wrote down both cars as gifts even though the women paid for them.

"They could say your house belongs to your family, too," maintained Blong.

Or did he mean that my house would also be written down as a "gift," as part of the dowry I get from my family? The elders tell me that this list is meant to inflate the dowry for the sake of getting "face." That is, it shows the in-laws how much the bride's family loves her and has given her to start a new life. *Niam* said the written record is necessary so that the in-laws can never question where the items came from.

"What? That's my house legally," I said.

"It doesn't matter. At the *rooj tshoob*, they'll have to 'give' it to you or they may just say, 'Be a good girl and give it to your mom and brothers.'"

I knew what the elders were thinking: "You don't need a house where you're going." Traditionally, Blong and I would live with his parents, but since they lived in Merced, California, I did not have to worry about that. And since Blong already had a house in north Minneapolis, I would just move in with him. The elders were right.

"They can't do that. It's mine. I bought it by myself. I pay for the mortgage."

"I'm just telling you how it works in Hmong marriage negotiations," said Blong. "You didn't know that?"

"No. I'm not privileged to have that information."

I WAS ANGRY WITH MYSELF. Why had I not known it? Was it my own fault for not knowing, or could I blame someone else? Kids from other ethnic groups had cultural lessons on Saturday mornings, but Hmong people did not. With so many things vying for our attention, when and to what should Hmong kids be paying attention? There were not *Hmong for Dummies* or *Hmong 101* books. How did other Hmong kids learn these cultural rules and traditions? I was twenty-eight years old and should have known.

At St. Olaf, I spent a whole summer researching traditional Hmong medical practices. I spoke with shamans, massage therapists, and herbalists. Although my family was Christian, I spent time reading books about Hmong animist rituals and traditions because I believed they were important to know. *Niam* has always told me that we may have gotten rid of the animist spirits, but we did not get rid of our families. My family attended the *ua neeb* (the shaman's healing ritual), *hu plig* (a soul-calling ritual), and animist funerals of our extended families. We helped out by cooking, eating, and cleaning. At the *ua neeb* rituals, I paid attention to the shaman, a spiritual healer, when he conducted his ceremonies.

MY FAMILY CONVERTED to Christianity when we came to Pittsburgh in 1981. At first, *Niam* was a typical "rice-bowl" Christian. The "rice" came in the form of furniture and clothes, English as a Second Language classes for the adults, and Sunday school for the kids. I was a Pioneer Girl, the Christian equivalent of Girl Scouts but with God and Bible verses thrown in. I memorized all the names of the books in the Bible, and I learned songs such as "Jesus Loves Me," "Trust and Obey," and "Kumbaya." My Sunday school teacher, Nancy, took the girls over to her big house in Allison Park, a suburb of Pittsburgh. We slept on sleeping bags in her sons' rooms with wallpaper of toy soldiers carrying bayonets. We saw photo albums of her and her husband at college, this mysterious place full of beautiful buildings and happy faces.

Over the years, however, I saw that *Niam* had become a devout Christian, calling on God in her times of need. The church became her "clan," taking care of all the things the clan did—weddings, funerals, visiting the sick in the hospital, settling disputes, and comforting the lonely. The only differences were that many clans belonged to one church, and the church was bound by the blood of Christ, not family. With the church, as one widow stated, "You can go directly to God yourself," as opposed to animism, where you have to call on a shaman to intercede on your behalf.

Niam and I never talked about how Christianity fits into the *rooj tshoob*. In fact, I had never talked to anybody—not my friends, not my pastor—about it. What did Hmong Christians do about the bride price? Did they do away with it or did they still ask for it? Did they do both the *rooj tshoob* and the church wedding, or did they roll them into one— the church wedding? At the *rooj tshoob*, did they still make the groom and his best man drink alcohol until they puked? Or did they substitute Pepsi (or any other pop) for it? Did they still make the groom and best man kowtow to the bride's parents, family members, and ancestors?

I was sure the answers differed based on whom you married and your church denomination. Perhaps within denominations, each church has its own policies about the *rooj tshoob* and bride price. And maybe within a church, each family has its own ideas about them. I wanted to know what my church, the First Hmong Baptist Church, thought about them. I remembered numerous talks between the pastor and the congregation. A couple of the talks were about how dancing could lead to sex. The youths' arguments of "But the Bible talks about how David danced for joy" were ignored. We even discussed interracial marriages. The youths' "Aren't Christians supposed to love all people?" was met with "We are Hmong first." I did not remember talks about how Christianity fit into the *rooj tshoob*. Or did the talks come out as, "Don't do this. . . . Don't do that" and so I tuned them out?

In Laos, where Hmong parents and kids lived more intimate lives, kids were able to watch what their parents did and then imitate them. It was as if, through osmosis, the knowledge seamlessly passed from parent to child. Here in the United States, the Hmong are minorities within the Asian minority in a majority culture. Hmong parents and kids live separate lives. During the week, our parents go to work while we go to school. When we get home from school, we take care of ourselves and our siblings, or the TV—nowadays YouTube or iPads or cell phones—take care of all of us. On the weekends, our parents spend their time at family functions at which we may or may not be present. Even if we are there, our parents are busy performing and participating in the traditional rituals while we chitchat, watch TV, or run around outside.

Here in the United States, sometimes young people learn Hmong cultural rules and traditions only when our parents yell at us or lecture us, after the fact. We learn from other young people's mistakes. Our parents tell us about these mistakes not as teaching moments in the Western sense but more as, "See, this is what happens when you don't listen to your parents!"

BLONG DROVE WHILE I sat in the passenger's seat, looking out the window. Highway 52 South was a smooth ride compared to the protest pounding in my head.

"Most Hmong girls who marry don't have a house, so you're a little unusual," continued Blong.

My thoughts drifted back to the Margaret Street house. Unlike the public housing or Section 8 homes we had lived in before, we got to choose the Margaret Street house. It had a porch to store the shoes of our guests, who took them off before stepping inside the house. A living room opened into the dining room, allowing us to put multiple tables together for family events. Our first home had many firsts for us—a bedroom for each of us, central air, two bathrooms, a two-car garage, and everbearing raspberries that Kai planted in the backyard. *Niam* also planted a few Hmong essential vegetables—cilantro, green onions, hot peppers, and greens—in the backyard.

"When I go to Hmong weddings, I'm in the kitchen, cooking, cleaning, and serving you men. Or I stand at the back of the room and watch the men at the table. How am I supposed to know?" I said.

I KNEW I WAS being snippy with Blong. It was not his fault, but he was a part of the good old boys' club that excluded me. It wasn't only the *rooj tshoob*. This club permeated Hmong life—marriages, funerals, clan meetings. At funerals, men took care of sending the deceased into the spirit world, including accepting funeral donations and thanking the donors. At clan meetings, men settled disputes between husbands and wives or between clans.

As with many other cultures, women were not invited to these meetings, the duties of which are seen as men's responsibilities. Certainly, wives accompanied their husbands to the meetings, but their purpose was to help the host wife clean, cook, and serve food and drinks to the men. At best, the women stood in the back of the room, to the side or in the doorways, and listened to the conversations and decisions made by the men.

We women were not at the table of decision-making. We did not help set the agendas. Growing up, I got the impression that Hmong men were not interested in our input or opinions. Not in public, anyway. But I'm sure later, in the privacy of their bedrooms, Hmong women told their husbands what they thought. However, by then it was probably too late. At that point, what could the husbands do if the clan had already decided to go one way or the other?

What Blong and I did not talk about was that, even here in America, Hmong people continue to adhere to strict gender roles. Boys are the spiritual carriers and performers of rituals, while girls are responsible for the house and children. From an early age, Hmong parents instill in boys the belief that they are important. Parents teach cultural information and rituals to boys so they can carry on the family line. Parents groom girls in housework and childcare so we will be good wives and daughters-in-law to our new families.

Niam had done her duty and properly trained me to be a good housewife.

Specific information about traditions such as the *rooj tshoob:* did I, the Hmong girl, really need to know all that? I was never going to be a *mej koob* or a representative for any parents. My role, if I was ever asked to officially participate in the *rooj tshoob*, was to be the maid of honor. As such, I followed the bride around to make sure no one did any bad things to her or she didn't run away or she didn't contact her old boyfriends. That was a no-brainer and did not require prior experience.

As far as other animist rituals were concerned, they didn't seem to be things I, the Hmong Christian girl, needed to know, right? As Christians, my family did not practice any of those rituals. And I didn't need to know about the animist worldview of souls because God the Father, Jesus, and the Holy Spirit, not the ancestral spirits, guided us.

However, not understanding the animist worldview meant I did not understand more than half the Hmong people. For the Hmong, the lines between culture or traditions and religion were often blurry. That is, it is not always easy to separate culture from religion. Thus, I think the "traditional" animist worldview is the base to which Hmong people refer. As a first-generation Hmong American, I needed to understand this worldview.

Doing the Right Thing

Most Hmong people thought I was an "old maid" at twenty-eight. Blong and I joked that perhaps *Niam* would be so relieved I was finally getting married that she would "give me away" for free. That is, she would not ask for a bride price.

Weeks after I asked Kai to tell *Niam* I did not want a bride price, she said, "Why is it that I always hear you say you're marrying Blong? I haven't heard him say he wants to marry you."

That was when I asked Blong to come to my house and talk to *Niam*.

"She wants to hear that *you* want to marry me," I told him. "Come and ask for my hand in marriage."

"Heck, no. I'm not going there by myself," exclaimed Blong.

He knew that Hmong culture dictated that he could not just show up at my house to talk to *Niam* about marrying me. He needed to come with his *mej koob*. This was the appropriate Hmong thing to do. My brothers, uncles, and their *mej koob* would be waiting at my house to start the marriage negotiations.

All that did not matter to me. No, that was not true: it did matter. It just did not seem as important or as big as the scenes in the romantic comedies my friends and I loved so much. At the moment, all I wanted was for Blong to go talk to *Niam* himself. Yes, ask for my hand in marriage just like my American friend Eric had done with my pastor. Eric had met my cousin when both their fathers attended Bethel Seminary. They'd lost track of each other after their fathers graduated and Eric's family moved away. Years later, in college, Eric moved back to town and they reconnected. I remembered that Eric was nervous because he'd called me before he went to meet with my pastor.

Before another cousin and her Hmong fiancé got culturally married, she too thought it was a good idea for him to ask her father for her hand in marriage. Although this was a very non-Hmong thing to do, the fiancé, who loved my cousin, agreed to do it. He flew to Minnesota from California. They chose a top-scale restaurant worthy of this special occasion. When my cousin's fiancé asked her father for her hand in marriage, I imagined that "the scene" would play out with her father responding modestly, "My daughter is ugly; you may not want to marry her." This was the appropriate Hmong response. You were supposed to say the opposite of what you really meant so you would not attract the attention of evil spirits who may want to kidnap or harm your daughter. The fiancé, I was sure, insisted that he really did want to marry her.

At my cousin's *rooj tshoob*, however, her family fined the fiancé for inappropriately "negotiating" with his future father-in-law. He had to "right" this wrong by paying a fine to the in-laws. My cousin was shocked. She had only done what she thought was right. Besides, at the restaurant, neither of her parents gave any indication that what she and her fiancé were doing was wrong. I did not tell Blong this when I asked him to talk to *Niam*. In all honesty, I kind of forgot about that part of the story.

Blong, like my cousin's fiancé, came over to my house. He was Daniel in the lion's den. *Niam*, the lioness, paced to and fro, ready to bite off his head.

Years later, that evening still seems like the nightmare of running in slow motion, not being able to get away. The details are fuzzy. I do not remember what *Niam* said or what I said. I remember sitting on the cool leather sofa bed with Blong, facing *Niam* and my older brother, Kai. It felt like sitting in the dentist's chair with my mouth open and both hands gripping the arms. Only when I exhaled did I realize I had been holding my breath. Even the molecules in the air had been holding their breaths. Held captive, I wondered who was going to say what first. We all waited to see what would happen. This was uncharted territory for all of us. We waited for one of my uncles, the designated "holder" of culture and rituals, to come to our house. *Niam* and Kai had invited him without letting me know. I prayed that he would not show up. I was relieved when Kai informed us that he was held up at a funeral.

I remembered Kai's questions: "Are you Hmong? Hmong people follow their culture and customs."

Since Blong is an attorney, I was sure Kai expected him to understand and follow the laws and rules of the Hmong culture. Blong must have said something along the lines of, "If that's what Mai Neng wants, that's what we'll do."

"Are you a man? Men don't let their women tell them what to do."

Had it not occurred to my brother that Blong was a good man, someone who wanted to honor what his sister wanted?

Somehow, the interrogation ended. Blong and I survived. He got up to leave. I saw his red face as he walked out the door. I felt his silence heavy as a mule's pack. I followed him out the front door and onto the porch.

"Are you leaving now?" asked *Niam*, her voice shaking.

She was not talking to Blong; she was talking to me. She seemed scared that I might leave right there and go home with Blong. Blong and I had planned a church wedding. I did not need to run off with him. As I told Blong, "I have my own car. I know where you live. If I want to come over, I can come by myself."

"No," I answered *Niam*.

Did *Niam* think Blong was "negotiating" with her? Probably. But I hoped she heard what she wanted to hear—that Blong wanted to marry me. That, after all, was the point.

Marriage Talks

I thought *Niam* and I never had the talks about love and marriage I imagined other girls had with their mothers. But we actually have. Ours were just different. They came in unexpected ways. Like the time when I wanted to buy a car, and she suggested I buy a minivan.

"A minivan? I don't want to buy a minivan, *Niam*. Why would I do that?"

"So when you have kids, there'd be enough room."

"Kids?" I said, laughing. "*Niam*, by the time I have kids, the minivan would be dead."

With a loan from *Niam* and some money from my first real job, I bought a used 1998 Toyota Camry instead. *Niam* and I never discussed the minivan conversation again, but I knew what she was up to.

Just like the time when I invited a friend to the house to make dinner. *Niam* was on her way to the garden when I introduced her to my friend. I told her that he lived in Minneapolis, but his mom lived in Georgia.

"Oh, *neb niam nyob nrad* Georgia *los*?" she asked.

My friend, who was not Hmong, did not understand the question. *Niam* had asked, "Oh, your mother lives in Georgia?" but she had used the plural form of "your," implying that it was "our" mother. That is, that we were already married. I gave her a look that said, "You know better than that." *Niam* smiled with a gleam in her eyes.

"No, *nws Niam nyob nrad* Georgia," I corrected her, emphasizing that it was *his* mother who lived in Georgia.

Niam has always told me how not to get married. "You must marry a man who loves you more than you love him," she said.

"Really? Why's that?"

"Because that way, your marriage will last."

I think she meant, if he loves you more than you love him, he will be more patient with you. He will let you get away with more things. He is more likely to do what you ask.

Another time, *Niam* said, "One day, I'll just hear that you've run off to get married."

What she meant was, "Don't just run off with some guy."

She warned, "If you run off with a guy, they'll say, 'Oh, look at her and how much she wants to marry them.'" She should have spelled it out for this Hmong American kid who could not decipher the Hmongspeak: "Even if you really want to marry a guy, when you are too eager, it is embarrassing. When things don't work out, the family will say, 'Well, we didn't want to marry you, anyway. It was you who came to us. You may leave now.'"

She should have explicitly told me that reluctance and resistance were face-saving tactics appropriate for use in strategic situations. Should the marriage fail, the bride could say she had been uncertain about the prospect all along. Her parents, too, could claim that they were not responsible for her failed marriage.

Niam said, "If they really want to marry you, they will come to your house to negotiate with your parents. If they do this, you save face, you save your parents' face, and you bring honor to your clan."

This was, of course, very different from my cousin whose mother told her she did not want anyone to come to the house to ask for her daughter.

"My heart cannot give away my daughter. It is not proper," said this grandmother.

Although my cousin's mother was not my grandmother by blood, Hmong custom dictated that I call her such out of respect. In her opinion, if the groom and his *mej koob* came to the house, the family literally has to say, "Here, you take her," as if forcing their daughter to go. So, on the day my cousin was to marry her fiancé, he came to pick her up as if they were going out on a date. Yes, she just ran off with him. And that was what her mother wanted.

Although my cousin and I belonged to the same Moua family, our mothers had different ideas of who they did not want us to marry. An example of this is the story of how Moua women cannot date or marry Thao men. Of course, I found this out only after I started dating a Thao man.

"You know our daughters can't date Thao men, right?" said *Niam* the first time she met my Thao boyfriend.

Later, when I was home alone with *Niam*, I asked her why. I really did not know.

"A long time ago, there was a Thao woman married to a Moua man. The *nyab* [daughter-in-law] was very mean to the mother-in-law. The *nyab* was going to a party. The mother-in-law, who was blind, couldn't go to the party, so she said, '*Nyab*, please bring me some meat to eat.' When *Nyab* came back, she handed the mother-in-law some meat. The mother-in-law was old, and she had lost all her teeth, so she gratefully accepted the soft meat. Soon her grandson walked by and said, 'Grandma, what are you eating?' The mother-in-law said, 'Meat your mother brought me from the party.' Her grandson said, 'Here, let me see what it is.' The mother-in-law pulled out the soft meat from her toothless mouth. Her grandson took one look at the meat and recoiled in horror. 'Grandma,' he shouted, 'it's not meat. It's a caterpillar.'"

I shook my head. That story did not even make sense. How could the mother-in-law not tell the difference between a piece of meat and a caterpillar?

"*Niam*, that's not true," I said, smiling.

"Yes, it is."

She was not laughing.

"The mother-in-law threw up and kept throwing up. She was so upset, she cursed her daughter-in-law by saying, 'When I die, *Nyab* will have to bury me.' Soon enough the mother-in-law died. Her sons took her to the gravesite on a wooden platform.

"When the sons got to the gravesite, they couldn't take their mother off of the platform. They tried to cut the ropes off. They twisted and turned the platform, but nothing worked. Finally, someone remembered the mother-in-law's curse, so they asked the daughter-in-law to try and get the mother-in-law off. As soon as she touched the mother-in-law, she couldn't let go. As much as people tried to pry *Nyab* off, nothing worked. Finally, after a couple days, the mother-in-law was starting to rot. So they had to bury *Nyab* with the mother-in-law."

"*Niam*! What kind of story is that?"

"A true story! Since then, the Moua have been forbidden from dating or marrying the Thao."

I did not really believe *Niam*. I mean, if this was a true story, why had I not heard about it until now? Besides, how could a body get stuck to another body, a decomposing one at that?

When I saw my cousin, I said, "Hey, did you know we can't date or marry Thao men?"

I told my cousin the whole story, just as *Niam* had told me.

"That's not the version my mom told me. The story is that Moua men can't marry Thao women, but Moua women can marry Thao men."

"What?"

"Moua men cannot marry Thao women, but we women can marry Thao men," repeated my cousin.

That was the exact opposite of what *Niam* told me.

"So what story did your mom tell you?" I asked.

"The Thao *nyab* was up, making some sticky rice cakes. Her father-in-law was smoking by the fire. He asked *Nyab* for some sticky rice cakes. Instead of walking up to him and handing him the rice cakes, she flung them from across the room. One landed with a big *plop* on the father-in-law's forehead. The father-in-law was so angry, he said, 'From this day on, no Moua men can marry Thao women. If they do, they'll be poor all their lives or they'll die.'"

I laughed at the image of the sticky rice cake flying across the room and landing with a *plop* on the father-in-law's forehead.

"But I don't get why the father-in-law cursed his own sons. I mean, why would you want your sons to be poor or die? Shouldn't he be cursing the *nyab*?" I asked.

My cousin did not know either. As girls who were born in Laos but raised most of our lives in America, we had forgotten that Hmong men, especially the oldest, had to take care of their parents. That is, their wives had to take care of their parents. Whomever they married, Hmong men needed to make sure their wives would fulfill this duty. The father-in-law was so concerned about his own well-being that he was willing to risk his sons being poor or dying. He wanted to make sure none of his sons ever married Thao women.

When I got back home, I confronted *Niam*.

"*Niam*, I told Cousin the story you told me, and she said the Thao *nyab* was mean to the father-in-law. The *nyab* flung sticky rice cakes at him, and one landed on his forehead."

"That's right!" said *Niam* with a smile. "The *nyab* was mean to both the mother-in-law and father-in-law. That's why you can't date or marry Thao men."

Needless to say, I did not believe *Niam* and continued dating my Thao boyfriend for three years. We finally broke up when his ex-wife came back into the picture. Sometime later, I reconnected with a different Thao man. He and I met at his high school prom. Although we were attracted to each other, we came with different dates and so nothing happened. Somehow, we both landed in Northfield, Minnesota, for college. He went to Carleton while I attended St. Olaf. Nothing happened between us during college. When we reconnected after college, he was single. I was single. We planned a date. We were both excited and looking forward to it. Then, a couple hours before the big night, he called.

"My whole family is sick, and we have to *ua neeb*," he said.

Ua neeb is a healing ritual where a shaman comes to the house and heals the sick person(s). The shaman does this by traveling in a trance to the spirit world and finding the lost souls of the sick person. He or she brings the lost souls back home to the body. When all the souls are back in the body, the sick person is well again.

I did not know what to say to him, so I said, "Okay." I wanted to know what his family had, but I did not ask.

"I need to help with the *ua neeb*," he explained.

I knew he was needed at home to help prepare the meal for his extended family members who would be coming to support his family.

"I won't be able to go out on the date," he said.

He did not explain that part of the *ua neeb* was for the family to quarantine themselves inside their home and exclude folks who do not have the same spiritual practices from coming inside the house. Without saying it, he was keeping his spirits away from me in order for his family to get well.

"Hey, I get it. Take care of your family. We can always go out at a different time," I reassured him.

I was convinced his animist ancestors did not like my Christian spirits of God the Father, Jesus, and the Holy Spirit. I mean, nothing happened in high school and college. Three years after graduation, we were both single, and now this?

"Dude, your spirits don't like my spirits!" I pronounced.

He laughed. I was not sure what his laughter meant. Did he believe me? Or did he think I was crazy?

"I'm serious! I mean, your whole family gets sick right before our big date? This date was seven years in the making!"

I decided it was divine intervention. Although we had promised to reschedule, we never did. Years later, I saw him at a community event. He was single again, after a divorce. As it turned out, I had just started dating Blong.

Are Moua men and women forbidden to date or marry Thao men and women? Was the Thao daughter-in-law evil to both the mother-in-law and the father-in-law? Did my friend's animist spirits and my Christian spirits prevent us from dating? All I know is, I am married to a Yang, not a Thao.

Damaged Goods

There is a black and white photograph of me that I can't look at even now. It is a self-portrait of me on peritoneal dialysis (PD). In the photo, I am standing against the wall after one of the PD exchanges. The catheter with its red and blue marks dangles out of the right side of my stomach. My right hand holds up two bags—the empty bag of dialysis solution rolled up in a ball and the 2.5-liter bag of yellow urine. My left hand hangs loosely at my side. On my face is an expression that says, "It is what it is" or "What?" Some may call it the resting bitch face, an Internet meme for an annoyed-looking blank stare. I am shirtless, wearing only white underwear. It wasn't a pretty picture.

"I don't know why you've taken this picture," said *Niam* when she discovered the framed photo in our shared bedroom. "We are Christians. We don't do this." *Niam* shook her head from side to side. She scrunched up her face so there were lines on her forehead.

I nodded with understanding. I didn't tell her that the framed photo would be part of an exhibit at a local coffeehouse. I didn't tell her, or any of my friends, that anyone who went to the coffeehouse would be able to see it for months.

After the exhibit, I didn't hang it up anywhere. I hid it in the back of the closet, facing the wall. There it sat for years, until I married Blong and showed it to him.

"Why did you take this photo?" asked Blong. "It's kind of disturbing."

"I know. Even I can't look at it. It's so raw." I took a deep breath. Then, remembering his question, I continued, "Because I wanted myself to see what it was like to be on dialysis. I needed to display it all—the good, the bad, the ugly parts. I didn't want to hide behind my clothes."

IN MY WRITING, I am most honest with myself and others. I write everything down—the good, the bad, the ugly—because I want to see it all in its true colors. I need the space, the many blank pages of a book, to lay it all out. When I am done writing the stories, I want to be able to hold them up and challenge myself and others to look at them from multiple sides.

Home for the summer of 1994, I went to get a physical exam for the Term in Asia, one of St. Olaf's semester-long study-abroad programs. I had been planning on this since my first year when I met returning students whose experiences abroad changed their lives. With the home stay in Thailand where my paternal grandfather lived, the Term in Asia was perfect. I would be able to travel throughout Asia, visit my grandfather, and get credit for it.

At the clinic, the doctor said, "You have really high blood pressure for someone your age. Has anyone ever told you that?"

I shook my head. "No."

I did not think much of the doctor's question and went out with my girlfriends. When I got home at midnight, *Niam* told me a doctor had been calling me all day. I called the doctor back. Although I do not remember his exact words, it felt as if he said, "Your kidneys are really sick. You're going to die." I remember thinking, *Who is this guy? Why is he saying this to me?*

The doctor told me to immediately go to the emergency room at St. Joseph's Hospital in downtown St. Paul. We lived ten minutes away on the west side of St. Paul. Silent tears streamed down my face as I drove to St. Joe's with *Niam* next to me. I heard *Niam*'s, "Don't worry. I am still here. As long as I am alive, I won't let anything happen to you. Nothing will happen to you."

At the ER, the doctors took urine and blood samples and ran a series of tests. They told me my kidneys were too sick and I could not leave. And so started the crash course into kidneys and kidney disease. I knew nothing. Given my ethnicity and age, the doctors diagnosed me with IgA nephropathy, a disorder that happens when IgA, a protein that helps the body fight infections, settles in the kidneys. After ten to twenty years with IgA nephropathy, 25 percent of adults develop total kidney failure or end-stage renal disease.

"What happened between my first year in college when I received a clean bill of health and the summer of 1994?" I asked the doctors. "Why did my own body attack my kidneys?"

All they could tell me was that it was an autoimmune disease. There were not any major signs. Toward the end of spring semester my junior year, my face was puffy in the mornings, but the puffiness went away during the day. I was tired, but what student was not tired during finals?

By the end of summer, my kidneys were sick enough that I ended up on emergency dialysis and could not go on the Term in Asia. It felt like things were going along so well and then someone snapped the rug from under me. I landed with a thud and could not get up.

By the end of that summer, I decided I needed to know how sick my kidneys were. The doctors suggested a biopsy.

"It's a simple procedure. We give her general anesthesia. We numb up the area real good. We take two small needles, insert them in the back and take out small samples of tissue. We do this all the time," explained the nephrologist.

None of my family members wanted me to do dialysis. They certainly didn't want the biopsy. They didn't really care to listen to the doctor. They waited patiently for him to be done so they could talk amongst themselves. They wanted me to go back home and try herbal medicine first. Surrounded by uncles and my immediate family, I was outnumbered. Out of the group, there was one uncle who thought the biopsy was a good idea. They saw the biopsy as a last resort. I argued that we were already at the last resort.

"That's why it's called end-stage renal disease," I stated.

I must've sounded like a smartass to my family. Finally, one uncle said, "If you're not going to listen to us, then why are we here?"

I didn't say anything. I hadn't asked them to come. But of course they would come. It was at times like this that my uncles were supposed to step up and take care of things. They were being responsible uncles taking care of their brother's kid.

"You're an adult," said the nephrologist. "It's your decision."

My uncles disagreed with him. I decided to do the biopsy. It was my body. My creatinine levels were too high. Creatinine is a waste product of normal muscle contractions that is filtered out by the kidneys. The level of creatinine in your blood reflects muscle mass and kidney function. A high level means the kidneys are not able to filter out waste efficiently.

I needed to know the condition of my kidneys. But since my uncles were so scared, I wondered if I should be afraid, too. I cried to Kai, who comforted me by saying, "Don't worry, Maaaai. People like us, we don't die easily." We laughed before the doctors sedated me. They inserted needles into my back and took out the tissues they needed.

The results of the biopsy showed that my kidneys had shriveled up. *Niam*, however, prayed they would magically regenerate. She hoped that, like dried beans soaked in water overnight, they would come back to life. That was why she did not want me to do dialysis or the biopsy. She did not want anyone tampering with my kidneys.

An aunt whom I had not seen for years called me in the hospital after the biopsy. Having just woken up from general anesthesia, I was still groggy.

"Why would you do such a stupid thing?" asked Aunt, referring to the biopsy.

"Aunt, I just woke up. I'm tired. Could I call you back?" I asked.

As soon as I hung up the phone, I threw up. The bitter taste of anesthesia ran down the sides of my mouth.

Niam WANTED TO HEAL ME with herbal medicine. She went around town, telling everyone about her sick daughter who had kidney disease. She spent hundreds of dollars on herbal remedies promised to cure me. I pleaded with her to not waste her money, but she said, "Money, you can earn. Your life, you can't get back." I took the doctor's medications, but I also drank and took all of *Niam*'s herbal medicines. Then one day she told me about the herbalist who had asked for the gold chain around her neck as payment when she confessed she did not have enough money. I told her I could not take any more.

Niam wanted me to stay home so she could take care of me, the sick one.

"I didn't take out all those loans to just quit now," I told *Niam*. I was determined to finish my undergraduate studies if it was the last thing I did. I returned to campus to a lonely single room; my roommate was fulfilling her dream of going to Tanzania. A refugee like me, she was not able to return to her home country of Liberia, but at least she would be on the same continent as her ancestors.

I spent my senior year balancing classes and part-time work with peritoneal dialysis, PD. On the right side of my stomach, a four-inch incision spewed a six-inch catheter. Through the catheter, I drained 2.5 liters of dialysis solution into my body cavity. This fluid dwelled in my body for several hours so that an exchange could take place between my blood and the dialysis solution, cleaning the blood of toxins that could no longer be filtered out by my kidneys. After three to eight hours, I drained out the used dialysis solution and replaced it with another 2.5 liters of solution. I did this four times a day: morning, noon, evening, and before bed. This was what I had to do to live.

The dialysis solution made me "fat." It seeped into my face, hands, and legs, making me puffy. Fluid-filled, I no longer recognized myself. The scariest thing about being on dialysis was that I felt I had no control over my body. That was hard. To feel disconnected from myself. It was strange to think my own body was a stranger to me. I was no longer intimate with my body. I could not get attached to it because I was afraid I would lose more of it.

Though I did not drink, I had a beer belly. After each exchange of dialysis solution, I carefully taped the catheter to my abdomen. My pants hung underneath the catheter. I tried to be "normal" like all the other college kids, dating and going clubbing in Minneapolis. However, there were days when my steps dragged and my lids were heavy as lead and I slept, curled up in a fetal position in St. Olaf's Lion's Den.

I sought help from others. I asked my pastor to meet with *Niam*, me, and the nephrologist to broach the topic of a transplant. *Niam* had gotten mad at the young Hmong woman whose mom and I shared the same nephrologist and who had come to talk to us at my request. While I wanted to know everything about kidney disease, *Niam* believed that if we talked about it, I was sure to get it. I needed someone else on my side, telling *Niam* it was okay to get the transplant.

Having kidney failure meant I was anemic. Little vials of erythropoietin (EPO) arrived in my mail. I was supposed to give myself shots of EPO on my legs, stomach, or arms. Though the needle was small, I couldn't stab myself. Besides, they hadn't put a buffer in the EPO, and the shots stung like a bee. I asked the school nurse for help. Every Friday afternoon after class, I went to her office, where she warmed the EPO in her hands. She distracted me with questions about classes and quickly shot my arm. As I fought back the tears, she rubbed my shoulders. Sometimes I did not go in for the shot and got a call from the nurse on Monday morning.

I finished my last year at St. Olaf and graduated with my class. A few months later, after I had worked up the courage to do it, I moved out with my college roommate. *Niam*, like others in my extended family, had not wanted me to move out. She never stepped foot inside any of my apartments.

"It's okay. I'll wait in the car," she always said.

I did not know how to translate into Hmong words the need to be independent, especially since, it seemed, my life was going to be on dialysis. I did not want *Niam*, my brothers, or my uncles to worry about taking care of me, the sick one. I needed to learn how to balance dialysis with work and paying bills. It was important for me to learn how to live on my own. Living on my own, however, meant that when I got an infection and the bag of yellow urine turned into curdled milk, I drove myself to the ER to get antibiotics.

My nephrologist worried that the multiple infections might be scarring my peritoneum, and thus making PD less effective. He switched me to hemodialysis. I called *Niam* to tell her I was going in for surgery— to take out the old PD catheter because it was probably infected and making me sick, and to put a new permanent catheter in my shoulder so I could do hemodialysis instead of PD dialysis.

She said, "It's up to you. Whatever you want to do."

What had I expected her to say? *Don't do it. I know a better way?* Shouldn't I have been glad she gave me permission to do what I wanted? All my life, it seemed, I'd been fighting for this exact thing. But then I thought, *Please care. Tell me what to do. Don't say, 'It's up to you.'* Sometimes when she said this, I felt like she was punishing me. An angry *Well, you chose this path, so why are you asking me what to do?* A *Well, you didn't listen to me. See what happens?*

I was on my own on PD and now, with hemodialysis, I was still on my own.

Hemodialysis is a process where a dialysis machine cleans your blood. Each session took four hours, and I did it three times a week at a clinic.

It was a part-time job whose payment was my life. On hemodialysis, I saw a glimpse of my future: an old maid asleep while the nurses hooked me up to the dialysis machine—the machine that *Niam* called my "opium."

"If you don't do it, will you die?" she had asked.

"Yes," I told her.

To Save a Life

The nephrologist told me the best match for a kidney transplant was a sibling. I said to myself, *They know I need a kidney. If they want to give me one, they'll get tested. I shouldn't have to ask.* I did not want to hear "No" to my face. I convinced myself that it was okay that my brothers did not give me a kidney. Except that, every time I talked about it, every time I read a "kidney" poem, I cried. I knew people only did things that made sense to them. I did not have to agree with them. I just had to understand it from their perspectives. I spent years rationalizing my family's decision to not save me:

They are afraid they could die.

Organ donation is so new in the Hmong community, and they don't know a lot of people who have done it.

As Blong would later tell me, "They're not any different from other Hmong families. If I were sick, my parents probably would've done the same thing."

He was right. I have three first cousins, on *Niam*'s side of the family, who also have kidney disease. One of them has ten siblings, and a brother offered his kidney. She refused, saying her life was not as valuable as his. She'd lived her life already, and his life had not started yet. My cousin loved her siblings, and so she told all of them not to give her a kidney. After five years on the waiting list, she finally got a cadaver kidney. My other two cousins are men. The Hmong community values men more than women, so I thought maybe their families would save them. They did not. At first I was puzzled, but then I remembered that at the reception for my kidney donor and me, Kai said, "Now, that I've seen this, I know you won't die if you donate a kidney." He really believed he could die if he gave me a kidney, and that family probably did, too.

If the choice was saving yourself or someone else, most of us would save ourselves.

I know all this. Still, it hurts. The result is the same: my family did not save me when they could have. Like a wound with its scab peeled off, this knowledge is still red and raw. The truth is, it was not okay for my family to not give me a kidney. I can be mad at them for not saving me. I can be mad at them for abandoning me. I was on my own. After a decade, there is still a part of me that is not sure I can count on them for other things, even small things.

One day, my cousin and her boyfriend, Eric, visited me and my roommate at our apartment near Macalester College. I asked Eric to get me a box of dialysis solution from the basement. When he asked what it was, I told him that both of my kidneys didn't work so I had to do dialysis to live. He offered me one of his kidneys. At first, I did not believe him. *Why would this man offer me one of his kidneys? He's not family*, I thought to myself.

"Why would you do this," I asked him later.

"Because I can," he said.

"What happens if your one kidney fails?"

"Then my dad will give me one of his, or my two brothers, or my uncles or my cousins."

"Will it make you weaker or slower?"

"No, you only need one kidney. It can do the work of both."

"Will it affect your chances of being a cop?"

"No, I just can't be in the FBI or CIA."

"Well, what do your parents think about your decision?"

"It's up to me. It's my decision."

"Yeah, I know, but what do they think? How do they feel about it?"

"They're happy for me. They're happy that I would want to do it."

"What does your girlfriend think?"

"She's fine with it, too."

"Are you sure?"

"Yes, I want to do this. I've wanted to do this ever since I carried that box of dialysis solution up the stairs for you."

I told *Niam* about Eric's offer. "How are you going to repay him?" she asked.

It was an important question. I did not know. I would offer him my arm, but it was on the skinny side. I suspected he would not take it.

"How do I repay you?" I asked Eric.

Eric shook his head and smiled. "You don't need to."

Months after he had made the offer, I had not accepted.

"Is it because I'm white that you don't want my kidney? Is my kidney not good enough for you?" asked Eric.

The truth was when my own brothers would not give me their kidneys, I'd spent years convincing myself it was okay for them to make that choice. It was also okay for this friend to not give me his kidney. I had a hard time believing he was serious. And if he was, I could not accept his gift because I could not repay him.

Once I said "Yes," Eric got himself tested. It was not the best match, so the doctors told us to wait six months to see if anything came up on the transplant list. When nothing did, Eric went back for more lab work. Finally, the doctors set August 7, 1997, as the transplant date.

I BLINKED A COUPLE TIMES at the bag of liquid at the top of the table. I didn't have my glasses on, but I knew that bag had not been there before.

"What's that?" I asked the nurse.

"That's your new kidney making urine."

I sat up. "Really? Already?"

"Yes!"

The bag of light yellow liquid was the sun waking up.

It felt like I'd just closed my eyes, and yet I knew it had been hours since that early morning ride to Hennepin County Medical Center. Eric's parents and my family were there. My pastor and cousin were there also. I knew our families were nervous, but Eric and I were ready.

I reached down on the right side of my pelvis. There it was, my "new" kidney, just below the skin. It hadn't settled in yet. My right hand lay gingerly on top of it. It was huge, stretching the full length of my hand, it seemed. I could feel its warmth, pulsating with life. It was strange to think that Eric's kidney was now in me.

I cradled my new kidney and whispered a little prayer to it: "Please. Stay. You and I are one now. Stay. We will learn to live together."

While Eric was recovering from the surgery, I skipped into his room to see how he was doing. I don't remember any pain, only excitement that the new kidney was already making urine. Eric's nine-inch scar on the right side wrapped from the back to the front. Post-surgery, he was laid up in bed for six weeks. The pain became bearable without medication after two months. Even now, pain is still there once in awhile.

My aunts, uncles, and members of the First Hmong Baptist Church came to see Eric and me. It seemed we had an endless stream of visitors who came to pray for us, brought us food, or just came to sit with our families. For as many days as we were there, they came or called. Our family members took over one end of the hallway. With so many family surrounding me, for the first time I did not feel like a lonely orphan. I felt loved.

It Takes a Family

When Blong and I started dating, one of his relatives, who had not been in touch with his parents for over two decades, called them. She told Blong's mom to not let him date me, the sick one. She offered healthy daughters for him.

This relative was married to a man from *Niam*'s Vue clan and lived in Wisconsin. Though I did not know them, they knew my family well. Years later, Blong and I accompanied his aunt to visit this childhood friend of hers. On her wall, I saw pictures of my maternal grandfather and uncles, their leaders.

"Ask Blong nicely for her telephone number," said *Niam* when I asked her if she knew this specific Vue woman. *Niam* did not know the woman, but it was not hard to find out who she was from *Niam*'s Vue relatives in Wisconsin. *Niam* was angry that a *nyab* from her own clan would cast *Niam*'s daughter aside so easily. She wanted to call and give this *nyab* a piece of her mind.

"I hope they get renal disease. And I hope there's no one to save them," cursed *Niam*.

I understood *Niam*'s anger. She was a mama bear standing tall, screaming at anyone or anything that threatened to harm her cub.

Because I had kidney disease and a transplant, Hmong people were convinced I would not be able to conceive. I explained that my kidneys were sick, not my womb, and that both were in different parts of the body. They were not convinced. They believed that even if I was able to have kids, I would pass kidney failure to them. A young Hmong woman on dialysis was even told that if she had kids, her kids would be retarded. Hmong parents feared I would die tomorrow or I would not be able to take care of their son or them. They did not want me anywhere near their sons.

For these reasons, the bride price was even more important to *Niam*. In her eyes, I was damaged goods. To her, if Blong's family paid the requested bride price, it meant they wanted to marry me. It meant they would treat me right despite kidney failure and a transplant.

"*Niam*, Blong and I are marrying each other. I'm not marrying his family," I said.

"Mai, you're wrong," said Kai. "That's not how it is."

I knew what he meant. As with many other groups, for Hmong people, when you marry, you are marrying his or her whole family. This affects how young Hmong people make decisions about our mates. It certainly did for Kai and me. Kai, as the son most likely to take care of *Niam*, knew he had to find a wife who could get along with her. His future wife had to be okay with *Niam* living with them. She had to accept the responsibility of taking care of *Niam*.

In Laos, it took a whole family or clan to marry a woman. The groom would not have the resources to cover the requested bride price, monetary gifts for the bride's family members, money to "right" offenses or settle old clan problems, payment to the family members who will go to the *rooj tshoob*, and expenses for food and drink. Thus, he needed his parents and uncles to pay for his wife.

Even if the groom has the money for the *rooj tshoob*, he can't marry his bride on his own. If he is animist, before he can bring her into his parents' house, an elder needs to *lwm qaib*. In this "chicken blessing," the elder moves a live chicken in a circular motion above the couple's heads. The elder chants words that sweep away wandering evil spirits, sickness, and misfortune. He asks for children who will come with the spirits of fortune, prosperity, cultivation, nurturing, and kinsmanship.

With the bride securely inside the house, the in-laws send two messengers to inform the bride's parents that she is safe with them and they intend to marry her. Then three days later, the family conducts a *hu plig* for her. *Hu plig* is a soul-calling ritual that welcomes, introduces, and incorporates the bride's souls into the spiritual domain of the groom's family. This means she no longer belongs to her family of birth but that of her husband's family. It is done so they are all joined spiritually as well as physically.

Hu plig involves family members tying white strings around the bride's and groom's hands while whispering blessings such as children, good health, and money. It concludes with a meal to introduce the new *nyab* to the extended family members. All these things must be done before the *rooj tshoob* can take place at the home of the bride's parents.

The *rooj tshoob* can be a two-day process. In addition to the bride and groom, you need two elders (one from the bride's side and one from the groom's side) to be in charge of the *rooj tshoob*. They watch over the process and listen to everything. Next, you need *mej koob* from each side to negotiate the terms of the marriage, including the bride price. These negotiators represent the wishes of the parents. Then, you need the best man to help the groom drink and kowtow to the bride's family members, and the maid of honor to watch over the bride. Finally, the bride's parents summon the important men of their clan to sit at the table as witnesses.

The *mej koob* have to know when to sing the appropriate songs or chants that accompany each of the different types of *rooj tshoob* (from the ones for a single woman to the ones for divorced women versus widowed women). They may need to be skilled at conflict resolution or at speaking "sweet words" that could win people's hearts. This is especially important in situations where there has been a lot of supposed wrongdoings between the two clans or families. Sometimes, these wrongdoings even include things that happened a long time ago and have nothing to do with the current couple who happen to be from the same two clans.

Once negotiations are completed, the bride price is paid.

The *rooj tshoob* is then typically followed by the *noj rooj tshoob*. The bride's family spends days preparing a big feast for their extended family members and neighbors who come with gifts for the bride (dowry). The *noj rooj tshoob* gives the bride's family "face" since all who come are witnesses to the marriage. The bride's brothers, male cousins, and uncles welcome and introduce themselves to the groom with shots of alcohol. As *Niam* said, "If you don't do this then people don't know what to call you." The drink is an official acceptance of each other. The more male relatives, the better since it shows the strength of the family/clan. This is an opportunity to test the new brother-in-law.

At the end of the *noj rooj tshoob*, the groom, the bride, and their entourage return to the groom's parents' house. The groom's family then thanks everyone on their side with a meal and gifts (usually cash).

This is how Hmong parents show that they love you; they do all this for their kids. For their sons, they pay the bride prices which don't need to be paid back. For their daughters, extended family members contribute gifts toward her dowry so she may start her new life. Family members love you by showing up to cook, clean, eat, and be witnesses to the marriage.

The newly married young man may not know it yet, but all of this obligates him to his father, uncles, and clan. They will not let him forget that they got him his wife. For this, he and his wife are indebted to them, sometimes forever.

A way for the couple to settle the debt is to live with the in-laws and repay them with their services. This is a chance to incorporate the daughter-in-law into the husband's household. In reality, it's an opportunity for the mother-in-law to instruct the *nyab* in how she wants to run

her household. The family then will guide the newly married couple in
their responsibilities.

Animist Hmong parents live with their sons because not only did they
pay a large portion of the *rooj tshoob*, but they will also help their sons set
up their lives. After all this, the sons are obligated to take care of their
parents in their old age and after death.

For a long time, I did not understand why Hmong parents could not
live with their daughters, especially the single ones who were gainfully
employed and had their own homes. It seemed to make the most sense,
since mother and daughter would get along better than mother and
daughter-in-law.

Were Hmong people just sexist pigs who did not value women? I
wondered.

What I failed to understand was the issue of religious beliefs and practices. Hmong parents need to live with their sons because only they share
the same religious performance of rituals. This distinguishes one family
or clan from another. It means you can die in each other's homes without
offending the spirits.

For Hmong parents, the sons are the ones who can ensure that the
relatives conduct the funeral rites correctly. This is important because it
guarantees safe passage of the soul of the deceased to the spirit world,
where they will reunite with their ancestors and be reborn.

In addition to strict adherence to the funeral rites, after the burial of
the body, there is the "soul-release" ritual that the sons need to conduct
to release the soul of the deceased for rebirth. After this ritual, each son
then has to perform the *nyuj dab* for each parent. As an uncle told me,
"Every parent owes their son a wife, and every son owes their parents a
nyuj dab." *Nyuj dab* is a ritual where a cow is sacrificed for each deceased
parent when they request it. The parents communicate their needs via
dreams. Or they could make you very sick or bring bad luck and misfortune to your family. A shaman then will be called and may determine
that it is your parents requiring a *nyuj dab*.

Finally, because the animist Hmong believe that the deceased still need food and money in the spirit world, the sons provide these offerings on special occasions such as the New Year and weddings through the *laig dab* ritual. This is a ritual where, before the family can eat, a little bit of meat must be offered to the deceased ancestors who are called back by name. Only the sons can perform ancestral rites such as *laig dab*.

In theory, Hmong parents who are Christians could live with their single daughters. However, if their daughters marry animist men, they can't live with them anymore. That's because when Hmong women marry, we leave our families and live with our husbands. We take on their family's religious rituals. Animist Hmong believe it is a violation of religious practices for people of different religious rituals to live in the same house.

As a church girl, I know that if I marry an animist man, I would have to give up belief in my God. This is the expectation. At my cousin's *rooj tshoob*, the men counseled her to conform to be like her new family when they said, "If they are a family of thieves, you become a thief like them." That translation is too literal, but they said it in a way that Hmong American kids such as me would understand.

Certainly, if the daughter married another Christian, the parents could hypothetically live with the couple. But they would be moving into their son-in-law's house. Thus, Hmong parents would rather live with their own sons.

Divorce is problematic for Hmong women. When we divorce our husbands, we also divorce our husband's spiritual world and religious rituals. But since we've left our family of origin's spiritual world, our souls do not belong there either.

Divorced Hmong women are then left in this void. In Laos, they came back home to their parents and lived in a separate shed nearby. But their souls were never incorporated back into the family's spiritual world.

They could make themselves desirable again so other men will marry them. This way, their souls can belong to the new husband's spiritual world.

Or if they have a son, they could continue to live with him after the divorce. When they die, that son will carry on the religious rituals of his father for them. If a woman has no sons, however, no one will claim her. There is nowhere to send her soul. She will wander in the land of darkness with no ancestors to return to.

Finally, a divorced woman could become Christian, thus bypassing the animist rituals. As a Christian, she doesn't need anyone to send her spirit to God the Father.

Spinsters and widows without male children are in the same situation as divorcées. They too are menless women. As such, they have the same options. This is why spinsters, divorcées, and widows without male children are always looking for a place to die, a place where their spirits may rest.

LIFE AFTER DEATH is a very important issue for Hmong parents. Animist or Christian, it is hard for them to change these long-held values just because they now believe in different spirits.

As the mother of two young daughters, I now understand why Hmong parents always urge me to have sons. I thought they were annoying, telling me how to live my life. It was I who didn't understand that they were concerned about the well-being of my husband and me in our old age and after death.

And this is why Hmong parents value males more than females. Only the sons can conduct the funeral and other mortuary rituals to ensure safe passage of the deceased's soul to the ancestors so that it may be reborn. Only they can perform other ancestral rituals to feed the souls of the deceased.

Not Good for the Family

Growing up, on TV and in the movies I saw plenty of "American" church weddings with the white wedding dresses. I've also been a bridesmaid in a handful of American weddings. In my cousin's case, she had the *rooj tshoob* first. Then a year later, she had her wedding ceremony outside a nice restaurant where she also had her reception.

My other cousin and Eric had a church wedding. Her father, who was my pastor at First Hmong Baptist Church, said, "This wedding belongs to you. Do what you want. Let me know what you need. We'll come and enjoy it."

My cousin didn't have to decide if she was going to run off with Eric or get "kidnapped." Eric met with Pastor Vang and asked him for permission to marry his daughter. Pastor Vang chose to not go through the *rooj tshoob* process with the *mej koob, lwm qaib* (chicken blessing), and bride price. Instead, my cousin and Eric had a ceremony in the church and a wonderful reception with family and friends. And afterward, we went to Eric's parents' house to open up wedding gifts.

I, too, wanted an American church wedding where the focus was on the bride and groom.

I thought perhaps *Niam* would listen to Pastor Vang. We'd known him since we came to the United States in 1981. He had helped our family through many things, including the transplant. I also thought maybe *Niam* would listen to Uncle Naw-Karl, one of the few uncles with whom *Niam* has not argued or fallen out of favor. He immigrated to France instead of the United States. I did not meet him until 1985, when his family moved to Minnesota. Uncle was also an ordained minister.

Like young Hmong men who consulted with their fathers and clan leaders when they wanted to get married, I consulted with my leaders in the church. Both had met Blong and liked him. I do not remember what I said to them, but it must have been something along the lines of, "Blong and I want to get married. *Niam* wants to collect a bride price. I don't want one. What do I do?"

I asked both to come talk with *Niam*, Kai, and me. Pastor Vang, Uncle and Aunt Naw-Karl, *Niam*, Kai, and I met at the Margaret Street house. *Niam*'s main concern was that I had kidney failure and a transplant. We all knew what Hmong people thought of me.

"When Mai Neng was sick, we were not able to save her. Now that she's been saved, the wedding should be a happy occasion for us to celebrate life," said Pastor Vang.

Pastor Vang and Uncle calmed *Niam*'s fears about Blong's family not wanting to marry me. We settled on not collecting a bride price. We decided to let the church take care of the wedding.

Kai worried that since we had not invited the other uncles to be part of the discussion and decision-making, they would be upset. But *Niam* said that since we had already made our decision, we did not need to involve them in the talks. We would invite them to the wedding and reception. We agreed that the next step was for me to ask Blong for his father's telephone number so that Uncle Naw-Karl could call him and work out the details of how to do the *rooj tshoob*.

Three days after the discussion, Kai approached me.

"Mai, the decision you made is not good for the Moua family. It's only good for you and your pastors."

Uncle Naw-Karl had not had a chance to call Blong's father yet.

"What are you talking about?" I asked. "*Niam* agreed to not collect a bride price."

"No, Mai. You did," said Kai. "What you want is not good for the Moua family."

And who the fuck is the Moua family? I wanted to scream, but Kai had already walked away.

Kai wasn't wrong. With my father's death, Hmong culture dictated that my uncles assume responsibility for my brothers and me. This meant making decisions about important things such as illnesses and the *rooj tshoob*. Talking with my leaders in the church about marriage had deeply offended my uncles. I didn't understand that even though I was Christian, being Hmong superseded that. As some of own church leaders have said themselves, "We are Hmong first." Hmong people believed that my membership in the Moua clan still prevailed, and thus, I should not have ignored my clan leaders (even if they did not share the same faith).

Leaving my uncles out of the marriage conversation meant that we did not think they were important. It meant that we thought we could make this decision on our own. Truth is, in Hmong culture, wedding negotiations are not done by two women and a young man. They are made by *mej koob*, designated representatives of both families. Furthermore, my uncles did not agree with the decision to not collect a bride price. They were livid with all of us.

Later, *Niam* told me that she, too, had been angry with my pastors and me.

"If we were in the middle of the *rooj tshoob* and the pastors came and told me to not collect a bride price, that's one thing. But Blong's family hadn't even come yet, and there you all were, telling me to not collect a bride price," said *Niam*. "It was so backwards."

After the discussion at my house, Kai and another uncle or uncles who had not been invited to the meeting drove down to *Niam*'s garden to talk to her. They made the one-hour drive there because *Niam* was hardly ever home.

But none of the uncles said a word to me. In their eyes, the marriage negotiations were not between them and me. They were between them and Blong's family. There was no need to talk to me.

None of these uncles called or yelled at Uncle Naw-Karl directly, either. Instead, they called his stepbrother to get him to exert pressure on Uncle. I remembered Uncle's story of how, at the request of an animist family, he went and talked to them about God the Father. One of the family's relatives, however, complained to his stepbrother. The stepbrother called Uncle and said, "If you do that, you're dividing the families spiritually." Uncle said he was doing his job and then acknowledged that Christians and animists are divided spiritually.

For the most part, the uncles were passive-aggressive, ignoring Uncle Naw-Karl, not inviting him for family functions, or, when they saw him at a family function, refusing to shake his hand. The handshake is an acknowledgment that says, "I know who you are. I see you, Hmong man." It recognizes both as equals on the same level.

One of the uncles, however, called up Pastor Vang and accused him of trying to "steal" my family into his clan. This uncle told my pastor that he had no right to talk to us about the *rooj tshoob*. Although I did not know the full extent of their conversation, I could hear Pastor Vang saying, "I am their pastor. They asked me to come and talk to them as they have done in the past. I am doing my job. When they ask, I come." Not only did this uncle call and yell at Pastor Vang, but some members of his own congregation gave him grief about it, too. Something along the lines of "meddling" in another clan's affairs.

Apparently, Uncle Naw-Karl's opinion did not count as much as the other uncles'. Although he is one of the sons of our late clan leader, he was not the oldest. He was also a pastor, while most of the other uncles were animists who practiced ancestral worship and shamanism. While Uncle Naw-Karl called on God the Father for guidance, my other uncles called on the ancestors. Some of my uncles were even shamans who, with the help of shaman spirits, traveled into the spirit world in search of the lost souls of sick people. This skill was highly respected, as it is only when the shaman brings the lost souls back to the body that the sick person recovers and is whole again. Although we were family, we each believed in our own religious systems. We were separated spiritually. Thus, Uncle Naw-Karl's opinions were only valued on matters that dealt with the church and God. Most of the uncles, even his own stepbrother, believed he had no say on issues that dealt with traditional Hmong rituals or cultural practices such as the *rooj tshoob*.

With so many uncles in the Minneapolis–St. Paul area, who was the one in charge here? Was it the oldest one? I was not even sure who that was. Was it the loudest or most argumentative? There were a couple of those. Was it the most educated? I did not think so since people did not listen to Uncle Naw-Karl. Was it the richest uncle? I was not sure who that was. Was it the most respected? Most respected by whom—non-Hmong people, Hmong men, Hmong women? Was it the most capable? Capable of what? Most skilled at talking? The one who knew traditional Hmong rituals the best?

I had no idea how to navigate this minefield. Besides my two pastors, I did not know whom to talk to or what to do next. With every step I took, I was afraid I would land on a mine that would blow me to pieces. Since our clan leader passed away in 1992 in Laos, ideally the next person in line would be his oldest son, who lived in Thailand. But was his leadership strong enough to reach all the way here in the United States? Was it relevant here?

When the uncles got involved in any issue, the issue was no longer an individual one, but a clan one. Whether *Niam* wanted a bride price became moot. I could hear my uncles literally saying, "This is our responsibility. Let us take care of our business."

One of Blong's good friends talked with her dad before she asked her fiancé to come to the house to ask for her hand in marriage. Her father was a military official in General Vang Pao's army. She asked him to not collect a bride price. He promised he would not. She trusted him. There was no reason to think he would lie to her. When her fiancé came to her house with the *mej koob*, everything changed. As the marriage negotiations progressed, her uncles pressured her father into collecting a bride price. Although he stood firm in his promise, the uncles stated that he was a well-respected military officer. It was appropriate to request a bride price for his daughter, who had graduated from college and was making good money as a consultant for an international firm. They told him that it was wrong to not collect a bride price when the rest of the Hmong world did. There was not much her father could do or say against the uncles, especially since one of them was negotiating on his behalf. Blong's friend's fiancé and his family had come to her house to ask for her hand. They obviously wanted to marry her. In the end, they acquiesced to a rather large bride price. If a well-respected military man could not change the collective will of the clan, a woman had no chance.

Captured

What do you do when you do not know what to do?

What **do** you do when you **do not know** what to do?

What do **you** do when you do not know what to do?

In frightening situations, people fight, flee, or freeze. When the talks with *Niam* and Kai broke down, I did not know what to do or whom to talk to, so I froze. The uncles wanted Blong to do the *rooj tshoob* and pay a bride price.

"As long as you can guarantee that you won't collect a bride price, I'll ask Blong to come," I told Kai.

"No, Mai," said Kai.

I had no choice, it seemed.

"Just get it done. The most important thing is to get married, right?" asked my cousin.

Although Kai was the only one who said it, I knew everyone else was thinking the same thing: "Most Hmong couples have to pay a bride price. Why not you and Blong? What makes you so special that you should not have to do it? Who do you think you are?"

Who? One of the lucky survivors who did not die in the Secret War along with the estimated thirty-five thousand who did. One of the hundred thousand who became refugees in their homeland. A three-year-old who lost her father, her paternal grandparents, and uncles on both sides of the family in the Secret War. The child of a war widow who worked her ass off so her kids would not die of starvation or disease along the way to the Mekong River or in the refugee camp in Thailand. The daughter of a woman whose bride price has been an anchor weight around her neck, threatening to sink her to the bottom of the ocean. A girl who, when she heard her mother's stories of the bride price, made a vow never to have one. A transplant patient who knows that Hmong parents do not want their sons anywhere near her. A Hmong American woman who dares to ask, "Why can't I?" A Hmong American who has spent twenty-one of her twenty-eight years in the United States.

"What is this really about?" asked a therapist friend to whom I had been crying.

"I don't know," I said.

My mind was a glass of dirty water. There was so much going on. I could not let the dirt in the water settle down. I kept stirring it and stirring it, hoping to see through to the other side.

"My relationship with *Niam*," I concluded.

If that was true, then I should go ahead and give *Niam* what she wanted. I decided to try to convince Blong to *tuaj nqis tsev hais* and pay the bride price.

"Are you doing this because you want to?" asked Blong. "Because your mom wants you to? Your uncles? I thought you didn't want a bride price."

I did not want a bride price. *Just tell me what to think, what to do,* I wanted to tell him. I was tired of fighting. I wanted Blong to take control, but he did not. Perhaps, even back then, he knew that when we were old, he did not want me to blame him for what happened. He did not want me to say, "It was your fault. You told us to do it this way."

I talked to *Niam* about the uncles.

"All our lives, we've not needed those people. What have they done for us? You've fought with all of them. They've broken your heart. Now, at this critical moment, you're going to let them make this decision for us? Don't give them this power. We can do this on our own."

But it was too late. The clan had taken over. What I wanted did not matter. What *Niam* wanted did not matter. What Kai wanted did not matter. We did not matter. It was about the clan asserting its power and authority. The clan was the Borg, a collective from *Star Trek* that took other species and forced them to function as drones of the collective. The Borg is the juggernaut against which "Resistance is futile."

I called to consult with Uncle Naw-Karl. Aunt told me that Uncle was in Thailand on a missionary project. For weeks and then months, I tried unsuccessfully to reach him. It was only later that I learned what happened to him.

In mid-May 2003, Uncle went to Thailand to build a church. While there, he met Belgian journalist Thierry Falise and French photographer Vincent Reynaud. He became their interpreter, and the three of them went to Laos toward the end of May. In northern Laos, they visited the Hmong Chao Fa, former soldiers who fought with General Vang Pao and the CIA against the Communist Pathet Lao and the North Vietnamese. This group included women, elderly, and children. They had old weapons and ammunition and little access to medical facilities, food, or other basic services. They were reportedly too afraid of retribution from the Lao government to lay down their arms and surrender. Amnesty International and the United Nations High Commissioner for Refugees have confirmed human rights abuses against this group by the Lao government.

In early June, Uncle and the two journalists were arrested by the Lao government for "obstructing security forces" or possession of weapons or both. The charges stemmed from an incident in which Hmong Chao Fa clashed with local security forces. In early July, all three were sentenced to fifteen years in prison after a two-and-a-half-hour trial. After intense pressure from the Belgian, French, and U.S. governments, they were released and returned home in mid-July.

I finally connected with Uncle after his release. When I told him what had happened and asked for his help again, he laughed and said, "Oh, I thought you had taken care of that already."

"I wish I had, Uncle. I wish I had."

I knew my issue of the bride price paled in comparison to being captured at gunpoint, thrown in jail, and then sentenced to fifteen years in prison without due process. I wanted Uncle to work a miracle. I, too, wanted to be released. But my uncle and I did not have the same authority as the Belgian, French, or U.S. governments. I certainly did not have anything my other uncles needed or wanted. I had one of two choices: go ahead with the planned American church wedding, or cancel it and wait for my family to work out the details of the *rooj tshoob*.

"Do you have to get married?" asked Pastor Vang when I consulted him.

What he meant was, *Are you pregnant?* but Hmong culture prevented him from being that blunt.

"No, I don't have to get married. I want to," I assured him.

Pastor Vang advised me to give Blong a test by asking him to *tuaj nqis tsev hais*. "If he really wants to marry you, he'll do it," he said.

I understood his logic, but coming to my house meant that Blong's family would pay a bride price. I did not want that. I decided not to give Blong the test.

Niam threatened me: "You don't do a *rooj tshoob* for us, we may not come to your [church] wedding."

"Wait until we do the *rooj tshoob*," she said. She asked me to change the August 2003 date of the church wedding.

Niam kept herself busy, working on her garden and sleeping at the farm. She did not want to waste any time making the hour drive between St. Paul and Lonsdale every day. Kai and I were lucky to see her twice a week when she came home to get more supplies. Yia had his own apartment, so we did not see him much. Kai and I were home, but we did not speak to each other.

Kai threatened me: "If you don't do a *rooj tshoob*, we won't tell people you're married. We'll just tell them you ran away."

He meant, since the *rooj tshoob* sanctifies our wedding, no *rooj tshoob* meant no wedding. He would tell people that I was living in sin or that I ran away like some worthless girl.

He warned: "Don't *tu siab* if we don't come to the wedding."

Literally, *tu siab* translates as "broken liver." It is the equivalent of a broken heart. Really, though, *tu siab* signifies an even deeper wound with deep longing. It is the lonely orphan with no one to help him or her.

My rational mind understood that, for Hmong people, these rituals and traditions were synonymous with their identity. It was probably impossible to change their minds. Still, I was hopeful, ever so hopeful. I kept trying to think of ways to make things work. If I had gone straight to *Niam* and conspired with her, could we women united (assuming I was able to get *Niam* on my side) have convinced the uncles to not collect a bride price? Could *Niam*, Kai, and I (assuming I was able to get Kai on my side) have convinced the uncles to not collect a bride price? If I thought hard enough, could I have found a way to compromise? If I waited long enough, would people have changed their minds?

Everyone told me, "We are Hmong. This is what we do."

There was no middle ground between the bride price and no bride price. I was stuck.

But Blong and I did not want to wait. It had been three months since the conversation with Pastor Vang and Uncle Naw-Karl. Blong and I had taken care of what we had control over: reserving a church and reception hall and sending out the invitations. Our friends from Arkansas, California, New York, and Indiana had already purchased plane tickets. Besides, I did not know when or if the *rooj tshoob* would ever take place.

Being Hmong and American

My collection of Hmong clothes consisted of four outfits. There was the White Hmong skirt, the Green Hmong skirt, the simple black satin pants, and the green-flowered pants with their matching shirts and aprons. Each outfit came with red and green sashes and either a traditional maroon headdress or a hat with coins and *paj ntaub* ("flower cloth" or needlework) on the sides. There were the four appliqué and reverse appliqué moneybags. With the exception of the skirts, *Niam* had made all of it. Then there were the accessories: the two-pound silver neckpiece and twenty-four-karat gold earrings, bracelets, and necklaces. The value of this whole ensemble was thousands of dollars. It took years to sew, buy, and collect the different pieces.

I never learned to sew the traditional Hmong shirts and pants. The closest I got to making one was when Eric married my cousin. As a gift, *Niam* and I wanted to sew him a Hmong outfit. We went to the Hmong store and bought yards and yards of plain black satin cloth. *Niam* cut the cloth for the pants for me, and using her Singer sewing machine, I stitched it together. Since my family is Green Hmong, the pants look like M.C. Hammer pants—baggy in the buttocks and narrow at the ankles. White Hmong pants do not have the baggy crotch. For the shirt, *Niam* borrowed a male cousin's black shirt to use as the pattern. She cut the cloth and then asked me to sew it. All I saw was two sheets of black cloth in a heap on the floor. Without a pattern or step-by-step instructions, I did not know where to begin.

"You're how old now? How come you don't know how to sew this?" demanded *Niam*.

"Because I never learned how to do it. How many girls my age know how to sew a Hmong outfit? I'm not the only one."

"You're going to be a wife and a mother soon, and you don't even know how to sew."

"No, I don't know how to sew a Hmong pant and shirt. You've always made them or we've bought them from the Hmong store. When have we sat down together to make one?"

"Oh, so now it's my fault."

"Yes."

It was partially *Niam*'s fault for not forcing me to sit down and do it. But the truth was that I was too busy with school, extracurricular activities, and work on the weekends. Even these things sound like lame excuses as I write them now. I guess I did not pay attention when *Niam* was sewing because I did not think I needed to know how to do it.

Niam snatched the materials out of my hands and sewed the shirt herself. I watched her do it, but I still did not get it. She then asked me to lengthen the two *paj ntaub* sashes to which the two moneybags were attached. Men wore the sashes across their chests. At five-eleven, Eric was taller than the average Hmong man. I had to add several patches of red and green cloths to the sashes to make them longer. It was easy to spot where *Niam*'s small-as-an-ant work ended and mine—the fat stitches of a child—began.

In Laos, Hmong girls spent hours sewing *paj ntaub*. Skilled *paj ntaub* sewers, like *Niam*, made their stitches small and consistent like a sewing machine. Using bright red, green, orange, or blue threads, they sewed intricate needlework in styles such as embroidery, appliqué, and reverse appliqué. I loved reverse appliqué the most. It was when you layered a piece of white cloth on top of a colored cloth. You then cut different patterns on the white cloth, folded back the edges, and sewed the edges in place onto the colored cloth. In this way, different patterns revealed themselves on the colored cloths. For example, many Hmong *paj ntaub* have the jagged patterns of mountains or the swirls of snails. I read somewhere that the mountains were protective barriers and the snails stood for the different generations. A non-Hmong friend said she had heard the spirals were tigers' eyes. I did not know. I did not sew *paj ntaub* and thus did not know the significance of the patterns. To me, they were just geometric shapes in pretty colors.

Girls sewed *paj ntaub* on the rectangular collars attached to the back of the shirts, on the aprons, the sashes, and the moneybags. If you were Green Hmong, the green and red skirt would be covered with *paj ntaub*. A girl's skill or laziness showed in the quality of her *paj ntaub* on her Hmong costume, which she wore at the Hmong New Year for all to see. No Hmong man wanted to marry a lazy girl.

In the United States, few girls sewed *paj ntaub* or made their own Hmong clothes anymore. We did not have the time. Besides, since Hmong families had more money now, we bought them from relatives in Laos or Thailand. Or you could easily find them at Hmong stores, the Hmong New Year, or the July Fourth Sports Tournament at McMurray Field in St. Paul. You could even find them at Hmong funerals, where women sat, gossiped, and sometimes passed around *paj ntaub* for sale during the three days the audience was held captive. This was as tacky as the men playing cards, I thought, but what did I know? I did not go to the funeral all day, every day for three days straight.

The morning of the wedding, I woke up at 6:00 AM and drove downtown to the St. Paul Farmer's Market. I looked for *Niam*'s blue cargo van. Unlike the other Hmong farmers who drove white trucks, *Niam* drove a former glass company van. Although the "Free Steaks & Glass" words had been removed from the side of the van, their imprints were still visible.

"What are you doing here?" asked *Niam* when she saw me.

"I came to help you," I said.

Niam did not refuse my help. As usual, she was by herself. Neither of my brothers were there helping her. *Niam* was still setting up her table. There was usually a morning rush of early shoppers who came at 7:00 AM. *I should be here every week, helping her*, I thought with some guilt. I crouched down near the bucket of green beans. I could tell from the fresh leaves in the bucket that *Niam* had picked them the night before. I grabbed a handful of beans, stacked them like sardines in the green tray, and then set the tray on the table. Four trays of green beans in a row in four neat rows.

"How much for the green beans?" asked a middle-aged white woman.

"They're three dollars a tray or two trays for five dollars," I answered.

"When were these picked?"

"Last night."

"They look really nice."

"Yeah, they're nice and young. Would you like to try one?" I picked out a green bean and handed it to the woman. She snapped it in half and ate one of the halves.

"Mmm. They're really good." The woman nodded. "I'll take a tray, please."

I threw the three dollars into a small basket on the ground. I grabbed the empty tray and plopped a handful of green beans inside. I shook the beans in place and set the tray on the table in the open spot.

"*Niam*, would you allow me to wear my Hmong clothes for the wedding?" I asked.

Blong and I were Christian, and it was important for us to be married in a church. Instead of the white wedding dress and tuxedo, however, we wanted to be married in our Hmong clothes. For us, it was a blending of our two worlds—Hmong and American—into one. *Niam* continued throwing empty buckets in the back of the van. She did not look at me. She did not answer me.

"Why would you come and ask for such a ridiculous thing?" asked *Niam* after what seemed like ten frozen minutes. "You've decided to do the American wedding. You've asked an American pastor to come and do everything. Why would you wear your Hmong clothes in an American wedding?"

Niam looked straight at me. There was no gleam in her eyes. Her mouth was in a straight line.

I wanted to say, *Because I am Hmong. Because it is important to me. Because I want to,* but I did not. The words were logs lodged in my throat. It was not that I did not know how to say them in Hmong. It was more that those words seemed shallow and insufficient to express the enormity of the feelings. To explain why I wanted to honor both

my Hmong and American identities at the same time. *Niam* was right.
Those words were ridiculous. They could have been the same words
she used to explain why she wanted Blong to do the *rooj tshoob* and pay
a bride price.

Why should I have to pay a bride price when I marry? I imagined myself
asking *Niam*.

Because we're Hmong. Because it's important to me. Because I want you to,
I could hear her say.

I begged *Niam* with my eyes, but she did not blink. Certainly, I could
have taken the clothes and worn them for the wedding. *Niam* had spent
a quarter of a century collecting, sewing, and buying the different pieces
specifically for me. They were mine. I had worn them for many Hmong
New Year celebrations at the St. Paul Civic Center. I knew that *Niam*
kept them in the suitcases in her room. But the Hmong ensemble and
accessories were usually given to the bride at the *rooj tshoob* as part of
the dowry. I wanted *Niam* to give them to me. I needed her permission.
She was not going to give either to me. I stood up without saying anything else to *Niam*. I left as I had come, empty-handed. I ran to the
car, got in, and locked the doors. Tears streamed down my face. I had
known there was a possibility that *Niam* would say "No." Still, antici-
pating the answer and getting it did not make it hurt any less. I resorted
to plan B and called my cousin to borrow her Hmong clothes for the
wedding later that day.

The morning of the wedding, Eric and my cousin picked up Yia. He
wore the new suit and shoes I bought him for the occasion. I prayed that
Niam and Kai would change their minds. It was not that I did not believe
their threats to boycott the American church wedding. It was just that
somewhere along the line, I fell for the non-Hmong idea of unconditional love. I believed that, out of their unconditional love for me, they
would come.

But my Hmong girlfriends and I knew better. "Not Hmong people,"
we said. "If you don't do what they say, or if you disappoint them, they're
cutting off that love."

As a writer friend said, "In an imperfect world, all love is conditional."

I knew *Niam* and Kai disagreed with me, but somewhere along the line, I fell for another non-Hmong idea: "We'll agree to disagree." I honestly hoped they would still come to the wedding. But I knew Hmong people believe in consensus even if it means strong-arming or forcing someone to "accept" a particular decision.

I tried to tell myself that *Niam* and Kai had the right not to come to the church wedding just as I had the right to decide that I did not want a bride price. Their not coming was one of the consequences I had to pay for standing up for my beliefs. I told myself whatever they decided, I had to live with it. I should not be mad at them; I could not be mad at them. Although I knew it was a long shot, on the morning of the wedding, I left the wedding invitation on the dining room table in plain view before leaving to take pictures.

The Wedding, Take One

In typical American fashion, Blong's bachelor party the night before the wedding lasted into the morning. He and his brothers were late to Loring Park in Minneapolis, where we were to take pictures at noon. I could not help but be angry at him. He seemed giddy and carefree, or maybe his head was still buzzing from the hangover. He had no idea of my conversation with *Niam* earlier that morning.

It was sunny and warm, but the wild wind, reflective of my soul, tousled my hair this way and that way. The bridesmaids looked beautiful in their black dresses. The groomsmen cleaned up nicely in their suits. Like a contestant in a pageant, I smiled my way through the pictures. These, I was told, would be memories I would cherish the rest of my life. I could not wait to stop pretending.

Then, it was time to go to Jordan New Life Church, three blocks from Blong's house in north Minneapolis. It was time for Blong and me to change into our Hmong clothes so we could take staged pictures of the ceremony. Somehow, I ended up in a room alone with my cousin's suitcase of borrowed Hmong clothing: black velvet shirt, white skirt, apron, red and green sashes, purple turban, moneybags, and silver neckpiece. I had never put the Hmong ensemble on myself before. *Niam* was usually the one who put me together. First, she tied the skirt around my waist. Then, she told me to slip on the collared white shirt and the long-sleeved black shirt over that. *Niam* usually pinned the lapels of the black shirt together and folded them back to show off their blue color. She folded up the sleeves to show off their matching blue. Then she tied the apron around my waist so that it hid my front area where the two ends of the skirt came together. Next, she wrapped the red and green sashes around my waist so that the right color hung in the right place. I could never remember which color hung in the front and which one in the back. After the sashes, *Niam* tied the moneybags around my waist—one in the front and one in the back, or if there were four, the last two would go on the sides. Then I squeezed my head through the silver neckpiece. Finally, *Niam* carefully wrapped and rewrapped the turban around my head until it was evenly balanced on all sides. To complete the turban, she wrapped a zebra-colored sash around it so it looked like bee eyes. Then she tied a colorful scarf around my neck. I remember the too-long scarf with a hot pepper pattern that caused an argument between my pregnant bridesmaid and the photographer, something about how to tie it. The whole ensemble, however, was not complete until one slipped on the gold necklace, bracelets, and earrings. But I did not have these.

Luckily, Blong's aunt was available and made sure all the pieces were in the right place. Finally dressed in Hmong, I smiled my way through the role-play of the ceremony so we could take pictures. I did not have time to think about the absence of *Niam*, Kai, or my aunts and uncles.

There was no one to give me away. In my borrowed Hmong costume, I walked myself down the aisle to the altar, where Eric's dad was waiting with my bridesmaids, the groomsmen, and Blong. The coins on my Hmong costume jingled as I slowly approached Blong in his Hmong costume. The walk down the aisle was brief, and then I was at his side. Blong reached for my hand and gave it a quick squeeze.

The Wedding, Take Two

Four years after the church wedding, I still had not printed one picture of my wedding day. No pictures of the walk down the aisle in traditional Hmong clothes. No bride in her ivory off-the-shoulder dress from Macy's. No bridesmaids holding their bouquets of silk flowers made by the maid of honor. No groom surrounded by his groomsmen who were, I was sure, thinking, *This is your last moment of freedom. You sure you want to do this?* No bride and groom cutting the cake quilt, sixteen six-by-nine cakes baked by sixteen willing volunteers. No just-married couple facing the sea of mostly Caucasian faces.

It was not that we did not take any photos. Our photographer took hundreds of photos of us setting up the sanctuary and dining hall, the rehearsal at the church followed by the barbecue at Blong's house in north Minneapolis, the wedding party at Loring Park, and the ceremony. There were pictures of family and friends from near and far. There were even pictures of the Hmong dinner of eggrolls, beef laab, rice, and salad topped off with a purple orchid. These captured images sat undeveloped on a CD locked away somewhere in the house.

Why had I not developed the photographs? Was it because I was too busy? Was it because they would be too expensive? Was it because I was ashamed of what I had done and was hiding the evidence?

When *Niam* and Kai did not show up to the church wedding, when I heard that my uncles banned everyone in the family from coming, when I could count the family members at the wedding on two hands, I questioned my decision.

I had second thoughts when my family did not call me for a year, when Blong and I were not invited to family functions, when extended family members purposely asked if Blong was my boyfriend. When my family did not call Blong by his proper titles of *Vauv* or *Yawm Yij*, when I was most sad, I wondered if I had done the right thing.

Sometimes my extended family members looked at me as if they wanted to kill me, as if they could not stand the sight of me. I understood that they were being supportive of *Niam*. They were angry for her. They were feeling her pain and made sure I knew. None of them ever said a word to me. But their eyes told me that what I did was worse than living "in sin" with a boyfriend, marrying a non-Hmong man, having a child out of wedlock. It was even worse than marrying a black man. I know I am indicting a whole culture here, but most Hmong parents have a hierarchy of preferences when it comes to whom you should marry: Hmong first, then Caucasians or other Asians, and lastly black Americans. It did not seem to matter that I got married when I was twenty-nine, not fourteen. It did not matter that I married an attorney, a member of one of the professions toward which Hmong parents push their kids.

I was ready for a fight. Like *Niam*, I was quick with my tongue. It did not matter if my words came out in Hmong, English, or some combination of the two. My opponents would feel the venom. I knew enough dirt on all their kids that I was a pit bull ready to bite at the drop of a word. I stared back at the family members, daring them to say something to me. They never said anything to my face. Behind my back, however, they gossiped about what a bad daughter I was, how I thought I was so smart and didn't need to listen to anyone, what a bad example I was setting for younger cousins.

There were days when I fantasized about the huge weddings of other Hmong couples I had heard about or been to. These weddings were held at fancy hotels, where both families were happy for the couple. The ones where leaders such as General Vang Pao or Dr. Yang Dao, the first Hmong to earn a PhD, showed up. The ones who had a wedding party of thirty: twelve bridesmaids, twelve groomsmen, two ring bearers, and four flower girls. The ones that had five hundred guests. Although the couple did not know all the guests, as *Niam* stated, "They came because of the parents." Hmong people loved to show off that they could afford to feed five hundred people, all witnesses to their lavish weddings. These weddings were a way of giving face to the parents. Yes, it was superficial, but I wanted others to brag and gossip about my big wedding, too.

It was not that I wanted the headaches of a wedding party of thirty or the expenses of feeding five hundred guests I did not know or care about. Nor did I need Hmong leaders to validate my wedding. What I wanted was to give face to *Niam*. *Niam*, who of all parents deserved the most thanks, the most praise, the most respect. This was my one opportunity to show *Niam* off. She, too, should have her daughter's wedding at a fancy hotel. She, too, had earned the respect of Hmong leaders and five hundred witnesses. I wanted all those people to say, "Mai Neng's mother is a widow, but she was able to pull off a wedding as big as other parents." I wanted a wedding that *Niam* could have been proud of.

After four years of being married, as I looked at the hundreds of photographs of my one-month-old baby, for the first time I understood why I never developed the wedding pictures. Like the wedding videos that I could not watch or, rather, "watched" but did not see because, as Blong stated, "You bawled through the whole thing," the photos were a reminder that *Niam*, Kai, and all my Moua relatives did not come to my church wedding. Absent from the happy faces was the most important person: *Niam*.

If I did not have the photos, I would not have to be reminded she was not there. If I did not have the photos, I would not have to deal with people's questions of, "Oh, where's your mother?" *Niam*'s absence was a slap in the face. Years after the church wedding, I can see the imprints of her white hand on my red face. It stings still.

You May Now Begin Your Life

"Marry so you may begin your life," counseled my aunts.

I knew they were worried about me since I was still single in my late twenties. But they said it as if I did not have a life or my single life did not matter.

My youngest uncle married "late" in life—he was probably in his late twenties. I remember family meetings where the other uncles were really worried about him.

"Put everything else on hold," said one uncle.

"Getting married is your number-one priority now," said another one.

"Who do you want? We'll go get her for you."

Never mind that my uncle may not have a girlfriend or does not want to be married right now. He may want to travel the world first. He may have a business he wants to start. It was very serious business that my uncle was not married yet. All the other uncles were willing to step up and help in any way, even resorting to possibly kidnapping a bride for him.

Since my uncle was still single, no one took him seriously. Traditional Hmong hierarchy was in the order of gender, marital status, and age. My uncle could have been a doctor or lawyer. He could have been thirty, but since he was still single, people did not take him seriously.

Hmong people talk about marriage and children as if it is the ultimate goal in life. It seems that if you are not married, your life is not worth living. In the slash-and-burn agriculture of the Hmong in Laos, this made sense. One could not survive by oneself. You needed a partner to help chop down trees that could then be burned. The ashes acted as fertilizer for the crops, which required a partner to help plant. And yes, a household of kids was necessary to help clear the weeds and harvest the bounty. In a country with a high mortality rate, you needed to have a household of kids so that half of them could survive. The only problem was, by the time I got married in 2003, the Hmong had been in the United States for almost thirty years. We did not live a slash-and-burn lifestyle. Hmong people were nostalgic about their lost lives in Laos and hopelessly old-fashioned.

Growing up, I thought marriage, especially marriage to a Hmong man, was prison. Well, maybe that was a little dramatic. It was a necessary evil. Something that you had to do but you would not like or enjoy. I knew young Hmong women who were forced to marry men they did not date or would never marry on their own. These women did not control whom or when they married. I am not judging their current happiness. I am just saying that the fact that these women were forced into marriage traumatized me.

Growing up, I had heard stories of men and women who did not marry their loved ones because other men had "stolen" them. These individuals suffered great loss and walked around with holes in their hearts. Common were the stories of husbands cheating on wives. And when the wives complained, they were told, "That's what men do. As long as they come back home, it's okay." And when men wanted to "marry" second wives, the first wives could not stop them. Or when men beat up their wives, no one helped the battered women. Sure, the wives followed Hmong custom and complained to their husband's people. The clan leaders and uncles counseled the husband to be good, but nothing changed. Since both families did not want the couple to divorce, they told the wife to go back to her husband despite her broken ribs, black eyes, or split lips. Sometimes people wondered what she did to deserve the beating.

I did not often hear stories of men and women who chose their own mates or married their lovers. There were not a lot of stories of husbands who stuck by their wives who could not conceive even though relatives told them to "marry" second wives. Or the husbands who married their wives despite the rumor that they were from a clan that had a leper in the family many generations ago. And where were the husbands who defended their wives who had kidney failure? Rarer were the stories of first and second (or third) "wives" who did not hate each other. I didn't hear many stories of daughters-in-law and mothers-in-law who loved each other and got along.

Although I did not know what it was like to be a daughter-in-law, I did not want to find out. I was terrified of being a Hmong *nyab*. In the kitchens where women cooked and gossiped, I heard rumors of bad *nyab* who could not do anything right. While the United States has stories of evil stepmothers, we Hmong have stories of evil daughters-in-law. Hmong women were destined to be bad daughters-in-law early in life and evil mothers-in-law later.

"Do you want to go up to International Falls?" asked Blong a month after the church wedding.

This was the annual trip north to spend the weekend playing bridge with Blong's friends, most of whom were Oles—graduates of St. Olaf—like me. Although Blong had graduated from the University of California, Los Angeles, one of his classmates at the University of Minnesota Law School was an Ole.

Before I got married, I had to give this kind of out-of-town request some serious thought.

Did I really want to go? Was it worth it to lie to Niam? *What excuse should I use?*

"Just tell her you're going out of town for work," suggested a friend.

Work was a convenient excuse for these out-of-town trips. Before that, I used college. It was not that I did not go out of town for school. I just went on a couple more trips, that was all. It was a terrible thing to do to *Niam*, I know. I felt bad about lying to her. But I had to. My girlfriends and I knew Hmong couples who came back home "late" from a date and were forced to get married.

When Blong and I were dating, I never stayed over at his house. Even if it was 2 AM, I made that sleepy half-hour drive home.

"It's your house! They're living in your house, so why can't you stay over?" asked Blong.

"Because I'm a Hmong girl. Because I live with them. Because those are the house rules."

Blong shook his head in disbelief. "How old are you?" he asked. He knew I was twenty-eight.

"It doesn't matter how old I am. Those are the house rules. Look, when you have a daughter, don't you want your daughter to respect your rules? I mean, if you don't want to follow the rules, then don't live at home with your parents, right?"

"I guess," said Blong. He understood my dilemma, but he wanted me to be more "American" so I could do things that benefitted him, such as stay over or live together before marriage.

"Just tell them you're staying over," Blong persisted.

I shook my head from side to side.

"Why can't you?" he asked.

It was not that I could not. It was that I did not want to. The part of me that was still very Hmong said, *Why do I need to rub it in their faces? Niam*'s rule of "Don't ask, don't tell" worked well for me.

The one time I stayed over at Blong's house, when I got home in the morning, Kai was waiting in the living room for me. *Niam* was so mad at me that she could not even look at me or talk to me. To this day, we have never talked about it. *Niam* believed I was acting like an "easy" woman and had brought shame to her.

"Look, Mai, if we're like other parents, we could make you marry him," said Kai.

In this day and age? Really? was what I wanted to say. Nevertheless, I nodded and never stayed over at Blong's house again.

"Do you want to go up to International Falls?" Blong asked again.

Yes, I did. And this time, after the marriage, I did not have to lie to *Niam*. It was the first time I felt I was living the life I wanted to live. I remember thinking, *I am my own person. My time is my own. My weekends are my own.* My aunts, uncles, grandmas, and *Niam* were right about marriage, at least this aspect of it.

A Knot Between Two Clans

Months after the church wedding, my father-in-law (whom I now called *Txiv*, Father) was still trying to untangle the problem of the *rooj tshoob* and the bride price. As Kai explained, by not doing the *rooj tshoob* and not paying the bride price, Blong and I had created a knot between the two families. No, it was not just a knot between the two families. It was a knot between the two clans, the Moua and the Yang.

A decent Hmong father would not allow his son to "steal" a Hmong woman without so much as a word to her parents, uncles, or clan leader.

He was required to do a *rooj tshoob* and pay a bride price, even if his son objected or refused. That is how most Hmong people marry.

My uncles took *Txiv*'s refusal to do the *rooj tshoob* and pay a bride price as a slap in the face. But because Hmong people consider confronting each other rude or hostile, my uncles never directly talked to *Txiv*. Instead, they searched their social network to see who would have more influence over him to make him do what they wanted. They talked to Moua leaders in Minnesota who talked to Yang leaders in Minnesota who talked to Yang leaders in California who talked to *Txiv*. They threatened that if he did not pay a bride price for me, it would cause problems for all future Moua-Yang marriages in the United States. That is, because a Yang man from California did not pay a bride price for a Moua woman in Minnesota, in the future, all Moua men in the United States who marry Yang women would not have to pay bride prices.

Good! I thought. *We'll get rid of the bride price.*

The Yang leaders told my father-in-law that if Yang fathers wanted bride prices for their daughters, they would have to collect from him.

Honestly, none of it made sense to my Hmong American mind.

Every other weekend for months, *Txiv* called and tried to convince us to go to the *rooj tshoob*. For nine months, we had the same conversation.

"Tell them it was our decision to not do a *rooj tshoob*, not yours," said Blong.

"You can't say that, son. It's not your decision," said *Txiv*. To him, Blong and I were not above Hmong law. No one was, not even him.

Blong told *Txiv* to publicly disown him. But what father wanted to disown his oldest son who was a lawyer?

"Tell them we're bad kids who won't listen to you," suggested Blong.

When *Txiv* could not make Blong go to the *rooj tshoob*, he appealed to me. "*Nyab*, go with us to the *rooj tshoob*."

"*Txiv*, go and do what you need to do to save yourself. But Blong and I are done. We're not doing anything else."

"*Nyab*, don't say that. You and Blong have to go. That's how it is."

"*Txiv*, I've been consistent on this from the beginning. I am done. I am not doing anything else. But please go and do what you need to do."

"I know you say that, but we are Hmong. We still have to do our part."

Then one Saturday morning as I was about to go to the Minneapolis Farmers Market, Blong's cell phone rang. He was still asleep, so I answered it. I walked to the kitchen so I would not wake him up.

"*Nyab*, it's your father. Go with us to the *rooj tshoob*."

"*Txiv*, we've been over this. Blong and I are not doing anything else."

"*Nyab*, you have to go."

"No, I don't."

"You are Hmong, aren't you? We are Hmong. This is how Hmong people get married."

Then, maybe because I was in a hurry, maybe because I was PMSing that day, maybe because this had been going on for months and, like a broken record, we always said the same thing to each other, I blew up at my father-in-law.

"Why are you forcing me to do something I don't want to do?" I yelled. "I am so angry at you."

The words were concrete in my throat. I spat out each one with a thud.

"I . . . am . . . so . . . angry . . . at . . . *Niam*. . . . You . . . all . . . make . . . me . . . so . . . mad."

I screamed at *Txiv*, but I was also shouting at *Niam*, my uncles, and Hmong culture.

"I am done with this conversation!"

With shaking hands, I hung up the phone. I left *Txiv* holding the line in disbelief.

"She hung up on me" was all he managed to whisper to the room of open mouths. His first *nyab* did what none of his kids had ever done: screamed at him at the top of her lungs and hung up on him. "Good" *nyab* did not do this.

Later I found out that, in the past, *Txiv*, in anger, had smashed two telephones. This time, however, the shock of his *nyab* yelling at him stopped him in his tracks. No woman, not even his wife, had ever yelled at him before. The cell phone he was holding was saved.

I waited to see if Blong would come out of the bedroom to ask if I was okay or to give me a hug. He did not. I knew he had heard the conversation. I stormed out of the house. Angry, too, at the lump buried under the down comforter. How I wished Blong and I had talked more that morning. Why didn't he come out and comfort me? Or did he come out to find me already gone? I wondered what he thought of what happened. Was he proud of me for standing my ground with his dad? Or was he angry that I had yelled at him? To my recollection, Blong and I never talked about the incident. Or maybe we did, months later. At the moment though, I needed more emotional support from him, and I didn't get it.

What Is It Worth?

Blong and I lived on a corner lot with a good view of the man-made pond across the street. On one corner lived an older Caucasian lady who reminded me of *Niam*. After a snowfall, they both came out with their brooms to sweep the sidewalks. On the other corner lived a stay-at-home mom married to a Chinese man. They had one daughter. Across the alley from them lived an African American man married to a Caucasian woman. They had two kids. Next to them were longtime homeowners with a preteen daughter. Across the alley from us lived a single mom with a preteen daughter. These were homeowners who looked out for each other.

There were other Hmong families on our block, but Blong and I did not know them. You could always tell the Hmong houses, with the Hondas or Toyotas parked outside, the shoes in the entryway, the peach tree in the front yard, or the *zaub paj* and *zaub ntsuab* in the back.

I FIRST GOT TO KNOW Blong when I was starting a nonprofit to house a Hmong literary magazine. I was looking for a board member who was a lawyer. A mutual friend suggested I talk to Blong, whom I had met previously at a conference. Blong suggested I meet him at his house, where he would make me lunch.

"I don't know about that, Mai," said one of my cousins. "You should meet him in a public space where it's safe. You don't know this guy. He could be an ax murderer for all we know."

"Is he cute?" asked a second cousin. "If he's cute, I'd go."

He was cute, and I was curious about lunch. When I arrived at the house, there was a flurry of activity. Outside the back door, the unfinished deck needed more red bricks. Inside, the living and dining rooms were empty, as if work had just been done. Blong quickly introduced me to his two Hmong housemates and a Caucasian friend who was putting in the deck. We then went upstairs to the second floor where we could talk business.

After I convinced Blong to join my board of directors, I found out he was single. As his sisters and countless other Hmong women friends had done, I offered to introduce him to the single Hmong women I knew. He said something about how hard it was to date Hmong, especially at our ages—mid- to late twenties.

"I totally agree!" I said. "When I say that, Hmong men get really offended, like it's some personal attack."

We proceeded to outline how hard it was to date Hmong. Because you care what people think or say about you, you cannot just go over and visit, especially if they still live at home. (Most unmarried Hmong guys still live at home, even after college.) You cannot show up to their family functions. People automatically assume you will marry them. Even though you do not know the family, it is not hard for them to find out who you are or who your family is. You, however, do not have the network to find out who they are. Or if you do, you're not going to ask because it's embarrassing, as a girl, to ask. You cannot stay out late or stay over because you might have to marry the girl/guy. We agreed it was too complicated to date Hmong.

For lunch, Blong made his family's famous sour soup with cilantro, green onions, and freshly squeezed lime juice. Since he did not have furniture in the dining room, we ate lunch with his housemates and friend on newspapers on the floor.

Blong's Hmong housemates were nice but reserved. I was sure they were curious about my motives, visiting Blong at his house.

"Is he worth it?" asked my cousin.

"Yes," I said, laughing.

"No, I'm serious," insisted my cousin.

"I know you are," I said, looking around my new home in north Minneapolis.

She meant, was it worth all the trouble to not pay the bride price? I wanted to say *Yes*, but I was not so sure anymore.

"Isn't the important thing to get married?" continued my cousin.

"Yes," I said.

I wanted to say, *We're already married legally*, but I knew she would say, *Yeah, but you're not married in the eyes of the Hmong community*. And that, after all, was what this was about.

"Then why does it matter how it's done?" asked my cousin.

I did not know how to answer her.

I wanted to say, *Because I'm not a fourteen- or sixteen-year-old who doesn't care how it's done.*

I wanted to say, *Because I don't negotiate with terrorists.*

My uncles were not terrorists. They would be pissed if they knew what I called them. But that was how they made me feel. It was their way or no way. It was one of those scenes in the movies where the bad guys say, "Tell us or we'll kill you." The prisoner raises her hands in submission and divulges all information. Meanwhile, the viewer is sitting on the couch in the living room screaming, "Stupid. Don't you know? They're going to kill you." And they do.

"When we have kids, we won't collect the bride price," said my cousin's husband. He seemed proud of himself for having found a solution.

"But if we don't change things now, how are we going to change things in the future?" I asked. "What are you going to do when your son marries a Hmong woman and her family wants a bride price? Tell him to marry a non-Hmong?"

At one time I, too, thought that if I married a non-Hmong man, I could escape the bride price. Some Hmong parents did not ask for a bride price if their daughters married non-Hmong men. Perhaps this was because, being non-Hmong, they would not have a *mej koob* to negotiate on their behalf. Or maybe it was because the bride price would sound so strange to non-Hmong ears, so, to save face, it was better to just avoid the whole thing. Some Hmong parents, however, have asked for bride prices and the non-Hmong parents have paid them. When I asked a non-Hmong parent why she agreed to pay the bride price for her Hmong daughter-in-law, she told me it was the respectful thing to do. It was not her agreeing with the tradition. It was her respecting Hmong culture.

Once, after a public reading, a Caucasian woman came up to me and said, "My Hmong daughter-in-law is worth every penny I paid for her." Her son was lost, and her daughter-in-law got him back on track and made him the man he was.

If I marry a Hmong man, however, the bride price is automatic. Although I may feel like this is punishment for marrying a Hmong man, the elders tell me it is a mark of respect and good manners to conform.

"Just grin and bear it and get it done," suggested my cousin.

Even if they do not want a bride price, this is what Hmong women do. They are the women in Neto's painting, *Adelita*. Six women in uniforms with red scarves over their mouths and noses. Four have their hands at the top of their scarves, as if to pull the scarves down. Two little girls stand out. One clings onto an older woman with both hands as if she needs the older woman to hold her up. Another little girl has her hands in front of her in resignation or silent obedience. There is one woman without a scarf, but she is blocking her mouth and nose with one hand as if in shock. Or maybe it is to prevent herself from saying something.

Some Hmong women see my dilemma, but they only look. They may have many intellectual debates about it. They may say many things for or against it. But what could they do about it? In Hmong culture, they can never be the *mej koob* who negotiate the bride price.

When *Niam* and I Last Talked

It was two months after the wedding, and rent was two weeks late. *Niam* and Kai were still living in the Margaret Street house, but it was like pulling teeth to get them to pay rent. The previous month, I had to drive to the house to pick up the late check.

"Tell Kai to write me a check for rent," I told *Niam* on the phone. "I'll pick it up later today."

"Of course we can pay you. You're the one that won't pay us," said *Niam*.

Niam's statement stopped my pacing in front of the window. Like *Niam*, I was quick with my tongue.

"What debt of yours do I still owe?" I asked, trying to sound calm and steady. I could feel the bile rise like mercury in a thermometer from my stomach to my face.

"Since you didn't pay us a bride price, we don't have to pay you rent."

"If you guys don't want to pay rent, you better go find a different place to live."

This is business. This is business, I repeated to myself. *Don't let her get to you!*

"Since you didn't pay me a bride price, I won't give you your Hmong clothes," said *Niam*. "I'm going to sell them."

Niam's comment caught me off guard, and I could not think of a quick response.

She's not serious, is she? I wondered. I was not so sure. At this point, anything was fair game. The Hmong clothes and accessories were usually given away at the *rooj tshoob* as part of the dowry. But since there had been no *rooj tshoob*, *Niam* still had them. She'd been making, assembling, and saving my Hmong clothes for my dowry for a quarter of a century.

"Since you didn't pay me a bride price, I won't give you your Hmong clothes. I'm going to sell them," *Niam* repeated.

All of them? I wondered.

Suddenly, I felt like those orphans from Hmong folktales whose lives I had previously thought were too dramatic to be real. Orphans who lived with their grandparents or uncles who thought they were just extra mouths to feed. Ragged kids who had only one shirt and pant to their names, which they wore year after year, patching up the places that had ripped. Like Cinderella, they were stuck with all the dirty work. And since the men were poor and the women had no parent to give them a dowry, no one wanted to marry them. I was the orphan who did not have a single Hmong outfit to her name.

I wanted to scream, *But they're mine. You saved them for me,* but I did not. I was not going to show *Niam* the impact of her words.

"It's fine if you don't want to give them to me," I said. "Sell them so you'll have some money."

How much longer can I go on, pretending her words do not hurt me? I wondered. The dam was about to break loose, flooding the world with my tears.

"*Niam,* I don't want to say more," I said, slamming the phone in its hook.

Niam and I did not speak for a couple months. When we did, we were bitches biting at each other. It took me days to prepare for a call to *Niam.* Before the call, I paced up and down. I ran in place. My hands sweated. I practiced what I wanted to say again and again. I role-played *Niam's* response and my comeback. I forced myself to breathe slowly and deeply. And even then, after the calls, I was exhausted and angry for days.

Then one day, *Niam's* voice mail said, "I know you two have not sold the house yet, but I want you to start making monthly payments to me."

I had borrowed some money from *Niam* when I refinanced the Margaret Street house. In previous conversations, Blong and I had told her that we would pay her back when we sold the house. She had agreed to that plan.

"Look at that. She's not answering the phone now," said *Niam.* "She knows it's me. That's why she's not answering the phone."

Niam sounded far away.

"I would like you to start paying me so I can buy a small car for myself. I'm tired of driving the van all the time. It's too hard to park."

Niam's vehicle was a fifteen-passenger van without windows. But a couple years ago, Kai and I talked to *Niam* about buying a smaller car for her. She did not want one then. I did not know where Blong and I were going to get the money.

"If you don't pay me soon, I'll have to start charging you interest. If I'd left the money in the bank, I could've made more money by now," persisted the voice.

Many Hmong elders did not leave their money in the bank. Instead, they hid it in suitcases or underneath the mattress or even in coat pockets. *Niam* was not like these people. She gave her money to the First Hmong Baptist Church to keep in their savings account. That way, they could use the interest from her money to take care of church business.

"How much money would I have made each month from the interest?" continued the voice.

I wondered who was filling *Niam*'s head with this information.

"Hmong parents don't usually ask for their money back in that way," said my cousin when I told her about *Niam*'s voice mail message.

"I think she's just mad at me so she wants it back. That's got to be it. It's the one thing she can still hold over me," I explained.

I deleted the voice mail. I decided that if one of my friends told me this story with her mother, I would tell her to not talk to her mother for awhile. I did not call *Niam* back. After a couple weeks of not talking to *Niam*, I had dreams about her. In one of my dreams, she was a big tiger, slowly circling the house, waiting for me to come out or searching for a way in. For the Hmong, tigers are significant. From cursing that a tiger will bite you to stories of Hmong people turning into tigers that stalk you, people were afraid of them. Even in dreams, I figured, tigers were a bad omen. I had other dreams about *Niam*. In them, she was human, but she was mute. *Niam* and I did not talk for a year, two months, and twenty days. Eventually, I stopped dreaming about *Niam*.

PART II

Hu-Plig (Soul-Calling)

. . . as tellers of ghost stories, it is imperative that we always look for "something more" in order to see and bring into being what is usually neglected or made invisible or thought by most to be dead and gone—that is, to always see the living effects of what seems to be over and done with. We need to *see*, and then do something with, *the endings that are not over*.

—Professor Yến Lê Espiritu, Ethnic Studies,
University of California, San Diego

When you are inside the myth, it makes perfect sense and when you are outside the myth, you ask, why would anyone believe that?

—Joseph Campbell

When *poob plig* or soul-loss occurs, one or more of your souls have left your body. To get well or be whole again, you must do a *hu plig* or soul-calling ceremony. This can be done by an elder who knows how to perform it. In more critical cases, the family must call a shaman to do it. In this soul-calling ritual, the shaman travels to the spirit world to find the lost soul. She or he may have to barter with, bargain with, or fight evil spirits to free the captured soul. Sometimes, in order to free the captured soul, they may have to swap it with the soul of a chicken or pig. Only when the lost soul returns home to the body will you become whole again. Only then can you move on.

In addition to being performed for a sick person, *hu plig* is always conducted for newborns and new brides. It summons the soul of the newborn into the body and to join the house of its new parents. In the case of new brides, the *hu plig* cuts her off spiritually from the birth family. It joins her soul to her husband and his family's spiritual domain.

Finding Grandfather

I made plans to visit Thailand to see my paternal grandfather, whom I had not seen or talked to since my family left Ban Vinai in 1981. Grandfather Ka Neng Moua and I, Mai Neng Moua, share the same root name: *Neeb* (Neng), the Hmong word for shaman.

Niam has often told me the story of how I acquired my name.

"When you were a baby, you cried and cried. And you wouldn't stop crying until we called a shaman. He performed an *ua neeb* and divined that we gave you the wrong name. He renamed you, Mai Neng."

"Did it work?" I asked.

"You stopped crying."

"What name did you give me when I was born?"

Niam told me many times, but I could never remember my original name, *Ntxhi* ("Whisper"). It seemed to disappear the second after she told me. Finally, I wrote it down. Captured on paper, I wondered at it. Anyone who knows me now would laugh at *Ntxhi*. Even when I am quiet or silent, I am not whispering. Although I may not speak the anger aloud, it is in my face and in my silence. Even as a baby, I knew *Ntxhi* was not my name. I protested it because it was not me.

There are two occasions when Hmong people change their names: If someone has a continued sickness or misfortune, the new name will confuse the spirits so they will leave the sufferer alone. And after a man marries and has kids, his in-laws give him an "older," more mature name. As in many other cultures, the name change is a marker of life that delineates the end of youth and the beginning of adulthood.

Grandfather Ka Neng was a *txiv neeb* or shaman. When he *ua neeb* or conducts a shamanic ritual, he transforms into the powerful Shee Yee, the first Hmong shaman, to battle evil spirits in the spirit world. Although I have not seen Grandfather since 1981, and I have never seen him *ua neeb*, I have seen other shamans in action. I imagine Grandfather standing on his wooden bench. The bench is his "horse," carrying him into the spirit world. His assistant stands behind him, spotting him so he does not fall off his horse when he is moving up and down on the bench. Although Grandfather is eighty-three years old, when he becomes a shaman disguised in a red cloth mask, he can shake continuously for hours. On his steed, he searches for the lost soul. When he finds it, he wrestles with, bargains with, and pays off the evil spirits in order to bring the lost soul back to the sick body at home.

Grandfather does not always need to *ua neeb* to find the lost soul. Sometimes he simply conducts a *hu plig*. He stands at the front door, shaking a metal rattle in one hand, announcing his arrival to the spirits. With his split buffalo horn in the other hand, he hits the left side of the door and then the right side of the door.

"This is the door," he says to the lost soul. "I am calling you home. Come here. Come this way. There is food for you to eat and water for you to drink. Come back home!"

He throws the buffalo horns on the ground to see if the lost soul has come back. Only when it has returned to the body does he stop.

On his journeys, Grandfather is guided by *neeb* spirits who chose him, many years ago, to be a shaman by making him so sick that nothing could heal him. Only after a veteran shaman divined that *neeb* spirits were calling him to be a *txiv neeb* did Grandfather become better. After years of apprenticeship with his master, he was transformed into a full-fledged shaman. In overcoming pain and suffering, he was now able to heal others with empathy. In doing so, he wasn't much different from a Western psychotherapist, identifying what a person's psyche is missing and helping to restore it.

As payment for his work, he received the head and leg of the pig used for the ceremony. By today's standards, this may seem modest. Back in Laos and Thailand where Hmong people ate meat only on special occasions, getting paid in meat meant you were able to feed your family.

A year and three months after the church wedding, Blong accompanied me on my trip to Thailand. It was the first time back for both of us. For me, it had been ten years since I got sick and could not go on St. Olaf's Term in Asia. I was traumatized by that experience. Even after the transplant, when there were no longer any medical issues holding me back, I was stuck in time, thinking I could not go abroad.

The Lonely Planet guided us on our trip to Thailand. I packed the camera bag with a camcorder, thirty-six hours of tapes, a digital camera, memory for the camera, and rechargeable batteries. We had cell phone numbers for my uncle in northwest Thailand with whom Grandfather Ka Neng lived. I also had a list of questions for Grandfather. I spent days writing out questions in English and then translating them into Hmong. My plan was to interview Grandfather about my father. Connecting with Grandfather would be as close as I could get to my father.

Before we left for Thailand, my cousins had cautioned that Grandfather was very sick and might not live past the New Year. At eighty-three, he was also losing his memory. I thought about calling him to tell him that I was coming to visit, but I thought it would be easier and cheaper to wait until I got to Thailand. Armed with my brand-new camcorder, I told Blong that every night we would record our impressions of the day. Just like the reality TV shows. That way, our feelings and insights would be fresh and immediate.

Because he did not know how to write, Grandfather sent spoken words via cassette from Thailand to family here in Minnesota. This was how our relatives in Laos and Thailand communicated with us. The cassettes were always full of life and emotions. When *Niam* popped one into the tape recorder, the roosters crowed, the dogs barked, and the children yelled in the background. I imagined that the parents and children gathered around the tape recorder in much the same way they sat around the fire at night. Sometimes you heard the parents chastising the children, "Stay back! Don't sit so close to me" or "Stay still so I can talk." They gave updates of their families and other relatives. They gossiped and asked questions of rumors they had heard. They reminisced about their lives back in their beloved mountaintop villages in Laos. They cried and talked of their longing for their relatives in America. They cursed themselves for their bad luck, Secret War refugees stuck in Thailand, not able to return to Laos and not able to come to America. They described in detail their miserable lives. Then they pleaded for money.

Grandfather did not often mention me in his spoken letters. An afterthought, I came at the end of the sentence that started out with my brothers. It was all right. I did not often think about Grandfather either. But perhaps he remembered the Christian songs I sent him.

When I was in junior high school, *Niam* recorded cassettes to relatives in Thailand. When she had said all she needed to say and there was still space to fill, she asked me to sing songs on the sixty- or ninety-minute cassette. I did not know how to sing *kwv txhiaj*, traditional Hmong folksongs. I did not know any pop or R&B songs, so I sang the songs I learned from the Christian and Missionary Alliance Church in Pittsburgh. Christian songs in English such as "Jesus Loves Me," "Father, I Adore You," "Kumbaya," and "Trust and Obey." *Niam* said these were fine songs. I took the tape recorder into my room. I practiced the songs, recorded, and rerecorded them to make sure they were perfect for Grandfather. Never mind that he and my relatives in Thailand were not Christians. Never mind that they did not understand a word of English.

To save money, the relatives would simply record over what was on the cassette and send it back. They would make good use of it by having several people send messages to different family members here in the United States. They would mail the cassette to one family in St. Paul or Minneapolis. After that first family had listened to it, they would pass it on to another family.

In late December 2004, on the eighteen-hour Korean Air flight, the attendants handed me warm, almond-scented towels like those you get at expensive salons. I knew they were for my hands, but I wiped my face and neck as well. They gave us warm blankets and pillows. They offered water, juice, pop, or wine. They served food familiar to my taste buds—rice, fish, and seaweed salad. Even the silverware was admirable—unbreakable plastic forks, knives, and spoons, which I kept. The faces of those on the plane reminded me of my own family members. I could easily pretend these were my people, traveling with me to visit our homeland.

Grandfather and I were blood—but strangers, really. I did not remember him. Recent photos of him showed a man with white, wild hair, much like Albert Einstein's. Grandfather was light in complexion like my father, my two aunts, one of my nieces, and me. Since he was so light, it looked like he often had a red nose. Or, at least I remembered a red nose. My youngest uncle, who I thought looks like Bruce Lee, looked like Grandfather. Beyond these physical features, was he the talker or the quiet one who listened more? Did he speak slowly and softly? Or did he sound like a woodpecker with a constant staccato that gave you a headache after a while? Or did he speak like the aunt who barked at you when she talked, the one who makes you rush to do things for fear she might yell at you?

My one memory of Grandfather, and I thought this was my own memory, was of the time when we had left our mountain village. We were walking on foot through the jungles of Laos to the Mekong River. It was 1979, four years after the Secret War had officially ended. My father had died. I was maybe six years old. I did not know how many people were in our group, where we were in Laos, or how long we had been traveling. I did not remember where *Niam* or my brothers were. All I remember was a still darkness lit by the moonlight. I was walking with Grandfather and then fell and scraped my knees. I wanted to cry, but Grandfather had his hands over my mouth. In front of us, a line of Lao soldiers walked by. I saw their shadowy shapes in the darkness. Crouching on the side of the road, we hid behind tall trees.

What I knew of Grandfather came from *Niam*. She told me that after my father died, someone took his watch from her bedroom. One of the other daughters-in-law confirmed that she saw Grandfather go inside

Niam's bedroom when she was at the garden. The watch was the last memento *Niam* had of my father. She never got it back.

Then there was the time Grandfather locked *Niam* and me out of the house. Grandfather asked another shaman to *ua neeb* to heal the whole family. They didn't tell us when they were going to do the *ua neeb*, so *Niam* and I went to the garden. Before we could return, the shaman started the *ua neeb*, cleansing the house of all evil spirits, and told Grandfather to not let people enter the house. The shaman believed that if people entered the house they might bring in bad spirits with them and make those inside sick. He also didn't want those inside the house to come out. When *Niam* and I returned home two nights later, green bamboo leaves on a stick marked the door, warning people not to enter.

"He knew we were coming back. Why didn't he wait to *ua neeb*?" asked *Niam*. "He purposely did it to keep us out!"

We were starving by the time we got home, but when we begged for some food, we were told, "We'd rather throw our food away then give it to you two." Later, Kai snuck out and brought us three finger-sized sticks of rice.

"We were hungry so we asked them for some rice and this is what they gave us," he said. "We didn't eat them so we brought them for you."

Niam and I finally went to my maternal uncle's house to eat. His family lived only a few houses away from Grandfather's house. That night, we slept at our next-door neighbor's house. The next day, we got up early and walked a couple hours to the garden to dig up some yams.

I want to know Grandfather beyond *Niam*'s stories. How many brothers and sisters did he have? Did he go to school? How did he meet my grandmother? How old were they when they married? Was he ever a soldier? Why didn't he come to America? What did he think of *Niam* taking his grandkids to America? After Grandmother died in 1991, what was his daily life like?

I long to look into Grandfather's eyes and touch the face that gave life to my father. Sitting next to him by the fire at night, I would love to hear stories of life in Laos or the Secret War. I want to witness Grandfather, the shaman, in a trance, battling evil spirits in the spirit world. Or him in his everyday life, feeding his chickens and pigs, weaving a basket, or making a stool. I wish for Grandfather to stroke my hair and say to me, "Daughter, it's been so long. The last time I saw you, you were only this tall. Look how you've grown!"

I want to know what Grandfather remembered about me. What happened on the day that I was born? Was it true that my father did not come home from the military base to see me because I was just a girl? I want to hear about my older brother who died when he was just a baby. *Niam*'s story of this brother consists of three lines: "He cried for days. We rubbed hot pepper paste over his body. He died."

I would like to know what my father was like as a child and a young man. Did he have many girlfriends? What kind of jobs did he have? When and where did my father die? How did Grandfather and our clan leader come to the conclusion that my father should go get *Niam*? What happened at their *rooj tshoob*?

Meeting Grandfather is the closest thing to meeting my own father.

Two days after we left San Francisco International Airport, we finally made it to Bangkok. Dressed in shorts, T-shirts, and sandals and carrying big backpacks, we were easy targets for scammers at the airport. While waiting for a small plane to Chiangmai in northern Thailand, we decided to take a taxi to get some food. We thought forty baht (one dollar) was cheap for a cab ride, but later learned that the driver charged us four times what he would have charged a local.

My St. Olaf advisor and his wife were leading the Term in Asia students. Their monthlong home stay was in Chiangmai. We planned it so Blong and I could stay with them for a week. I figured it would give us a good introduction to the language, culture, and place. It would also give us time to figure out how to get to Grandfather's village.

On December 26, 2004, the tsunami hit southern Thailand. It killed about 5,400 people. In Chiangmai, way up north, Blong and I were safe. Jet-lagged, I could not sleep that morning. Up early, writing at the kitchen table, I felt the earth tremble. Although the house was not near a big street, in my American mind, I thought a Mack truck had driven by.

After a couple days in Chiangmai, I finally called the uncle with whom my grandparents lived. He was the one who stayed in Thailand and took care of them because, at that time, he was the only one who was married with children. The other two uncles were single young men who had decided to go to America. I called every day for four days with no luck.

Why didn't I call Grandfather and Uncle before I came? I shook my head, mad at myself. I guess I was scared. After all the drama with the *rooj tshoob*, I was afraid to call because I thought they would yell at me, too. I thought they would not let me come. So, instead of calling, I figured I would just show up. What could they do then?

When I could not reach Uncle, I called my cousin in Minnesota to make sure I had the right number. I did. I then e-mailed Uncle Naw-Karl to see if he knew what was going on. Later that day, I received this e-mail from Uncle Naw-Karl: "Your grandfather died. Your uncles have buried him."

Uncle Naw-Karl's words were a tsunami. The blood drained from my face. The cold wave crashed over me in that sweaty Internet café on the streets of Chiangmai. I swallowed my grandfather's death, and it filled my lungs. I could not breathe.

Grandfather is dead? The man I have not seen for twenty-three years is dead. The reason for this ten-years-in-the-making trip is dead. I have hundreds of questions. With Grandmother's death, Grandfather is my last connection to my father. What am I going to do now?

Walking back to the house where Blong and I were staying, I felt as if I were drowning in quicksand. I walked as fast as I could, but it felt like I was moving in slow motion. The sounds of cars, tuk tuks, and vendors selling mangoes and noodles seemed far away.

I later learned that Grandfather died the day Blong and I flew out of San Francisco. My uncle buried him the day we landed in Bangkok. Five days later, I finally reached my uncle.

"Hello. I am Mai Neng, the daughter of Tong Chee," I introduced myself.

Uncle did not seem to know who I was. It was understandable. It had been four years since he had visited the United States. He had stayed for six months with his first wife and six children, who had come to the United States a decade earlier. During his stay, I saw him once at a family gathering. There were so many people in the house, we did not say much to each other.

"I am Kai and Yia's sister," I explained.

Then Uncle remembered, but he seemed surprised that I, a girl, made it to Thailand before her brothers.

"Grandfather has died," said Uncle, his voice cracking. "We have already buried him. You have no luck and thus you did not see Grandfather."

Although Grandfather was dead, Blong and I decided to fly to the airport nearest the small village where Uncle lived. We had not been able to get a hold of Uncle because his cell phone only worked in the city. Blong and I happened to call on a day when he and Aunt were in the city, dropping off my youngest aunt and her husband at the airport. They had come to visit Grandfather, had stayed for the funeral, and were returning to Minnesota.

Uncle's village is in Tak province in northwest Thailand. Although I did not know the history of the village and did not see opium anywhere, I guessed the village had been named for opium. This is a crop that, at one point in time, Hmong people grew for both medicinal purposes and cash. From the small airport, the village was a good hour drive up and down the mountain on a narrow two-lane road. Uncle drove fast and hit the brakes hard at every curve. Without seat belts, Blong and I slid from side to side in Uncle's Toyota pickup truck. We dug our fingernails into the seats to steady ourselves.

Uncle's village is situated on the side of the hill on what feels like a forty-five-degree incline. It made me think of mountain goats and how they could walk on such unsteady grounds. Even in Laos, Hmong people lived in mountaintop villages away from the cities, away from other ethnic groups. Perhaps when the Hmong migrated from China to Laos, these were the only places left. Perhaps Hmong people chose these places so they could live in peace. Or maybe in previous lives, the Hmong were mountain goats who often rested on rocky cliffs so that predators could not reach them.

Like many young Hmong Americans who changed their names from Nou to Stacey or Ka to Kris or Tou to Danny in the 1980s, to survive in Thailand, the Hmong Thai adopted Thai names. The Hmong Thai college students Blong and I met at Chiangmai University all had Thai names. This was the only way to get accepted in Thai society or to find work. The Hmong Thai students interested in law complained that no Thai person would use your services if you were not Thai. It was easier to pass as Thai with a Thai name.

Like the Hmong American kids who spoke Hmong with a mix of Hmong and English, the Hmong Thai kids also spoke a mix of Hmong and Thai. I thought since they were closer to the motherland, so to speak, their Hmong would be better than mine. Some, however, did not speak any Hmong.

This need to survive sometimes went as far as what my uncle and his family did in their village. As undocumented immigrants, they had to purchase, from the village leader, the identity of a Hmong Thai citizen who had died but whose death was not officially recorded or reported. My uncle became this dead man. Everyone, from the leader to the villagers, had to be in on it. Everyone knows but no one says anything except to confirm, "Yes, this is so and so." If all are in, all win.

In the village, the very poor lived in simple thatched-roof houses with thatched siding. People who had relatives in the United States or some other country had the nicest houses and cars to drive. Their houses were like Uncle's, sturdier structures with tin shingles and bamboo siding that could withstand the wind and rain. Uncle even constructed covered parking for his Toyota truck. His kitchen was separated from the rest of the house so that the smoke from the cooking fire did not permeate the living room and bedrooms. Finally, there were the rich folks whose houses were Thai-styled homes made with bricks and stucco roofs. These houses were walled off with a gate high enough so you could not see into the yards.

I did not know Grandfather had remarried. I met my new grandmother when Blong and I arrived in Uncle's village. As we walked alongside my new grandmother, she pointed out one such house.

"That woman, her husband is a Hmong American. He comes to visit her once or twice a year," said Grandmother.

Some people would probably call this woman a mistress. We Hmong called her "wife" because there had been a *rooj tshoob* and the Hmong American man had paid the bride price. She now belonged to him. He was responsible for taking care of her and her children.

Blong and I talked about the reasons why a Hmong Thai woman would marry a Hmong American man who only came to visit her once or twice a year.

"Why not?" I said. "You get a nice house, maybe even a motorbike. Unlike the suckers slaving away in the hot fields, you don't have to work because he sends you money. You can have your own life, your own lovers here. And you only have to deal with him once or twice a year."

"I guess," shrugged Blong.

Like others in the community, Blong and I had heard the stories of Hmong American men coming back to Laos and Thailand. Old men on Social Security Disability income, dressed in suits, pretending they were rich. Married men who lied about their marital status and how many houses, cars, or even restaurants they owned. Grown men who made promises to marry the young girls if they had sex with them. College-educated men who told each other, when they were in Laos and Thailand without their wives, "The girls here are cheaper than a bowl of noodles." Hmong men preying on the poverty of the people who want to come to the United States so they can save their families.

Back in the days when Hmong people lived in small villages in the mountaintops in Laos, it was easy to find out the backgrounds of the men. This was not the case now. Hmong American men coming back to Laos and Thailand could be anonymous. It was difficult to find out about their families and backgrounds. As one Hmong Thai man told us, "He said he wasn't married, but we didn't know."

Although Blong and I did not know the details of the Hmong American man's marriage to the Hmong Thai woman, I hoped she was getting something out of it.

Although we had traveled across oceans to Uncle's village, he talked only when he called Blong and me to eat. Even if Uncle hadn't wanted to talk to me, I had expected Uncle to, at least, talk to Blong. Hmong men usually make small talk with each other. In making each other's acquaintances, it would have been natural for Uncle to ask Blong about his clan leader, his father, if he was related to so-and-so or from what village in Laos his family came. The elders always asked these questions when they met you. They did not care who you were. You mattered only in so far as who you were connected to. But maybe, by then, Uncle knew all these details already.

Since Blong is a lawyer, Hmong men in the United States and Thailand ask him questions related to the law. I remember a conversation with the Hmong Thai men in the village near Phra Yao where we had gone with the Chiangmai University students. The men had heard rumors that American men could do "bad things to" Hmong women (they meant rape). And Hmong men were powerless to do anything about it. They had heard that if married Hmong women ran off and married some other non-Hmong men, they would not be able to do anything about that, either.

"Is that true?" asked the men.

Blong spent time discussing U.S. law versus the "right" or moral thing to do.

I had expected Uncle to be, at least, curious about us. But he did not ask any questions about our jobs, homes, or lives in the United States. He did not even ask about our American wedding versus the *rooj tshoob*. Not an angry, "You stupid kids! How could you embarrass your uncles like that?" Not a flippant, "Kids nowadays, they think they're so smart. They think they know it all." Maybe he did not talk to us because he was so mad about the *rooj tshoob*. Like the one time I stayed over at Blong's house and *Niam* was so mad at me, she had Kai talk to me. I could understand Uncle being mad at us; who was not?

But I guess I should not have expected anything different. My two uncles here in St. Paul did not talk to me much either. We have lived in the same town for seventeen years, attended the same church for half of those years, and yet my friends in church did not know we were blood.

It wasn't entirely my uncles' faults. Their behaviors were in line with the traditional Hmong mentality that men and women could not be friends. I grew up with the notion that men and women stayed far away from each other unless they were intimately interested in each other. In fact, when I was a little girl looking for a place to pee outside, *Niam* told me not to pee where the boys had peed or else I'd get pregnant. Though technically not true, her message was that I needed to stay far away from boys.

The one real conversation I had with one uncle was when he got an invitation to come to my church wedding and reception. He had suffered a stroke in 2001, and the left side of his body was paralyzed. He called me to ask about the invitation.

"Daughter," he said to me, "I got your invitation in the mail, but I have not heard Son Kai or your mother talk about it. What is going on?"

Although I am not his daughter, it is proper Hmong etiquette to call me such. I, in return, call him *Txiv* (Dad).

"*Txiv*, Blong and I are having a church wedding on August 23. I sent the card to invite you and your whole family."

"Why hasn't Son Kai said anything about it?"

"I asked them to not collect a bride price, and they're not happy about it."

I do not remember the rest of the conversation. He probably told me about some other Hmong woman's wedding where things had gone wrong because her family did not collect a bride price. He must have warned me to not make the same mistake. All I remember is that he did not seem angry with me. His tone was gentle. And I loved the fact that he had called me Daughter, a name I had not heard from his lips. He called me Daughter as if he were my father. It was sweet. It made me feel like a daughter who would do anything to please her father. It was the first real conversation I had with one of my father's brothers.

Perhaps the uncle in Thailand did not talk to Blong and me because he had been paralyzed by Grandfather's death. He had buried his father only days before our visit. What mood did I expect him to be in? How could I have expected him to be chipper and talkative for my sake? Besides, he did not have time to talk. He and Aunt were busy, cleaning up Grandfather's farm where he had a shed that needed to be dismantled. They had to dismantle the farmhouse. They had to transport the wood beams to their house and cut them up for firewood.

There were money issues with my new grandmother, which had to be resolved. There were disagreements between Aunt and Grandmother, two clucking hens, which Uncle had to mediate. Blong and I were yesterday's scandal. We were the least of his concerns.

Grandfather's death paralyzed me, too. I no longer had the desire to videotape my impressions of the day like the reality shows, public spectacles that made their money off of conflict and people's misery. I did not have the will to express myself on paper. My notepad was as blank as the emptiness in my heart. My sadness was a matter that I wanted to keep to myself. I did not know how to talk to Blong about it and so we did not talk about Grandfather's death.

In college, this kid "read" my palm and asked if I had ever been abandoned. No one had ever asked me that. When I asked him why, he said, "Your heart line is disconnected from your head line." I did not know what that meant then, and I do not know what that means now, but I do feel disconnected. Although people who look like me surround me, it is the emotional disconnect that I feel most profoundly. With Grandfather's death and Uncle's silence, I am back where I started: fatherless.

The day after Blong and I arrived in the village, Uncle took us to see Grandfather's gravesite. Uncle had buried him a mile away at the farm where Grandfather had raised chickens and pigs.

My introduction to Grandfather came in the form of Uncle saying, "*Txiv*, your granddaughter, Mai Neng, has come from America to see you."

I stood beside Grandfather's gravesite, which was an upside-down cement U. Like Uncle who did not have any substantive things to say to me, I, too, had no words for Grandfather.

In Hmong, when someone comes to your house, there are two ways to greet them: "*Tuaj los?*" and "*Los lawm los?*" The first, "*Tuaj los?*" is "You come?" To enter the house, the guest must answer in the affirmative, "*Aws, tuaj os,*" or "Yes, I come." Then permission to enter the house is granted. "*Tuaj los?*" is both a statement and a question. It is said as if the speaker is not sure if the guest is spirit or human. It is asked in case one is greeting a spirit.

Deep in the mountain villages in Laos, where the lines between the spirit world and human world seemed more permeable, people were afraid of spirits. This is especially true for a people who believe dead ancestors can still communicate with you and have the power to affect your everyday life. A people who believe bad spirits can scare or steal one of your souls. Although the Hmong no longer live in the mountain villages in Laos, as minorities in a majority culture, they know that many foreign things could show up at one's door. This, I think, is why we still ask, "*Tuaj los?*" when guests come to visit. This is the same reason that when *Niam* answers the phone she says, "*Leejtwg os?*" or "Who is it?" instead of "Hello."

When a family member, an insider, returns home from work, school, or running errands, you greet them by asking, "*Los lawm los?*" or "You've come back?" or "You've returned?" The important difference is that "*los*" is the familiar form of the word "come." To enter the house, the family member must respond, "*Aws, los lawm os!*" That is, "Yes, I've come back." By responding in this way, you are affirming, "I belong to you. I belong here. I am human." Once your humanity is verified, entrance into the home is granted.

I always thought that when I returned to Laos or Thailand, I would be going home. Finally, I would be in a familiar place where people looked like me. Since I understood and spoke Hmong, I wouldn't have to translate the sounds around me.

Like the collective memory of a people, some things were familiar. I felt myself saying, "Right, this is what the thatched-roof houses look like." At night when Blong and I slept on the bamboo beds, I imagined my own family must have slept on such beds in Laos when I was a little girl. At night, when I saw the world outside through the gaps in the bamboo siding, I finally understood the intrigue of the young lovers' evening courtships of which *Niam* had spoken.

But what I discovered was that the "home" of which *Niam* had talked existed only in the collective memory of her generation. That "home" to me was a nostalgic land that never changed. But the Secret War had changed everything. It had killed most of the men in my life. It had moved a whole people across many oceans to lands we had never imagined. It had destroyed that idealistic village in the mountaintops of Laos. The Hmong who did not escape to Thailand were no longer permitted to go back and live in those same villages. Corralled onto small patches of dry land in the city where the Lao government could keep an eye on them, they could no longer farm as they had before. Almost like pigs in a pen, some were even tourist attractions.

Although we Hmong like to talk as if we are one and as if there is only one way to be Hmong (and, depending on where you live, that is *the* way), it is not true. What it means to be Hmong is different here in the United States than in China, Laos, Thailand, France, Germany, or Australia. In the United States, it is even different from city to city and state to state (say, St. Paul versus Walnut Grove or Minnesota versus California or Texas).

When Blong and I were in my uncle's village in Thailand, my relatives greeted me with "*Tuaj los.*" Understandably, this is because I have married out. I am coming back as a guest. I also did not live with them, so I am not part of their physical family.

However, I really did feel that I had not returned home. I was a guest, an outsider. I was a tourist, visiting a foreign land that I had read about in *The Lonely Planet*.

"*Tuaj los?*" asked family members.

"*Tuaj os,*" I answered.

Finding Father

The only picture I have of myself as a baby is a faded two-by-three-inch black and white one. I am sitting on a stool (or is it a tree stump?). I cannot

sit by myself yet, and so, in the left-hand corner of the photo, an arm—
I do not know whose arm—holds me in place. I am still leaning to one
side, ready to fall over. I cannot hold my head up yet, and so I do not
look at the camera. Or, is my head down because it is too bright? In any
case, you cannot see my face. You cannot tell it is me. It is too small and
too far away. It is a baby in a dress. It could be any baby, but *Niam* insists
it is me.

In all five of *Niam*'s photo albums, there is no picture of my father
with my family. No picture of me in his arms, on his knees, or riding his
shoulders. No picture of him kissing or hugging me or holding my hands.
There is no picture of my father with my brothers. No picture of him
with *Niam*, either. Unlike other Hmong families who have pictures of
their father in his military uniform standing proudly next to his family,
there is no evidence of us as a family.

You can argue that these pictures that I want to see are very American—Hmong fathers do not kiss or hug their kids. But there is not even
a picture of us in the standard "Hmong" pose with everyone standing
like sardines, hands at their sides, no one smiling. It is as if my father
never existed in our lives.

We have only three black and white photos of my father. In the eight-
by-ten portrait, he sits on a big black leather chair. Like me, he is lighter
skinned than most Hmong. Wearing a crisp white shirt, clean-shaven with
slicked-back hair, he looks regal and sure of himself. In the second photo,
my father is with two friends, one standing on each side of him. He stands
tall and looks straight at the camera. He looks intelligent in his white
shirt, pressed black pants, and black dress shoes. He is young and hopeful.
He can be anything he wants to be. He can do anything. The third picture of my father is a wallet-sized headshot. In this close-up, he is older
and there are lines around his mouth and eyes. He and *Niam* are married,
and they have kids now. My older brother Kai looks like my father.

With my father's monthly salary as a soldier, they could afford the
pictures. When I asked *Niam* why there were no pictures of us as a family
or them as a young married couple, *Niam* said, "I don't know. He didn't
want to take any pictures with me. He said he didn't get the wife he
wanted."

This is hard for me to believe. Why did he go and get *Niam* then?

Or was it that *Niam* had to leave behind most of her photos when my family crossed the Mekong River? She was told to leave behind all unnecessary things to lighten the load on the canoe that transported our group to refugee camps in Thailand. They almost drowned.

The muddy waters of the Mekong have damaged the surviving pictures in *Niam*'s photo albums. Yellowing and water-stained, some have become superimposed on the backs of others. In some pictures you see only the feet. In others you see only the head. One photo now carried the images and memories of two. One group of people stared through the backs of another, hoping to be seen. Hoping to be remembered. When looking through *Niam*'s photos, you must remember to turn them over and look at the back. You must remember to ask about the backstory. You must remember that for every picture there are two sides to the story.

With my writing, I shall fashion my father, who died when I was three years old, out of the bits and pieces I know of him. Like a shaman, I shall search for him in the nooks and crannies of my families' memories. I shall assemble him from what *Niam* knows. In this way, I may know him so that I may be whole again.

I realized that I was angry with my father. *Niam* had told me that he had died in a farming accident. I was angry at him for "abandoning" *Niam*, my brothers, and me. For not coming home from the military base when I was born because, as *Niam* said, I was just a girl. For having mistresses when he was already married with children. I realized this was a common practice for Hmong men back in Laos, but I expected better from my father. He was educated and thus should have known better. But that education would have been why other women were attracted to him. He bought gifts for these other women. He should have spent his money on *Niam*, my brothers, and me.

Yia was several months old when our father died. He does not remember anything about him.

"All I know is that he looks like Kai," said Yia. "*Niam* said something about him dying when a tree hit him."

I asked Kai what he remembered about our father.

"Nothing," he said. "I never knew the man. He never came home; he was always at the military base. Even when he was home, he went to write letters for our clan leader."

My aunt and *Niam* described my father as a "slave" to our clan leader. Not literally a slave, but one who worked for his boss all the time or was at his beck and call. As *Niam* stated, "Your father was his feet and eyes."

"*Niam* took care of us by herself," said Kai. "When Dad died, I was at the farm with *Niam*."

"You were? I never knew that."

"I was five or six, old enough to go with *Niam* to the farm," nodded Kai.

"Where was I?" I asked.

"I think you were home with Grandma. Yia and I were at the farm. Yia was several months old, I think. Anyway, when Dad died, they came to get *Niam* at the farm. She left without me."

I could see *Niam*. The news that a tree had fallen on my father must have hit her like a hammer on a nail. A dragon with powerful wings, she must have flown across the field with Yia on her back. With the single purpose of getting to my father as soon as possible, she could not afford the slow gait of a child.

"Heavens, please don't let this be true. Please don't let my husband be dead!" begged *Niam* with each swoosh of her wings.

"How did you get home?" I asked Kai.

The farm was probably an hour's walk from home. Too far for him to walk home by himself.

"I think Grandma came and got me."

"What do you know about when *Niam* and Dad got married?" I asked.

"I think Dad was courting Aunt, *Niam*'s older sister."

That would explain why *Niam* has said, "Your father never intended to marry me."

"How did he end up marrying *Niam*, then?" I asked.

"Aunt got married so our clan leader told him to marry *Niam*. After Dad went to get *Niam*, they ran off to the jungles and hid out for awhile until things cooled down," said Kai.

This was starting to sound like a Korean drama with twenty parts instead of my parents' story. I made a mental note to ask *Niam* about the sequence of how things happened.

Being a soldier in General Vang Pao's army, my father was often at the military base. When he did come home, our clan leader needed him to write letters for him. In addition, my father still had to take care of everyday things, such as helping his relatives clear the land of trees so they could farm it. Hmong people were big on showing up and helping others so that when you needed help they would show up for you.

In those days, the men propped up ladders on the trees and climbed the ladders to chop the trees. You were supposed to chop the tree in such a way that it fell away from you. For some reason, my father chopped it so that it fell toward him. It was as if the bad spirits momentarily blinded his logic.

"It was a mysterious time," said *Niam*. "Even the animals knew something was going to happen." She said it was as if the animals and the land were holding their breath, waiting.

"Other people must've seen him doing this," said *Niam*, "but no one said anything to him."

The tree made a sound as if it were going to fall. My father jumped down. Nothing happened. He climbed back up on the ladder and gave the tree a couple more good whacks. The tree cracked. He did not have time to jump off the ladder. The tree fell on top of him.

Being three at the time of his death, I should have some memories of my father. I do not. I used to tell myself that I did not miss him. *How could I miss something I never had?* I thought. I told myself that *Niam* had been both Mom and Dad for me and that was enough.

The truth is I miss my father.

I missed him for *Niam*. She needed him when my family left our mountain village and hid in the jungles, surviving on palm hearts, tree grubs, and lizards. With his status in the military, we would not have had to live in Ban Vinai for two years before resettling in the United States. When we came to Pittsburgh in 1981, *Niam*, who spoke no English, had to navigate the social services system by herself. She needed my father when we got our first apartment by the Heinz factory. With three little kids by her side, she was so scared; she pushed the chairs and couches against the front door. When we moved to St. Paul in 1987, she could have used his help to find and pay for apartments that were not infested with roaches. When my brothers and I brought schoolwork home, she could not help us. When we were bad kids who did not listen to her, *Niam* had no one else to back her up. Maybe if she had a partner, *Niam* would not have had to work so hard since my father would have gotten a professional job.

I missed my father for Kai. He needed a male role model to take him to the clan meetings and show him what Hmong men were supposed to do. As he bought or fixed cars or did small repairs around the house, I wished he had my father to consult with. When *Niam* and Kai disagreed, it was too bad my father was not there to mediate. Kai could have used my father's help in college when he needed money for tuition. He especially needed my father's advice when he started dating and when he got married.

I missed my father for Yia. Of all the siblings, he needed my father the most. Kai had his role as the oldest son, and I had my place as the only daughter. Yia was a ship lost at sea without a lighthouse to guide his way. My uncles were never close to us, so they did not pay attention to Yia. In elementary school, Yia needed my father to teach him how to protect himself against the kids who threw him in trash cans. In high school, he bounced from school to school and finally ended up at the Area Learning Center (ALC), or as the kids at church called it, "Asians' Last Chance." Yia needed a father to enforce *Niam*'s advice to not start smoking, drinking, or hanging out with his friends whose grandfather smoked opium. He did not listen to *Niam*, Kai, or me, but he might have listened to our father.

I missed my father along the way to the Mekong River when I wanted him to carry me on his back like the other kids. In my senior year in high school, I could have used his help filling out the financial aid forms for college and determining what college to go to. As the first ones to attend college, Kai and I did not know how to decide on a major or how the majors we chose would translate to jobs. I wondered what my experience with kidney failure would have been like if my father were alive. When I graduated from college, maybe if he was alive, he would have thrown a big party for me, not that I needed one. I missed my father when my car broke down and I needed help finding a reliable mechanic or auto shop. When I had writing successes, I wanted him to be proud of me. I missed him on Father's Day when I saw my friends with their fathers. I wished he had been there to walk me down the aisle on my wedding day.

I have wondered many times what my father was like. But Hmong people do not talk about those who have died. When people did not talk about their fathers, I assumed it was because their fathers were dead. I assumed their fathers were dead even if they were just physically or emotionally not present. Technically they were not dead, but, to me, they might as well have been. Did Hmong people not talk about the dead because they did not want to invite those spirits or any other curious spirits to come around?

I thought everyone had forgotten about my father. No one ever talked about him. Not *Niam*, not my uncles, not my brothers, not even me. But one time after college at my uncle's *hu plig* for his baby, I heard my father's name. After the shaman conducted the *hu plig*, he went into the kitchen to *laig dab*. *Niam* had told me about this "feeding the spirits" ritual. I had also read about it in sociological journals for classes at St. Olaf. But this was the first time I saw *laig dab* with my own eyes. This ritual calls back the souls of our ancestors to come and "eat." It thanks them for giving the clan another son and for protecting all of us. The ancestors are "fed" first before we human beings can eat.

In the midst of women preparing food in the kitchen, men talking in the basement, children running around outside, and guests watching wrestling in the living room, the shaman sat on a small stool in the kitchen and conducted the *laig dab*. I stood in the entryway between the living room and the kitchen, straining my ears to hear him. He placed a spoonful of cooked rice and small strips of cooked chicken and pork on a small plate. He poured rice wine over the food and then called back each of the ancestors by name. I did not understand all the ritualized Hmong words. I did not recognize any of the names or know how many he called. I did not know if he called both men and women, but I assumed he did not call the women since women married out and did not belong to their birth families anymore. Then I heard my father's name: Tong Chee. His name was a sharp train whistle, piercing my eardrums. It woke me from my trance. The shaman had moved on, calling other ancestors, but I was frozen in place. *Did he really call my father?* I wondered. My eyes, on their own accord, watered and my throat tightened. I had not heard my father's name uttered in years.

I then realized that I was the one who had forgotten him. I was the one who did not understand how animist Hmong remembered their ancestors. Since my family converted to Christianity in the mid-1980s, we did not conduct any of the animist Hmong rituals anymore. Pastor Vang at First Hmong Baptist Church preached that the animist spirits were spirits who were against God, Jesus, and the Holy Spirit. We were told to choose sides, for we could not serve two masters. My Christian self had forgotten about *hu plig, laig dab*, and the other animist Hmong rituals of which I was no longer a part.

These rituals and beliefs still influenced older Hmong people's behaviors and attitudes. For example, although *Niam* has been a Christian since we came to the United States, I could still remember her calling, "Let's go! Let's go home. Let's not stay here," at the end of the church picnic at Battle Creek Park in St. Paul. My brother and I were standing right next to her, ready to get in the car. In retrospect, I realize that she was not talking to us. She was talking to our multiple souls who may have wandered off somewhere. She was calling them, telling them not to stay at the park. She was telling them to come home with us. Just like the time she spent four days in the hospital. When we were getting ready to go home, she said, "Let's go home. Do not stay here." She was calling her souls to go home with her and not get stuck at the hospital.

In my efforts to learn more about my father, after my trip to Thailand, I visited the oldest members of my extended family in St. Paul. When I got there, they had a visitor, a man holding a *qeej* ("kheng") between his legs. The *qeej* is a free-reed multiple pipe musical instrument made of bamboo. It has the ability to mimic the tonal sounds of the Hmong language. It is traditionally used to communicate with the soul of the deceased at a funeral. It turns common Hmong language into a ritualized language the soul of the deceased can understand. The sounds of the *qeej* lead the soul back to the ancestors in the spirit world. The man was at my grandparents' house to learn *qeej* from my grandfather, a master *qeej* player.

Although these were not my grandparents by blood, out of respect for them I called them such. As they are in the same generation as my paternal grandparents, it is proper for me to call them Grandmother and Grandfather.

These grandparents spent their days watching their grandchildren, a two-year-old girl and a five-year-old boy. The boy was at summer school, a short walk down from the grandparents' house. *Sesame Street* was on, and the girl was watching a little boy and girl make a sandwich. Next, Elmo was pretending to eat a pastrami sandwich. I watched *Sesame Street* with the little girl, who clung on to the arm of the couch and stared at me. I waited patiently for my grandparents to acknowledge me.

"What do you want to ask about?" asked Grandmother, holding the little girl in her lap. The girl looked up at me and then back at the TV screen. *Sesame Street* was over and *Caillou* was on.

"I came to ask you both about my father," I told them.

Before Grandfather could speak, Grandmother said, "We don't know a lot about your father. We didn't live with them."

"I thought we all lived together in Laos?" I asked.

"There was a war going on, so we all lived in different places."

"Oh, okay," I said, nodding.

"We lived in Long Cheng, and your parents lived in Phou Ma Thao. When we moved to Phou Ma Thao, your father had died already," explained Grandmother.

Long Cheng was the military headquarters the CIA established for General Vang Pao during the Secret War in the 1960s. At its height, it had forty thousand inhabitants, making it the second-largest city in Laos. I have no idea where Phou Ma Thao is in relation to Long Cheng.

"Oh, really?" I said, unable to hide my disappointment. "Who would know about my father? Who could I talk to about him?"

"I don't know," said Grandmother.

"I don't know, either," said Grandfather. He wore a black beanie to cover his graying hair. His face was wrinkled but kind. His voice was so soft I could barely hear him. I moved my stool closer to him.

"If your grandfather was alive, he would've known," said Grandfather.

"I went to Thailand to talk to Grandfather, but I missed him," I informed them. "He died the day we flew out of San Francisco. By the time we landed in Thailand, they had already buried him."

Everyone seems to know how my father died, but no one can tell me about his life, I thought.

"Your grandfather loved you," whispered Grandfather. He started to cry. "I am only crying because your grandfather is dead now. When we were running away from the Viet Congs, your grandfather carried you on his back, on top of whatever he was carrying. He held on to Yia's hands."

"Grandfather, what about Kai? Where was he?" I asked.

"Kai was big already. He could walk by himself," said Grandfather. "Oh, your grandfather loved you guys! No matter what he was carrying, he threw you on top of that," repeated Grandfather.

"Your grandparents were good people. They were very good. We saw it with our own eyes," said Grandmother. "Your mother did not love them. When you become someone's *nyab*, you must love them!"

I nodded in agreement.

"Your mother had a whole field of sugarcane and bananas. She brought them home, but she did not give your grandparents anything," continued Grandmother.

"But why would she do that? What happened? What did they do to her?" I asked. In my head, I thought, *What? She ate them herself?*

"Don't know. We were newcomers, so she loved us. We got to eat her sugarcane and bananas," said Grandmother.

I had heard of similar stories from *Niam's* perspective. She has told me stories of when she brought home cucumbers and no one touched them. "I never told them not to eat it," said *Niam.* "Grandmother instructed all her sons and daughters-in-law not to eat them. 'It's theirs,' said Grandma. Theirs?! *Theirs* is the people on the outside, not people on the inside."

"One time, your mother asked your grandfather and me to go and watch over the shaman who was conducting an *ua neeb* ceremony for your family," said Grandfather. "After the ceremony, your mother did not say one word to encourage us to stay for the food."

"They had to come home and cook their own food to eat," said Grandmother.

I did not say anything.

"I remember one time, when we were at the farm, your mother killed one of her big chickens, the really good ones, and cooked it. She called me to eat. I came and sat at the table. I saw your grandmother and I called her to eat. She said, 'Go ahead and eat.' I realized your mother had not called your grandmother to eat. I could only eat a couple spoonfuls," continued Grandmother.

"But why would she do that? Something must have happened. Someone must have done something to offend her. Before my father died, when my father died, did my grandparents do or say something?" I asked. I could not believe that *Niam* was intentionally mean without cause.

"Perhaps something happened before we got to the village. We don't know," said Grandfather.

"Don't know," said Grandmother. "People also say that your maternal grandmother was like that, too. She had fields of fruits and vegetables, but she never brought them home to eat. She ate them all in the field."

I thought to myself, *Please don't bring my maternal grandmother into this. You don't know her.* I did not say anything. I knew my grandparents did not intend to be mean, but I could not hear any more. I thought,

People behave rationally. There must be a reason why Niam *did what she did.* This was indicative of how my uncles and everyone else in the clan felt about *Niam.* They believed she did not love my grandparents or them. They believed she was evil.

I need to love Niam *even more to make up for all those who don't love her!* I thought.

The first year *Niam* married my father, she lived with him at the military base in Muang Mok, which was a half day's walk from Phou Ma Thao. That's when she had my older brother, Kai. After she gave birth, she came home to live with my grandparents in Phou Ma Thao's country-side. Every one or two months, my father came home, once for a week. Some months, he didn't come home at all. He stayed at the military base instead.

"There were soldiers who asked him, 'Why don't you go home?' He said, 'I didn't get a wife worthy of me going home.' So he'd rather stay at the base and talk to his girlfriends," explained *Niam.*

"Did he actually say that?" I asked. "How did you know?"

"The soldiers came home and told me."

There were those who said things, and then there were those who came home and told *Niam* what was said. Like the time when I was born, my father's girlfriend told him, "Your wife only had a girl. There's no need to go home." Later, when I got sick, he finally came home.

"Why did my grandparents hate you so much?" I asked *Niam.*

Similar to the Mouas-can't-marry-Thaos superstition, there was an even worse one for Vue girls. People said that if a man marries a Vue girl, either he was going to be poor all his life or he was going to die. Did my grandparents believe that? Did they think that *Niam* was, somehow, responsible for my father's death?

"I had you three already. Your dad was at the military base. Grand-mother didn't want me to touch any knives or sickle or anything sharp."

"Why was that?"

"She said it could bring harm to your dad."

"Really?" I'd never heard of that superstition. Hmong people had all sorts of superstitions. No hot peppers on your wedding day or your marriage will be full of heat—arguments, fights, etc. Some Hmong didn't eat duck because it'd cause the family to break apart and fly away.

"I couldn't use a needle to sew. I couldn't sweep the floors. When I cooked, I couldn't use a knife to cut the vegetables."

"Okay. Could you use your hands to break the vegetables in half?"

"No."

"Well, what are you supposed to do?"

"Boil them whole."

I shook my head at the ridiculousness of the situation.

"So, I sat there and didn't do anything," continued *Niam*. "Then they accused me of being lazy. 'Don't even know if she can cook or garden,' they whispered loud enough for me to hear. So then I decided, I'm just going to do it."

At first, *Niam* couldn't seem to do anything right. When she went to get water from the stream, Grandma said it was not "clean." When she went to get firewood, Grandma complained that the sticks of wood were too small, only good for drying one's clitoris. *Niam* asked her why she would say such a thing, said that these were not good words to use to discipline someone. They got into an argument.

"I told Grandma, '*Niam*, whatever I do is wrong. Perhaps only the *nyab* in heaven can be your *nyab*. Earthly *nyab* can't do it.'"

Although Grandma never gave *Niam* specific instructions, she paid close attention and watched Grandma and her two other *nyab*. On the mornings when it was their turn to fetch water for the household, she looked to see how many buckets of water they brought home. She made sure that when it was her turn, she fetched the same number of buckets of water. When it was their turn to make breakfast, *Niam* counted the number of bowls of rice they made. When they took the husks off of the rice, she made sure she had the same number of bags of rice as well. She worked hard to be done with her chores at the same time they were done with theirs. While my dad was at the military base, *Niam* toiled on her garden and took great care of her chickens, ducks, and pigs.

"You had three little kids. How were you able to garden?" I asked.

"Sometimes I left you home with your grandparents. Then I took Kai and Yia with me to the garden. I built a little lean-to shelter for them to sit under. Kai watched Yia while I worked on the garden," explained *Niam*.

AFTER TALKING WITH *Niam* one day, my aunt called me. I had translated many parts of the book to *Niam*. My aunt wanted to tell me which part upset *Niam* the most.

"Don't write the part where people are saying how bad of a person your mom is," pleaded Aunt. "She might not have told you but I can tell by her voice that it really hurt her."

"You know I didn't say it, right? I'm just writing down what other people said about *Niam*." I explained that Americans have the evil stepmother while Hmong people have the evil daughter-in-law early in her married life and then a bad mother-in-law later in life. The rumors about *Niam* being a bad *nyab* fit into the narrative.

"I know you didn't say it, but your mom is not as bad as people make her out to be," said Aunt. "I've lived with her. I know."

"Why did my grandparents hate her so much?"

"Everybody would work the field together, and then your mom, she wanted to do a separate plot for you guys. So they didn't like that."

True enough, *Niam* did tell me that my grandfather had told her, "Those daughters-in-law who do things I haven't asked of them, I'll never praise them."

"What I'm doing, I'm doing for my relatives," answered *Niam*. "One day, they will come and visit me, and I will have plenty for them to eat and drink."

"I TOLD THEM, 'You don't know how to use or benefit from my strength, what can I do?'" said *Niam*.

Niam didn't do what Grandmother did. She did not hide her prized sugarcane or cucumbers in the bedroom so no one else could have them. She did not tie the bags in a certain way so that if anyone opened up the bag, she'd know.

"I brought all my vegetables home and put them in the center of the house and left it for everyone to eat. Even if I boiled a pot of corn and called them to eat it, they'd say, 'Okay, we'll eat it,' but they wouldn't. When I left to go somewhere, then they'd eat them."

Niam didn't worry that they didn't eat her food.

"I figured I could feed it to my pigs so they can get fat."

One time when my father was home from the military base, Grandma encouraged him to hit *Niam*, who had gone to get water.

"It's because you're not a man, that's why she's bad like that. Step on her until her vaginal veins come out. Kick her so hard that you break her ribs."

They didn't think *Niam* was back yet, but she was outside the door, listening.

Bursting inside, she said, "If my relatives encouraged me to do bad things to you, would you be happy? My husband and I don't know how to fight. Why do you teach him to do those things to me? I tell you now, the day your son hits me, I will get all of you. I will not let you be. From this day forth, I will not be afraid of you. In the past, I thought I'd leave. But not now. I will be here."

Niam never knew what she did wrong because my grandparents never told her. When my father and *Niam* argued, she encouraged him to hit her so she had a reason to leave. My father had gone to see a monk who had told him, "You stole someone else's wife. Your wife likes to argue. But she's only doing it so she can leave," so he never hit her.

"I know they said those things. But I haven't done it," said my father.

I was sitting at the kitchen table at Aunt's house in Woodbury. This is the first wife of the uncle whom I had visited in Thailand. Although they were legally divorced, they were still culturally married. Aunt had just gotten home from work and was preparing dinner. I thought she may remember my father.

"Aunt, I want to know more about my father," I told her. "What do you remember about him?"

"When I married your uncle in 1976, you were already walking. You could speak already. How old is that? Two?" she said.

"Maybe," I said, nodding.

"When your mom and Grandmother finished cooking, Grandmother said, 'Mai, go tell your father to come and eat.' Your father was working for our clan leader as his slave, writing for him. They lived next to us. Our houses were separated by this far." She stretched out both her hands to indicate the distance.

"You went and knocked on the door, but no one heard you. They didn't open the door, so you sat down at the door and waited. After awhile, Grandma said, 'Why is Mai not back? Why is Chee not back?' Grandma went and found you sitting at the door, knocking quietly."

I smiled at the image of my young self, calling my father to eat.

"Your father loved you," continued my aunt.

"How did you know that?" I asked.

"One time, your father was in Nong Het. He brought back a whole basket of fruits. You were waiting for him at the door. As soon as he got home, he picked you up and sat you on his shoulders."

A lump rose in my throat, and I did not speak for fear that my voice would betray my emotions. One part of me, the doubtful part, felt like banging my head on the kitchen table and saying, *Of course your father loved you!* The other part of me wanted to jump up and down and scream, *My father loved me! My father loved me!*

"When Blong and I were in Thailand, Uncle didn't talk to us at all," I said.

"He's always been a man of few words," explained Aunt. "The kids would be fighting in front of him, falling back and forth over each other, yelling and screaming. He'd just look at them and say, 'Stop it, you two,' but that's about it. He didn't get in the middle and stop them. He didn't yell at them."

"Why was he like that?"

"Oh, he said that the good ones don't need to be yelled at. Each person has his or her own heart. They know death and life, and you don't need to yell at them like a hen clucking."

An e-mail from a cousin, whose older sister was married to one of the sons of my late clan leader, gave me some ideas about where we had lived in Laos: "The saddest thing is that I could only see one of the mountains located next to our old town where your father passed away. If you travel south along the Mekong River you will see a dark mountain shaped like a human nose and that's where you're born and where your father's resting place is."

This cousin and his family had also lived in Pittsburgh with us, and for many years we all went to the same church.

I did not know that my father and I would inhabit the same space someday. According to animist Hmong beliefs, when a son is born, the placenta, which we Hmong call the "birth jacket," is buried at the main house post. Like the central post that holds up the house, this act symbolizes the role the son plays in performing rituals. The daughter's jacket is buried under the parents' bed where it's most convenient.

When you die, one of your souls remains at the gravesite while another one travels to the spirit world to be with the ancestors. Before you can travel to the spirit world, you need to return to the village of your birth to retrieve your "jacket." When my spirit returns, I shall meet my father's spirit in the village of my birth.

How would my soul find any of the villages in which my family has lived in Laos, let alone the village of my birth? How would I find the house where my jacket is buried? I wondered.

Animist Hmong have a designated singer who chants the Showing the Way ceremony to lead the soul of the deceased to the ancestors. In this ceremony, the chanter guides the soul back to all the places where he had lived on earth. Finally, the chanter leads the soul to his natal village to retrieve the jacket. The chanter then tells the soul how to recognize his own ancestors so that he can be reborn into the same lineage. If the soul doesn't reach his own ancestors, he will become lost. He will wander and cause trouble for the family.

Although *Niam* has told me numerous times the names of the villages where we had lived in Laos, I could not remember them. Laos was one big mess of land to me. From what I could see, the names of Hmong villages were different from the official Lao names on the maps. I didn't know if this was because the Lao government didn't officially recognize any of the Hmong villages. Or if it was because the Hmong had different names for the same Lao villages. Or perhaps it was as one elder asserted: the names are the same but the Hmong do not pronounce them properly.

Perhaps if I wrote them down, the names of the Hmong villages would not escape me. Then I could ask *Niam*, my aunts, and my uncles to mark them on the map for me. That way, I could be grounded in the geography of the Hmong in Laos. If I had told them I was going to Laos and Thailand, if I had consulted with them, this exchange of information might have happened.

MY COUSIN TRIED to map this out for me: "The name of the village [where you were born] is called *Roob Dev Laus* or Phou Ma Thao. The human nose shaped mountain is located about some miles away, but it is the only mountain that is visible from the road along the Mekong going south."

Roob Dev Laus is literally "Old Dog Mountain." I had not heard this Hmong name before. I have, however, heard the Lao name, Phou Ma Thao.

For some reason, I confused Phou Ma Thao with *puag thaum ub* or "a long time ago." *Puag thaum ub* was what elders said before they told myths, folktales, or legends. They usually said, "*Puag thaum ub!*" with dramatic emphasis on the word "*puag*" or "long," as in, "A looooong time ago." It announced to the listener that what they were going to hear was a make-believe story; one conjured by the teller to explain or make sense of things.

It was as if I were so tired I could not think straight. Or maybe I was in that quasi-sleep stage where I could not tell if I was dreaming or awake. As if Phou Ma Thao was a place that existed only in the mind of my two-year-old self. Now awake, I understood that Phou Ma Thao was a long time ago, but it was a real place.

Sometime later, I received this e-mail from Uncle Naw-Karl: "While in Laos, you can safely go to KM52, which is 52 kilometers north of Vientiane, but never be able to go to your birthplace at this time."

"What is KM52?" I asked.

Uncle explained that KM52 was Village 52, a Hmong village fifty-two kilometers north of the Lao capital city, Vientiane. Where was Phou Ma Thao in relation to KM52? I had no idea of the lay of the land.

I could never go back to Phou Ma Thao even if I knew where it was. After the Secret War, after the Americans left, the Lao government corralled the remaining Hmong from their mountaintop villages into the cities. These Hmong were no longer allowed to farm the mountaintops by using slash and burn. They could no longer pick up and farm a new patch of land when they depleted the soil in one area. They were contained on one patch of land.

I inherited the gift of writing from my father. When I went back to Thailand to visit my grandfather, the uncles in my extended family told me the following things about my father:

1. My father was born about 1945.
2. He died in Phou Ma Thao in east-central Laos, the same place I was born.
3. In Laos, my father went to school in Muong Mok, which was a half morning's walk from Phou Ma Thao.
4. Although no one is sure how many years of school he had, my father was one of the few men who learned how to read and write Lao.
5. My father was the second oldest boy in a family of six boys (four deceased) and four girls (two deceased).
6. He married *Niam* in 1968. He was about twenty-three years old, and she was about eighteen.
7. His military rank was *xov neeb*, for which he was paid about eight hundred kip a month.
8. He had his first child, my older brother Kai, around 1969 or 1970. My mom was living with him at the military base in Muang Mok.
9. My father's second child, my older brother Phia, was born about 1970 or 1971. He died when he was just a baby.

10. He had his third child, me, about 1972 or 1973.
11. He had his fourth child, Yia, about 1974 or 1975.
12. While home from military base, my father died in 1975 when a tree fell on him while he was clearing the field for an extended family member.

This list may seem strange, even random. But when you do not have a lot of things to hold on to, you hold on to whatever you can to anchor you. Although my uncles may not have known it, they helped me call back my father's soul. They have given me precious pieces of him. He was starting to take shape and come alive for me.

"Talk to Uncle So-and-So," stated Uncle Naw-Karl when I asked who else, besides *Niam*, would know about my father's life. This "uncle" was part of my extended family. When one of my father's brothers died in the Secret War, he had agreed to marry my uncle's wife. He was a respected shaman, while his brothers and sons were pastors.

"But I thought he was younger than my father," I said.

"He is, but only by a couple years."

"Okay."

"Also, talk to Uncle So-and-So," suggested Uncle Naw-Karl.

Like my father, this uncle had worked for General Vang Pao. As one of the few educated men, he had worked with the Thai officials and USAID personnel in Ban Vinai, helping to manage the camp. Here in the United States, I didn't know what he did for work, but he was one of the noted Moua leaders. Growing up, I envied his daughters who accompanied him to Hmong parties and were shown off like trophies for everyone to admire.

"Say some nice things to him, and he'll warm up to you," suggested Uncle Naw-Karl. "This uncle worked with your father. He would know about your father's work."

When I got to Uncle's house, he'd just gotten back from working on his garden.

"Go and look around the garden," suggested Uncle. "I'm going to take a quick shower."

I walked out the back door to the patio and down the steps. Uncle's garden was the size of half a city lot. Uncle and Aunt had planted pumpkins, cucumbers, bitter melons, greens, hot peppers, cilantro, and green onions.

I imagined that if my father had lived, like Uncle's family we too would live in a stately home in the suburbs. I stood in Uncle's living room, looking up at the wall of photographs of him and his family. There are black and white pictures of him and his wife in their younger years wearing Hmong clothes. Pictures of them with General Vang Pao. I scanned the wall of men, and two pictures stood out. Uncle's two daughters beautifully adorned in sparkling Lao sashes and gold jewelry smiled at me. They must've been at some formal event. Their heart-shaped faces, the slight tilt of their heads, and their demure smiles said they were ready to be of service to their father. This was what I remembered most about them. I, the poor orphan at the back of the room, caught a glimpse of their entrance at their father's side. Like a scene from the days of kings and queens, the people parted to make way for them. They stood and smiled. They seemed so beautiful and important.

Then I saw the same black and white photo that *Niam* has in her album of my father with his two friends. They are young men dressed in their crisp white shirts, black pants, and dress shoes. They look straight at the camera. They're not smiling but they're not sad. They have a serious look about them like this is an important occasion.

I've stared at this photograph thousands of times. I walked closer and looked at it again. And then it occurred to me: the guy in the middle is this uncle! *Niam* must've told me, but I never made the connection until just that moment.

When Uncle joined me in the living room, I pretended I've always known the guy on the right was him.

"Uncle, who is the bigger guy on the left there? I don't know him."

He mentioned a name I didn't immediately recognize. "You know him; he lives in Wisconsin."

"Oh, he's still alive?" I asked.

"Oh, yes, you know him. He's the father of . . ."

Uncle mentioned two Hmong attorneys in town. And then, I see him. He still has the same pudgy face; he's just bigger now and shorter in person. He has always been kind to me. His wife being the sister of Pastor Vang, he knew my kidney story and always asked how I was doing when he saw me. And now I felt foolish for not knowing his name and for even asking if he was alive.

"I know him now. What year did you take this picture?"

"That was 1969–70. Your clan leader had a house in Long Cheng. We lived on the same road, just up and down from each other. Your father came to visit me in Long Cheng, and we went to Vientiane to take that picture."

"How old were you? You look so young."

"Twenty-three, twenty-four."

"Were you married already?"

"Yes, we had wives and kids."

From Uncle, I learned that my father's rank of *xov neeb* was second lieutenant. If he had lived, he would've eventually moved up to first lieutenant, then captain. If he had lived.

The Truth

Because the Hmong believe that a parent cannot negotiate for his or her own son or daughter, it is better to have some other family member negotiate on your behalf. Nine months after the church wedding, *Txiv* sent his first cousin from Merced to St. Paul to negotiate the *rooj tshoob* with my Moua uncles. We called *Txiv*'s first cousin *Hlob*, which I mistakenly translated as "The Big One."

Blong laughed when I told him my translation.

"It doesn't mean 'The Big One!'"

It seemed fitting to me. *Hlob* was big and round like a barrel.

"What is it then?" I asked.

"*Hlob* is Older Uncle."

Hlob was a title of respect you used for uncles who were older than your father. You were supposed to defer to them because they have had more life experiences, and so they know what's best.

Just as *Niam* did not attend our church wedding, Blong and I did not attend our own *rooj tshoob*. This was unprecedented, I was told. Not attending our *rooj tshoob* was worse than marrying a gangster or lowlife, worse than marrying a non-Hmong person, worse than dating or even worse than "marrying" someone from the same clan. All Hmong people know that it is taboo to date or marry a person from the same clan. It is the equivalent of dating or marrying your own brother or sister. After a Yang-on-Yang marriage in Merced, people said terrible things:

"They are worse than animals. They are ants. Ants don't distinguish amongst themselves."

"That father knew his son was dating that Yang girl. Why didn't he stop them? He wanted the girl for himself. That's why."

Although a bride price was paid for her, "The money was thrown down like purchasing a pig at the slaughterhouse."

There was no *rooj tshoob* and meal to celebrate the abomination. Both families told the couple to never talk about their story.

As bad as these "same-clan" marriages were, we all had heard of or even knew people who had done it. No one, however, had ever heard of a Hmong couple who did not attend their own *rooj tshoob*. Or was it that it has happened before, but the elders did not pass the story around? What elder would want that kind of suggestive, subversive story to circulate among the young people? It was dangerous. As Blong was told at a Lee clan gathering in a small town in Wisconsin when he was invited to talk about legal issues in the Hmong community, "Don't talk about divorce. You'll give the women ideas."

"There's got to be people who didn't attend their own *rooj tshoob*," I told Blong's sister.

"No. Never heard of anyone," said his sister, shaking her head. "Even if they said, 'Don't tell,' you know that person's going to tell someone."

When *Hlob* flew up for the *rooj tshoob*, he called Blong to tell him to go.

"If you're coming to our house to visit us, that's fine. But if you're coming to force us to go to the *rooj tshoob*, I'll call the police," warned Blong.

Hlob never came to our house.

One night at Kai's house, *Niam* said, "I heard you said you'd call the police on us if we did the *rooj tshoob*."

"What? I've never said that. I told them to do whatever they wanted to save themselves."

Somehow, Blong's conversation with *Hlob* had morphed from, "If you come to our house, I'll call the police" to "Mai Neng said, 'If you come to do the *rooj tshoob*, she'll call the police.'"

After Blong and I were married, we visited my in-laws in Merced. I spent time transplanting cauliflower seedlings with *Niam*'s older sister, who also lived in Merced. Like other Hmong truck farmers in the Central Valley, my aunt and uncle rented land and planted various vegetables to sell at farmers' markets in Merced and San Francisco. Every foot or so, Aunt dug a small hole with her Hmong hoe. I separated the clumps of cauliflower seedlings and placed one seedling in each hole.

"Does your father-in-law have two wives?" asked Aunt. "I heard that he did and that Blong lives with the younger wife in Minnesota."

"No, Aunt, *Txiv* does not have two wives," I corrected her. "He likes to talk to other women, but he has not married one yet." I laughed.

Later on when I told Blong about my conversation with Aunt, he said it was probably because people confused *Txiv* with *Hlob*. *Hlob* had one legal wife and two cultural wives. One of the wives lived in St. Paul. I could see the resemblance. Both cousins were charismatic men liked by many people. Both were short, stocky men with beer bellies and lots of hair.

Aunt went on to tell me about a conversation she overheard at a party.

"They kept saying, 'Our *nyab* had renal disease. Her mother and her two brothers didn't want to give her one of their kidneys, so she refused to do a *rooj tshoob* for them.'"

Aunt folded the dirt around the base of the cauliflower seedling and pressed it firmly in place. I followed with a watering can and slowly watered the plant.

"I didn't know who they were talking about, so I asked, 'Who are you talking about? Who is your *nyab*?' so they told me, 'Our *nyab* is Neng Moua.'"

Although my first name is Mai Neng, some family members call me "Neng."

"*Aub yau*! That's when I realized they were talking about you," exclaimed Aunt, turning toward me. She told them it was true that *Niam* and my brothers had not given me a kidney.

I told Aunt that my family's decision not to give me a kidney had nothing to do with my decision to not do the *rooj tshoob*. It was the easiest explanation, but it had not occurred to me until I heard it.

"Hey, how come we didn't attend the *rooj tshoob*?" I asked Blong, having forgotten why we did not go.

"Because you didn't want to go. You said we were done," answered Blong.

It was true. Every time Blong had asked if I was done with the *rooj tshoob*, I said, "Yes." Every time he had said, "We don't need to do anything more with it, right?" I said, "Yes."

So now he did not let on that he was annoyed at me. What he really wanted to say was, *Why are you even asking me that stupid question now?* but he did not. We did not talk more about my question and how it showed my lack of understanding of the *rooj tshoob*. In my mind, I thought that Blong had other reasons—his own reasons—for not going.

"So why did you support my 'No Bride Price Campaign?' My brother said terrible things to you. Your family and clan were pissed at you."

I didn't even want to imagine the things they must've said to him, especially since he's an attorney who's supposed to follow rules and laws. Some must have wondered if Blong thought he was above Hmong rules and laws.

Blong nodded and then shrugged. I gave him a scrunched-up look of confusion.

"I told my family, 'That's great. That means we don't have to pay!'" laughed Blong.

He wasn't wrong.

"Be serious now. Why did you do it?" I persisted.

Blong had supported my decision to keep my maiden name. That was easy. This decision to not want a bride price? I never thought it could actually happen. I knew of only two *rooj tshoob* where the girl's parents did not collect bride prices for them. One was my cousin whose late father was a major in General Vang Pao's army. He believed, as my cousin did when her daughter married, that his girls were priceless, that no amount of money could ever buy them. The other situation was when Eric married Pastor Vang's daughter. But Pastor Vang was one of the most progressive Hmong pastors I knew. Both situations did not apply to me.

In my extended family, I'd never been to a *rooj tshoob* where there was no bride price. I'd never seen one where the girl didn't want one, her parents supported her decision, and things worked out as planned.

If I were Blong, under all that pressure, I would've told my girlfriend to go ahead and get it over with. What was it that made him different? Why did he do it?

"I agreed with you. A woman should not be bought and paid for," explained Blong.

What he didn't say was that loyalty was one of his core values. Because he loved me, he was loyal to me and would stick by me no matter what happened.

I THOUGHT THE ELDERS needed the bride and groom to be there in order to do *rooj tshoob*. I thought that if Blong and I did not go, there would be no *rooj tshoob*. If there was no *rooj tshoob*, there would be no bride price. It was reasonable to think that you needed the bride and groom at a wedding ceremony.

I was wrong. The elders did not need us.

Maybe this was because we had already gotten legally married. I think, however, they did not need us because the *rooj tshoob* is not about us.

Marriage is a series of exchanges between two clans (the Mouas and Yangs in my case) leading to an alliance. *Hlob* flew up from Merced and took two other Yang men with him to meet with my Moua uncles. My *rooj tshoob* was a meeting where Blong's family paid a bride price of $5,000 and gave $800 to my family to hold for the *mov rooj tshoob*. Like the Yang-on-Yang *rooj tshoob*, money was thrown down like they were purchasing a sow. Technically, it was a formal transaction between the two families, without the customary *rooj tshoob* rituals. And since Blong and I weren't there, there was no *noj rooj tshoob* (meal) either.

Nine months after our legal marriage, Blong and I were finally married in the eyes of the Hmong community. This was the way I understood it. I had no idea *Niam* still waited, that she saw it so differently.

Finding Family

The night before, the ten o'clock news said today would be fifty-eight degrees with a 30 percent chance of rain. It looked more like 100 percent chance with the overcast late-November sky. November in Merced was perfect for growing vegetables that did well in cooler weather such as *zaub ntsuab* and *zaub paj*. Beyond the concrete porch and before the wood fence, my mother-in-law has beds of *zaub ntsuab* and *zaub paj*. I thought about stir-frying the *zaub paj*, light green in color with no flowers yet, with chicken or pork, garlic, and ginger.

The house was warm and dark like a cocoon. *Niam Tais*, my mother-in-law's aunt, was asleep on the couch in the living room. *Pog Koob*, Blong's paternal grandmother, was asleep on the love seat on the other side of the TV. Blong and I were sitting on the couch facing the TV, which was playing a *kwv txhiaj* video. Blong checked his fantasy football scores on my laptop. I watched the *kwv txhiaj* video while waiting for the laptop.

My mother-in-law (whom I now called *Niam*), *Niam Tais*, and Great-Grandma had been up since 7:00 AM. I heard them from the bedroom. *Kwv txhiaj* was on, but I heard *Niam* telling everyone to eat. The aunt was hard of hearing, so *Niam* spoke louder than usual.

"*Niam Tais*, what would you like to eat?" asked *Niam*. "Sticky rice or regular rice?"

"Is the sticky rice soft?" asked *Niam Tais*, who, in the rush to get to the airport three days ago, had forgotten her dentures in Milwaukee, Wisconsin. She chose the soft, warm sticky rice. The three ladies proceeded with breakfast before Blong and I woke up.

Great-Grandma and *Niam Tais* were thin like me at about a hundred pounds. A strong wind could blow all of us away. They were even shorter than me, and I was only five feet tall. *Niam Tais*'s purple scarf was wrapped around her head, hiding her short, salt and pepper hair. Great-Grandma wore a black winter cap and fuchsia-colored socks that had a space for each toe. The socks were a gift from her youngest daughter in Dallas, Texas. Great-Grandma's shoulder-length hair was pulled back and held in place at the nape of her neck with a white barrette. Although we did not know their "real" ages, both were in their eighties.

Great-Grandma was a homebody. She did not like to go out anywhere unless you forced her to. But it was only her youngest daughter who could get her to do anything. Great-Grandma, supposedly, did not know her numbers so she could not use the phone to call anyone. She did not know how to use the VCR or DVD player. "I am so dumb," she always said, but I understood that she was old, and she deserved to be pampered.

Niam Tais, however, would say, "I want to go, too!" as soon as she heard you were going somewhere. It did not even matter where. Like a child who was afraid her parents would leave without her, she had her shoes on and was standing by the door. Every November, like a bird migrating south for the winter, *Niam Tais* traveled to Merced from Milwaukee by herself and stayed with *Niam* for about three months. She carried with her a little black book of important names and phone numbers. She knew how to use the VCR and DVD player.

The *kwv txhiaj* was loud and filled the whole room. It was a video of a couple dressed in Hmong singing in a Hmong village somewhere in Laos. I could not catch every word, but when the songstress sang of the sun rising, there was a sun on the screen. When she sang of *yaj yuam*, I saw peacocks. I had to listen hard to understand the riddles and metaphors of the call and response prose poems of lovers courting each other. I caught phrases such as, "My parents didn't know how to give birth to me. They gave birth to a dark face" or "Like a peacock, I'll spread my wings out for you" or "Your words are so sweet. When I get you, I will love you to the end. Our lives will be one of love and riches." The young lovers were using that soft voice that agreed with everything. This was how young people were supposed to court back in Laos and Thailand. Or, at least, this was the sanctioned way to do it at the Hmong New Year.

Although *Niam Tais* and Great-Grandma were fast asleep on the couches, I hoped the *kwv txhiaj* transported them back to the lush green landscapes of their youths. I hoped that, in their dreams, the two widows were standing next to their lovers.

Niam was in the master bedroom, watching a Korean movie that had been dubbed in Hmong. It was one of those seven-part fourteen-hour (or was it twenty-one-hour?) series. Something about two lovers who could not be together because the girl's mother had already promised her to another man. *Niam* had started watching the epic love story last night while Blong and I were watching the ten o'clock news. The movie was so loud I could hear the syrupy sometimes Korean, sometimes Hmong music and the voices of the characters from where I was sitting in the living room.

When Blong's two brothers and two sisters were here for the weekend, the house was alive with noise. A football game was on in the living room with a Korean movie or *kwv txhiaj* playing in the master bedroom. Every available seat in the living room was taken up by a body. All the kids talked loudly in English while the adults had their own conversations in Hmong. Bursts of laughter erupted from the brothers and sisters who joked easily with each other. With only four people in my family, this felt loud, but their camaraderie made me feel at home.

Great-Grandma came and sat down on the wooden stool next to my legs. Fashioned by Hmong hands, it was low to the ground, good for sitting when washing dishes outside after big family gatherings.

"*Nyab*," she said in a soft voice, taking my hands in hers.

"What is it?" I asked.

"Allow yourself to have children," she said.

She said it as if I did not want to have children. It was true that Blong and I did not want to have children right away, but it had been only three years since we got married. Hmong people thought something was wrong with you if you did not have kids right away. With me, the situation was even worse because they blamed our decision to wait on my kidneys.

I nodded in response to Great-Grandma's request. "We want children," I said.

"Don't be like . . ." She mentioned some woman I did not know. She warned that because the couple wouldn't allow themselves to have children, when they wanted to have kids, they could not conceive. They had to beg a grandfather for help.

"Did it work?" I asked.

Great-Grandma shook her head.

"You must allow yourself to have four or five kids," she continued.

I understood this was not a lot of kids for the Hmong, who usually had an average of six to eight kids, but it was for me.

"Only three," I said. "That way, they'll fit in the back of the car." I laughed like it was a joke, but I was serious.

"Oh, no! Not three," laughed Blong's sister. "Three's trouble. Just look at . . ."

She mentioned two close relatives with three kids who have had trouble with their kids.

"Yeah, I see what you mean," I said. "Okay, two then."

I thought three would be hard because the kids outnumbered the parents. Yet, when I asked friends who have three kids, they said going from one to two was hard, but from two to three was not as hard.

"You must have kids," continued Great-Grandma, not understanding my side conversation with Blong's sister.

"Of course we want kids!" I reassured her.

It was hard for Hmong elders to accept that Blong and I did not want kids yet. They expected children immediately after marriage. What, after all, was the point of marriage if not to have kids?

Great-Grandma did not ask me what she wanted to ask, but I knew she was thinking it: *Is it because you can't have kids?* Not only did Hmong parents believe I could not conceive; they feared that if I did, I would pass kidney disease to my children. I was prepared for the question, but she did not ask it. I decided that if she was not going to ask it then I was not going to bring it up. It was the usual "Don't ask, don't tell" rule of dealing with things.

Now, with all the siblings back in Sacramento where they lived and worked and Blong's father visiting relatives in Laos and Thailand, time moved slowly here. The days were long. All day, every day, this was what they did. The day was interrupted by a walk out to the garden in the backyard, telephone calls from relatives, a trip to the Hmong store, or a visit to relatives. But for the most part, the American world was far away from this warm and cozy cocoon in Merced, the other main area of settlement for the Hmong in the United States.

"Are you coming back for Christmas?" asked Blong's uncle.

Although Blong had many uncles in his extended family, he had only one surviving uncle by blood. We were at this uncle's new house. Like a brand-new car, you could still smell the fresh paint. I saw Aunt's handiwork in the clean and spacious home. It was not cluttered with things like most Hmong homes, which made even new houses "old." A dark cherry mission style dining room table with six accompanying chairs sat neatly in the dining room. There was nothing on the table. It was not storage for bowls, pots and pans, napkins, or leftover food. Instead of taped-up or thumbtacked calendars from the Hmong stores or fam-ily pictures haphazardly hung on the walls, Aunt had a thirty-by-sixty professionally framed floral print on the wall above the dining room table. In the living room, a small TV sat inside a dark cherry armoire. Sitting on soft brown sectionals against the wall, we had a clear view of the TV.

"We might not be able to," answered Blong. "Mai Neng will have just started her new job."

"See if you can find some time to come again. I'd like us to do a *hu plig* for *Nyab*. She's looking a little pale," said Uncle.

He was smiling as if he were joking, but I knew he was serious.

I laughed out loud. I was lighter than most Hmong people, but Hmong people thought being light skinned was a good thing because it meant you didn't have to work in the fields. I had never thought of myself as jaundiced or sickly pale, but that was exactly what Uncle meant. Suddenly, I was yellow slime, lighting up the whole room.

"Who knows? The *hu plig* may help her," said Uncle.

What is this really about? I wanted to ask, but Uncle was not talking to me. He was talking to Blong. And even though I was sitting right there, I could listen, but I should not answer him. That was the proper thing for a woman to do.

"No, Uncle, we don't need to do that," said Blong.

It was at this moment—three years after I had been legally married and three serious conversations later—that I realized Uncle's comment was an excuse for them to do the *hu plig* they had wanted to do. Because of the complicated way Blong and I got married, my in-laws never did a *hu plig* for me. No *hu plig* means no real daughter-in-law, just a body with no spiritual belonging. My in-laws were looking for any excuse to do it now.

Although Blong's family was Catholic, they had their own version of *hu plig* (which they called *ua plig*). Instead of it being religious in nature, they see it as social, more as an introduction of the *nyab* to the extended family. They see it only as a blessing.

My church was Southern Baptist, and, unlike Catholics, we did not mix Christianity and animist rituals, such as *hu plig*. We believed, as Pastor Vang has stated multiple times, "You cannot serve two masters." The ancestor spirits were separate from God, Jesus, and the Holy Spirit. Thus, my church did not *hu plig*. And while we attended our family members' *hu plig* ceremonies, to my recollection, my immediate family had never *hu plig*. As a result, I had not realized my in-laws should have done a *hu plig* or *ua plig* for me. I might have been offended if I had known, but I had no idea.

Blong saw the *hu plig* as part of what we were giving up when we gave up the bride price. He understood this. As far as he was concerned, we had a church wedding and reception and we were legally married. We did not need to do anything else. He was of the mind that you make your decision and you stick with it.

Now, the conversations were coming back to me. The year before when Blong and I visited Merced for Christmas and stayed with my in-laws for a week, *Txiv* had talked to Blong about doing the *hu plig*.

"If we come to California and you do one, I'll leave," Blong had threatened.

At that time, I thought Blong was being a little dramatic. *Txiv*'s question did not seem that threatening. I did not see the significance of the *hu plig*. Besides, it was not my place to say anything. I was sitting not too far from Blong, but *Txiv* had not been talking to the both of us.

Suddenly, he turned to me and said, "*Nyab*, Blong said he doesn't want to do it, what do you say?"

I was not prepared for his question. What was I supposed to say? *Yes! I want a* hu plig*! You must do a* hu plig *for me!*? In my head, I heard my mother, *As if you're starving, begging for one!* I said the only thing I could say. "It's Blong's decision. If he wants to do one, then do it. If he doesn't, then don't do it."

That was not the last of it, however. A couple days later, Blong and I were ambushed. After a party at Uncle's house, we were told to go talk to Uncle and *Hlob* in the garage. It was typical for Hmong fathers to ask their brothers to talk to and discipline their kids if they thought their kids would not listen to them. Uncle and *Hlob* were already sitting down at the table in the middle of the garage. Two black metal chairs, the cold ones without cushions, waited for Blong and me. The room was filled with a dampness that got to your bones and made you cold from the inside out. While everyone else was inside the house, watching TV and laughing, Blong and I sat on the cold metal chairs in the garage and waited for whatever may come from our two interrogators. We were captives in the dungeon, and there seemed to be no way out. I wondered who was going to strike *first*.

"Your *Hlob* says he would like you to listen to *Hlob*'s words," he said, clearing his throat.

Hlob's slow speech reminded me of a turtle running. I was confused as to why he was talking about himself in the third person. He talked as if he was *Hlob's* messenger. I had never met anyone who talked about himself or herself in the third person. *Maybe this is not the same* Hlob *who came to St. Paul to "untie the knot" Blong and I had caused by not wanting to do the* rooj tshoob, I thought to myself. When he was in Minnesota for the *rooj tshoob,* he had gotten sick and ended up at St. John's Hospital. When Blong and I visited him at the hospital, he had said, "Live your life so as to not splash dirty water on the legs of the people nearby." As a writer, I could respect a good metaphor when I heard one.

It turned out that I was not confused. He was *Hlob.*

Hlob and Uncle wanted to know what we—no, not we: Blong—thought about doing a *hu plig* for me. I did not understand why they would even ask Blong for permission. Didn't parents just tell their kids to come home so they could take care of their Hmong business? Then I remembered that my father-in-law had talked to Blong a couple days ago and Blong had threatened to leave if they did one.

"We don't need to do anything. We're married now. It's done," said Blong.

"It's not like that, Blong," explained Uncle quickly, his voice rising. Uncle sported a spiky crew cut that reminded me of a drill sergeant.

"People would say we didn't do our part in welcoming *Nyab* to the family," continued Uncle.

"If we don't do a *hu plig* for *Nyab,* we won't be able to do a *hu plig* for your brothers' wives when they marry. If we did, it wouldn't be fair to *Nyab,*" explained *Hlob.*

"We don't care what you do with them. They have nothing to do with this," said Blong.

"No, Blong. That's not how it is," said Uncle, who was thinking about ramifications for the clan.

"Listen to your *Hlob,*" said *Hlob.*

Around and around the talks went as I sat quietly and listened to the men. Was this taking so long because *Hlob* spoke slowly as if every word mattered, or was it slow because they were repeating themselves like a CD stuck on one song? At one point, Blong suddenly stood up. Uncle, *Hlob*, and I looked in his direction.

Was he leaving as he had threatened? we all wondered. We held our breaths.

Blong walked to the long white plastic table at the side of the garage, which had held aluminum trays of food a couple hours before. He grabbed a Styrofoam cup and poured himself some water. He walked slowly back to his chair and sat down. We all thought Blong was leaving, but he had only gotten water. I almost laughed out loud to break the tension.

All I could think about was, *You're just talking about doing a* hu plig *for me now!* Blong and I had been legally married for two years. We had been culturally married for one year. In that time, we had been to Merced a couple times. Why hadn't this come up before? I was not angry that we were talking about it. I was mad that it took two years!

A small part of me wondered if I should have been angry. Blong's family might have felt they needed to do one so my soul belongs to their family. But I am Christian. *Hu plig* was not something my church or family did. It wasn't something I wanted, was it? So what did I care? Why did it matter that my in-laws had not done a *hu plig* for me? Was I mad that they didn't do a *hu plig* when they should've done one? Or was it because I did not know there was something else to be done? Yes, no, maybe, I don't know. It was all of those things all at once.

Then I knew why I was at the table. *Txiv*, Uncle, *Hlob*, and the other uncles had had some version of this conversation before. Being typical Hmong men who loved to sit and talk for hours about an issue that could have been resolved in thirty minutes, they had had multiple meetings on this issue. I did not know when, how many times, or if any of them had talked to Blong before.

This time, Uncle and *Hlob* invited me to be part of the conversation not because they cared about what I thought or wanted. I was there to be a witness to the fact that they had wanted to do a *hu plig*. The only reason they did not do one was because Blong and I did not allow them to do it. It was not their fault. If Blong and I divorced later on, I could not blame them for contributing to the divorce by not doing their part in welcoming me to the family.

"*Nyab*, you're our *nyab* now. We've heard from Blong. He doesn't want to do it. What do you say? If you tell us to do it, we will," said *Hlob*.

I could only imagine how "famous" that would have made me. Oh, how the Hmong in Merced would have talked about me. Like wildfire, those talks would've spread to Fresno and the other cities in California, then to Minnesota. Oh, how my ears would've burned from all the gossip.

"Did you hear about that Moua girl who was going to call the police on her family if they did a *rooj tshoob* for her?"

"What? That's crazy! Why would she do that?"

"She's mad because her family didn't give her a kidney. As punishment, she won't allow her mother to collect a bride price."

"That makes no sense."

"Well, they got married the American way, and no one in her family went to it, not even her mom. Nine months later, there was a *rooj tshoob*, but they didn't go to it. Two years after the American wedding, her in-laws haven't done a *hu plig* for her."

"Well, they didn't want her."

"Right, but she's demanding that they do a *hu plig* for her now."

"Does she not get it? They don't want you, girl! That's why they haven't done a *hu plig* for you."

"*Nyab*, what do you say?" *Hlob* asked again.

Hlob's question snapped me out of my thoughts. I gripped the cold metal chair to get a hold of myself. The room was cold, but I was sweating with anger.

"*Hlob*, I am only your *nyab*, an outsider," I said in the calmest voice I could muster.

In my head, I wanted to scream, *I don't know why you haven't taken care of this yet! Now, you want me, an outsider, a woman to tell you,* Txiv, *and Uncle to do something for me?*

Instead, I said, "This is a conversation you have to have with your son. If he says he wants to do it, fine, go ahead and do it. If he says he doesn't want to do it, I have no right to tell you to *hu plig* for me. It is not my place."

I knew I had punted to Blong, making him the bad guy. But I was not going to let them put me in a corner and pin this on me. I was not going to give them the pleasure of saying, *We didn't do the* hu plig *because* Nyab *said "No."*

This conversation was only happening because other Hmong people had been talking about how Blong's family had not done a *hu plig* for me. Extended family members had not had the opportunity to formally meet me, their "new" *nyab*. Did *Txiv*, Uncle, and *Hlob* really care about doing a *hu plig* for me? Maybe, but if they had really wanted to do one, like the *rooj tshoob* that Blong and I did not attend, they would have found a way. What they really cared about was their reputation. They were still Hmong, after all, and this was what Hmong people did. I now understood this was a cover-your-ass situation.

I heard *Niam's* voice: *You think you're so smart, but you can only read and write. You think you know it all so you don't need us elders. We show respect for people. We elders may not be educated, but we know traditions and rituals. We remember who's done what to whom. We hold each other accountable for past wrongs. We know when people are fucking us over.*

———

"Our child will grow up an orphan!" I cried.

Blong and I did not have kids yet, and I was being overly dramatic, but I was worried. In the three years that Blong and I had been married, *Niam* and Kai had never visited our house. Because we'd done what we wanted, not what they wanted, we'd rejected them. They, in return, denied us. After several months of nasty phone calls to each other after the church wedding, *Niam* and I were not talking. Only two cousins, both my age, had invited us to two family gatherings in three years. My Moua clan had cut us off.

Blong and I lived a very non-Hmong life in that it was just him and me in our house in north Minneapolis. We did not have the typical Hmong gatherings such as *rooj tshoob*, funerals, *ua neeb*, and *hu plig* to attend on the weekends.

Hmong people are big on you showing up to help your relatives at their events. This is so that when it is your turn, they will return the favor and show up to help you. What parents do not explicitly tell you (because they assume you know) is that showing up is not enough. You have to participate and pay attention. You have to get in there and do the work so you know how to do things properly (that is, according to your family's ways). These occasions are opportunities for learning the exact procedures of religious rituals and customs. This bonds the members to each other and reaffirms their identity as one family/clan. This is when young men discuss and debate the proper way to do things with guidance from the elders. Knowledge is not the same as knowing. In order to really know, you have to work (and sometimes fight for work) and get your hands dirty.

Blong had relatives here in the Twin Cities (even one family in north Minneapolis), but they did not call or invite us to anything either. As a young man, Blong was expected to call upon and get to know his relatives, not the other way around. Even though they never called or visited him, he needed to call and visit them. If he knew about any of their events, he was supposed to just show up and help them by doing whatever work needed to be done or by giving money. At the events, he needed to sit down and talk with the elders. In order to get something in return, he needed to sacrifice his energy, time, and money on his relatives. That was what a good or respectful Hmong person did.

As a young law student at the University of Minnesota–Twin Cities, Blong lived in Minneapolis on his own. Without his parents to connect him to his Yang relatives, his focus was doing well in school. He didn't have much time for other things.

Two years after law school, Blong and I married legally. Though his family did the *rooj tshoob* and paid the bride price, they had not done the *hu plig* for me. This meant I had not been incorporated into the family's spiritual domain.

Blong and I were a young couple without the connection of my in-laws. If they had lived here in Minnesota, things would be different. People would visit my father-in-law to talk about resolving different issues, problems, or cultural things. He would be invited to clan meetings, *rooj tshoob*, funerals, and *ua neeb* and *hu plig* ceremonies. Blong and I would be expected to show up with my in-laws. It would have been easy for the relatives to relate to us through them.

Without my in-laws in Minnesota, I was not sure how Blong and I were supposed to connect with his relatives. Call and visit them even though they never called or visited us? As an outsider who married into the family, what was my role in connecting with Blong's side of the family? Hmong people are supposedly rich in social capital because we have so many family members around. Since Blong and I had neither side of our families, I did not feel so Hmong.

My "family" consisted of my Hmong girlfriends and their husbands and our non-Hmong friends. Feeling so isolated reminded me of the time in Pittsburgh when Pastor Vang and the First Hmong Baptist Church moved to Minnesota. Other Hmong families moved to California, Wisconsin, or Georgia. My family was one of two Hmong families left in Pittsburgh. Without my cousins around me, all of a sudden I wondered who I was.

"Blong, I thought when I married you, I'd have more family. And now, I have even less family. We could die here in Minneapolis, and no one would know for weeks, months!" I yelled.

"What are you crying about, you crazy woman?" asked Blong.

"My family's disowned us. Your parents are in California. No one calls us for anything," I explained.

"So what? I like my weekends. I can sleep in. I don't have to go to some ceremony that takes up my whole Saturday or a funeral that takes up my whole weekend or some meeting that should've taken only a couple hours but takes the whole afternoon."

I knew Blong sounded selfish and very un-Hmong. I understood that Blong did not want to be claimed by the clan. It meant we were obligated to show up or give money at all the family or clan functions from births to funerals to graduation parties. It meant our weekends were never our own. But as an elder told me, "You can't get something for nothing." In order to have family, in order to get reciprocity, we had to do all the things a good Hmong person did.

Being on our own meant we lived a lonely life with just the two of us. I wanted to be close to my aunts, uncles, and cousins. Having grown up on the fringes of my Moua family, I longed to be at the center of the action. I wanted to be included. I wanted to be loved.

I told Blong to call his "uncle," one of my mother-in-law's cousins who had lived in the same village back in Laos. Although he was not an uncle by blood, for Hmong people, being related by last name and having lived in the same village in Laos was as good as gold.

We had stopped by Uncle's house a week earlier. Uncle and his two wives had gone to the Hmong store and left the oldest son, who was sixteen, in charge of the kids. He was both older brother and warden. We explained that one of Blong's friends was moving to Austin, Texas, and she had a sofa bed, bookshelves, tables, and lamps to give away, and we, too, had a sofa bed they could have. They were new refugees from Thailand, and we thought they could use the furniture. If they wanted it, we would rent a U-Haul truck and bring it to them. All they had to do was drive the twenty minutes from their house in St. Paul to our house to help us move the furniture into the U-Haul.

"You guys have a lot of guests. The two sofa beds would be good for you. You sit on them during the day, and they're beds for your guests at night," explained Blong.

"My mother said she wanted other sofas," said the oldest son. "The two you already gave us are dirty now, and the springs are coming out of them."

Blong and I looked at the two couches in the living room. One was so dirty you could hardly tell it was navy blue at one time. The other couch was missing a cushion.

"These kids go outside, play in the dirt, and then come and jump on the sofas. You yell at them not to do it, but the next minute, they're already at it," explained the son.

"Do you have friends who can help us load the sofa bed into the truck?" asked Blong.

"It's pretty heavy," I said. "You'll need three or four guys to lift it."

Blong and I were standing in Uncle's dining room. The hardwood floors had been scrubbed clean of their varnish. They looked like faded jeans that had been washed too many times. A small table with four chairs sat in the middle of the room with a pair of flip-flops and a sock underneath it.

"I have two or three friends that can help," said the son.

The son's Hmong Thai friends looked different from their Hmong American counterparts. They were shorter and skinnier, with long, high-lighted hairstyles that reminded me of the eighties. They wore their jeans low on their hips and dragged their feet when they walked so the bottoms of their jeans were frayed in the back. They were hip like the popular Thai and Korean movie stars they emulated.

On the day of the move, as we had planned, Blong and I rented a U-Haul and picked up his friend's furniture. We then drove the U-Haul to our house and waited for Uncle and his son. We waited and waited. Uncle never called us. They never made it to our house. In the end, Blong paid two big guys who were standing outside to help him move the sofa bed into the U-Haul. We changed plans and delivered one sofa bed to Yia and the other sofa bed and furniture to Uncle. On the way to St. Paul, we agreed we would not do anything else for Uncle and his family.

"Mai Neng, these people don't care about us! They never call us for anything. He has my business card; he knows how to get a hold of us. That party that we were invited to, it wasn't Uncle who invited us. It was an outsider!" said Blong.

It was true. Another Lee uncle from my mother-in-law's village had invited us.

"Uncle didn't even talk to us at the party," said Blong.

I did not see Uncle at the party, but I was busy in the kitchen, cooking with the women. Since the family's arrival in St. Paul, the only times we saw them was when we stopped by on our own. The only time they called us was when they needed something from us. They never invited us to any of their celebrations or rituals.

"We're not that important to them, Mai Neng. They have their own relatives they care more about. I'm not going to try that hard," said Blong.

I had invested so much emotional energy in Uncle and his family; I had been so hopeful. We had already given Uncle two couches, and now we were giving them more furniture. If this was not to build family, then what was it for?

"Blong, if you don't care about these people—your people—why should I care? Why am I trying so hard? This whole time, I was trying to connect us to them, trying to build 'family.' That's why I kept pushing you to call him. But, I mean, you're right. They don't care about us; they don't love us. So why should we care about them?" I said.

I wanted more family. Since my father's death, my family had always been on the outer circle of the Moua family. Until Kai was old enough to join the conversations, my uncles never called us for clan meetings. As a fatherless family, we were not useful to our clan.

A friend asked, "What did you miss out on?"

I missed being known by aunts, uncles, cousins, and grandparents who look like me, to whom I belong, people who remind me of who I am—a Hmong person. I missed out on these relatives demonstrating their love for me by showing up to the hospital and sitting with me for hours for as many days as I was there. And how nice it would have been to have these people come to see me at my house when I was sick.

I wanted to gossip with my aunts about who fought with whom, who cheated with whom or got divorced, who had babies, who bought what outrageous possessions, whose kid got locked up for what, which relative died, etc. How was I supposed to keep up to date with what was going on in the Hmong community?

I enjoyed being part of a kitchen of a dozen women, hands flying everywhere, making quick work of chicken noodle soup to feed fifty or a hundred people. I longed for Hmong dishes I did not know how or was too lazy to make:

Fresh beef boiled until the meat fell off the bones, flavored with
    lemongrass and ginger
Fancy *nab vam*, a sweet tapioca drink made with coconut milk
Sweet pork cooked with soy sauce and sugar until the fat slid down
    your throat

Pickled mustard greens with the fixings of cilantro, ginger, lime juice,
    and hot peppers
Squirrel cooked with fresh herbs and spices until the meat was soft
Fresh tofu made from soybeans soaked overnight, then blended until
    the juices run clear, slow-cooked with lemon or lime juice until tofu
    soft as cotton formed

Marrying the way I did, I didn't have the opportunity to eat these
dishes, which were typically served at Hmong parties, funerals, or *Niam*'s
house.

PART III

Made Whole

Disobedience, in the eyes of anyone who has read history, is man's original virtue. It is through disobedience that progress has been made, through disobedience and through rebellion.

—OSCAR WILDE

Deciding to remember, and what to remember, is how we decide who we are.

—ROBERT PINSKY

After the *hu plig* (soul-calling) is done, the lost soul has been returned to the body. The sick person is whole again. Or in the case of the newborn or new bride, their souls have now been incorporated into the family's spiritual domain.

The family prepares a feast to celebrate this restoration. Extended family members and friends come to comfort and support the sick. They welcome the newest member into their circle by helping to cook and eat the meal. Indeed, a house is alive when full of family and friends, eating good food.

The Garden Full of Weeds

"I called your mother, and it just made me more depressed," said Aunt Naw-Karl.

Blong and I were at Aunt's house. My uncle was in Thailand again, and she needed some legal advice from Blong. She had lost Blong's business card and did not know how to get a hold of us. She had called *Niam*, thinking that *Niam* or Kai would know our phone numbers.

I asked what happened.

"I said, 'Aunt, do you know Mai Neng and Blong's phone number?' She said, 'I don't know those two.' I tried again. 'I need to ask Blong some legal questions. I was hoping you would know their phone number.' She said, 'I don't know it.' I hung up the phone, and I just wanted to cry."

It was possible that *Niam* did not know my new cell phone number or home number. But she said she did not know Blong and me.

Another day I was at a grandmother's house when she said, "People at church say to your mother, 'We heard your daughter got married.' And she says, 'Oh, I didn't know.'"

Niam was true to her words: "Run off and get married and we won't tell people you are married."

To *Niam* and my uncles, marrying in a church without doing a *rooj tshoob* and paying a bride price was living in sin.

But nine months after the church wedding, *Hlob* had come from Merced to do the *rooj tshoob* and pay the bride price. Did *Niam* continue to deny that I was married after that?

"Grandma, you have a new perm," I said.

Blong and I were standing outside the church next to a grandmother who was waiting for her son to pull up the car. She was sporting a new perm that was a little too short and too tight. Someone had convinced the old Hmong ladies to cut off their long, straight hair in exchange for perms dyed too black against their graying skin.

"Yes, my daughter took me to get it. It was hot so I told her to take me to get a haircut, but she said a perm was better," said Grandmother.

"*Nyab* Kai told me you went to help *Niam* at the garden," I said.

"Oh, yes. Your mother's garden is full of weeds. I spent one day, from 7:00 AM until 9:00 PM, helping her get rid of the weeds."

"Oh, that's good."

"Your mother asked how much money I wanted for the day. I told her, 'Give me whatever you want.' You can't pay me enough to be out there all day. It's too hard."

Blong and I laughed.

"No one can beat *Niam*," I said.

"Her weeds were so tall and overgrown, I had to cut them with a knife first. I felt like I was back in Laos, cutting rice with a scythe."

I felt a pang of guilt. *I should be there, helping* Niam, I thought.

"This is the problem, Grandma. There's only one of her. Who's going to weed when she's busy harvesting or selling at the market?"

"She told me to spend the night down at the farm, but I couldn't. I asked her, 'Why are you working so hard? All your kids have their own lives. They are earning their own money now. You don't need to work so hard anymore.'"

"Everyone tells her that, Grandma, but she won't listen," I said. "It's as if we're still in the Secret War in Laos, and she has to work so hard so we won't starve to death."

Or as *Niam* stated, "So, I would never have to borrow from them." Or perhaps it is because she is the only parent and she has to be ready to help her children at a moment's notice. She had to help Kai with the bride price. Although he was married now, what if he needed help buying a home or a car? And there was still Yia, who did not look like he would get married anytime soon, but it was only a matter of time. Perhaps

Niam knew that although we were all working now, we could not save as much as her. *Niam* had always been the backbone of the family. Unlike other widows who waited for their husband's brothers to make decisions for them, *Niam* had always relied on herself to take care of her family. She had no one else to back her up. And there was no way she was going to be caught off guard.

The Year Without *Niam*

I had the opportunity to reconcile with *Niam* at my niece's *hu plig* several months before going to Thailand, but it did not happen. Kai had not called or invited me to the hospital, but a cousin told me that *Nyab* Kai had a baby girl. I did not see my niece for the first few months of her life. Kai finally invited me to the *hu plig*. While Blong did not want to go, and I did not try too hard to convince him, I was excited to see my niece. Because we were a newly married couple, I knew people would wonder what was wrong if I showed up without Blong. And in this case, people would really wonder if Blong did not like them, but as he said, "They don't like me and I don't like them, so why pretend?" He was not wrong. The few times when Blong met Kai and my youngest uncle, they did not shake his hand as was custom. They did not call him by his proper title of *Vauv* or *Yawm Yij*. They did not even acknowledge him. I contemplated saying the exact thing Blong told me if people asked why he was not there, but I did not have the guts to be so blunt.

When I got to Kai's house, the place was abuzz with my Moua aunts, uncles, and cousins. People from the First Hmong Baptist Church also came. Although Kai was not a member of the church, many were extended family members who came for *Niam*. Besides, as *Niam* has said, "We've given up the animist spirits, but we haven't given up on our people."

I had not seen these family members for months. I wiped my clammy hands on my pants and sat in the car, watching the kids running around the blue rambler. It looked smaller than the two-story Margaret Street house where *Niam*, Kai, and *Nyab* Kai had lived for six months. Kai had called to tell me they were moving out.

As I made my way to the backyard, no one talked to me. I saw Kai's seven peach trees that he had transplanted from Margaret Street. A white E-Z Up tent covered the patio where they had set up a table for the pho, papaya salad, and grilled steaks. People sat on black metal chairs scattered throughout the backyard.

Kai was the first one to acknowledge me. He gave me a hug. Like typical Hmong people who did not hug often, we were not sure who was going to go which way.

"Are you eating?" he asked. "Why are you so skinny? Go get some food!"

At five feet tall, I have been a hundred pounds for the last decade. But Kai always said the same thing when he saw me. It felt familiar and comforting. I saw *Niam*, and I knew she saw me. I waited for her to greet me, but she did not look my way. She did not say a word to me. With a pan in one hand, she walked by and entered the house. I was disappointed, but relieved. I exhaled, not realizing that I had been holding my breath. I had feared this silence more than any yelling, no matter how loud or how long it would have lasted.

"I'm yelling at you because I love you. The day I don't yell at you anymore, I don't care about you," *Niam* had said many times before.

My brothers and I used to roll our eyes at that, but now I understood what she meant.

"Why didn't you just go up and hug her?" asked my cousin later when I told her about *Niam* ignoring me at Kai's house. "What could she have done with all those people around?"

Nothing or everything, I wanted to say.

"Go see your mom. Talk to her," my cousin had encouraged me. "Just do it."

She was right. I was done being miserable. I hoped that *Niam* and I could forgive each other for the decisions we felt we had to make.

"They're our parents. They're never going to apologize, even if they did something wrong," said my cousin. "We have to apologize even if we didn't do anything wrong."

Apologize? That means I've done something wrong. I didn't do anything wrong, I thought to myself. Although I was tired of living a life in isolation away from *Niam*, it seemed disingenuous to apologize if I did not mean it.

"I called your mom when we didn't hear from you and Blong," my cousin continued.

I did not know she had called, but of course she would. The tsunami in Thailand had killed approximately 5,400 people with another 2,900 people reported missing. No one had heard from us via e-mail or telephone for a couple weeks. It was natural for her to call my family to see if they had heard from us.

"I asked if your mom had heard from you guys."

I held my breath.

"She was like, 'They didn't tell me they were going.'"

I waited for my cousin to yell, *You didn't tell your mom? Why? Are you crazy?* but she did not.

"They're our moms; they'll always love us no matter what."

I was not sure about that.

"I asked her how things were going with you. 'It has been a year, have you two talked?' She said, 'Ah, they've not called me.'"

I had not returned *Niam*'s last phone call. In fact, I could not listen to the voice mail without being upset, so I erased it.

"I told your mom, 'It's been a long time, so don't be so mad at her. Just love each other.' She didn't seem upset. She said, 'I'm not mad at them. It's they who are mad at me. Whenever they want to come and see me, they should.'"

I nodded to tell my cousin I was listening. No, *Niam* was not mad; she was beyond mad. I had no idea I could still visit *Niam* even though we had not talked for a year and two months. I just thought she did not want to see me anymore.

"It won't be as bad as you think."

You don't know Niam, I thought.

I wondered if being homebound in winter had given *Niam*'s face time to lighten up. As my cousin's mom said, "Your mom is as black as an African." It was true. By summer's end, *Niam* had a dark red farmer's tan, a dead giveaway that she had spent more than twelve hours a day in the field. I had bought her tubes of sun block with SPFs of forty-five, but in her haste to farm, she forgot to put it on. By the time she remembered, brown freckles had already formed on her face. By the end of the farming season, the wear and tear showed on *Niam*'s fingers, which had cracks so deep, lathering them with petroleum jelly and sleeping with gloves on did not help. Had they softened? Her fingernails, especially the thumbs and the first fingers, which she used to pick vegetables, were stained black. Her hands were curled in the shape of the letter "C," the position to pick vegetables. Was she still stretching them out every morning and evening?

I wondered if *Niam* was still limping. A couple years into the farming, she had injured her right knee while jumping down from her van. From then on, she walked as if her right leg was shorter than her left. She was taller than me, but her hobbled walk made her look shorter. I wondered if she still wrapped herbal medicine around her right knee. She pounded the green leaves into a pulpy mess and wrapped it around her knee with plastic wrap and then a piece of cloth. It stank terribly, and she left trails of the green leaves wherever she went in the house, but she insisted they worked. Like my maternal grandfather, *Niam* was an herbalist. In the winter, she kept a dozen herbal plants in gallon-size Kemps ice cream buckets by the windows. In the summers, she planted them in the backyard to soak up enough sun and air so they could survive the Minnesota winters.

I was not proud of going to Laos and Thailand for six weeks without telling *Niam*. It seemed everyone knew except her. I had thought about telling her for a long time, but I kept myself busy, tying up loose ends at work and packing on the day we were leaving. At the San Francisco International Airport, I again thought about calling *Niam*, but did not. It was one of those times when you had waited too long to do something and now you were too embarrassed or you felt it was just too late. *Niam* and I had not spoken for more than a year. Would she even care that I was going to Laos and Thailand for six weeks? What would she say to me? What was I going to say to her? I suppose I could have just called and said, "I know we haven't spoken in a year, but I wanted to let you know that Blong and I are going to Laos and Thailand for six weeks."

When the tsunami devastated southern Thailand, we were safe in northern Thailand, far away from the action. But like those around the world who called their relatives in Minnesota to make sure they were safe after the planes flew into the Twin Towers in New York, our family and friends in California and Minnesota worried about our safety. Two weeks after the tsunami, I called *Niam* from Blong's uncles' village to tell her that we were safe. Kai answered the phone.

"Blong and I are in Thailand. We're safe. We visited Uncle and now we're in Blong's uncles' village in Chiangrai. Tell *Niam*."

I felt foolish. My monologue was less than a minute. I was so nervous I even forgot to tell Kai when we were coming back home.

Two weeks after Blong and I got back home, I made plans with Yia to go visit *Niam*. My excuse was the pictures from Laos and Thailand and the gifts I had bought *Niam*, Kai, *Nyab* Kai, and my niece. I thought perhaps they had moved far away from the Margaret Street house, but it was only a five-minute drive.

I was glad Yia was standing outside Kai's house with me. I felt a little like we were the prodigal sons coming back home, but I was not a son, and I was not sure *Niam* would welcome us back with open arms, let alone throw a party in our honor.

Outside Kai's house, I stood beside Yia, whose five-seven frame easily towered over me. Although I was two years his senior, Yia, with his unkempt moustache and goatee, always looked older. With hands in the pockets of his green army jacket, he did not look nervous, although he had not visited *Niam* and Kai in their new house yet.

When they moved out of the Margaret Street house, Yia told me that they had not informed him or asked him to help. I suspected this was because there was no easy way to get a hold of him. His pay-by-the-minute cell phone was always out of minutes. There was not a telephone in his apartment, about a mile from the Margaret Street house. They could have called him at work, but there was no guarantee they'd get him since the number was a general number for the kitchen where he worked as a sous chef.

"I have Kai and *Niam*'s new address. You should go visit them," I told Yia.

"No," he said. "They may say, 'How did you know we lived here?'"

Yia did not curse anybody, throw a fit, complain, or cry. He stated it matter-of-factly. Although neither of us said it aloud, I felt a little hurt that *Niam* and Kai did not tell Yia they had moved or give him their new address. With only four people in the family, I did not think we could afford this kind of behavior, but who was I to talk? My own behavior was nothing to be proud of.

Yia had had his fallings-out with both *Niam* and Kai. Kai remembered always getting in trouble for him, even back in Ban Vinai.

"He'd go and play and not come home, then I'd have to go find him or *Niam* would just beat me," said Kai.

"He was not more than five years old. It was a refugee camp. How far could he have gone?" I asked.

"Far. It was a big place, Mai."

I did not remember it, but it was true. In my research, I found that, at its peak in 1986, Ban Vinai had about 45,000 people on four hundred acres. I could see how easy it would be for a naughty kid to get lost. I could also see how hard it would be to find him.

The year Kai and I both went away to college, *Niam* and Yia were the only two in the house. There was no one else to buffer one from the other. One time, I came home to Yia having been locked up in juvenile detention for carjacking. I remember sitting in his room, trying to act as if I was not troubled by his behavior. I calmly asked how many people were there, how they knew which car to take, and what they found in the car. He grabbed a stack of Christian CDs: Michael W. Smith, Amy Grant, and Steven Curtis Chapman.

"Here," said Yia, handing the CDs to me. "I knew you'd like these so I saved them for you."

I did not know what to say, so I just took the CDs.

It must have been my fault that *Niam* and Kai had shut Yia out, too. Maybe the last straw for them was the fact that Yia was one of the three males in the Moua clan who had come to the church wedding and reception. My uncles had organized two clan meetings to talk about me and banned everyone from attending. Yia had not gone to these meetings. One of the few times he showed up to a clan meeting, an uncle asked, "You still smoking?" Yia never attended another meeting.

At least Niam *could yell at both of us*, I thought.

Maybe if we did not talk back, she would not yell as much or as long. We could tune her out like we did in high school, but that did not seem right at this age. I prayed for a short lecture; however, there was more than a year's worth of material from which she could choose as ammunition.

As Yia and I waited in the snow for the door to open, my thoughts drifted to Pittsburgh, our first home in the United States. I had stayed at my friend's house near my elementary school too long. It was dark. I ran all the way home. The icy wind bit into my face, but I did not feel it. Although it was dark, I swore I could see *Niam*'s red face and the skinny switch by her side. We kids never knew where she hid the switches, but they magically appeared when she needed them. If we knew the hiding spots, we would have thrown those switches away because the skinniest ones sting the most. The bright kitchen light illuminated *Niam*'s dark shape in the doorway. I stood still, my stomach in a knot. I wanted to run away. I had on a T-shirt and jeans. I remember wishing I had worn several layers of pants and my thickest winter coat, which hung past my butt.

Another time, *Niam* was hitting Kai and Yia with a switch. I could not remember what they did that was so bad, but it did not matter. What was clear was the sinking feeling in my stomach. *Niam* was hitting them so hard. My heart screamed, *They're going to die this time*. I cried and begged *Niam* to stop.

"You want some of this, too," she shrieked.

My brothers ran around the room. It was a tornado of a bullfight. *Niam*, the bull, red in the face, fire and spit flying out of her eyes, nose, mouth. The bull hit every time it charged. My brothers, the unarmed matadors, cried and ran for cover. I, the clown, threw myself in her path. She shoved me aside. The bull was crying, too, but all she could see was red.

———

The weight of a year's silence sat heavily on my shoulders as I waited for the door to open.

"Oh, it's you two," said *Niam* in the doorway.

She looked surprised to see us. She stepped back, and Yia and I walked into the blue rambler on one of St. Paul's main thoroughfares, Johnson Parkway. Hmong elders liked ramblers because they did not have to deal with steps. You walked in and everything was right there. *Niam* looked skinnier, and her hair looked more gray and thinner. Kai and *Nyab* Kai were not home. *Niam* was watching my niece, whom I had not seen since the *hu plig*. Although my niece could not stand up by herself yet, she was able to crawl and sit.

My niece had never met Yia, but she was not afraid of him. She stood on his lap, pulled his mustache, slapped his face with her little hands, and giggled. I unwrapped the gifts I had purchased from Laos and Thailand. I put the Hmong Thai skirt on my niece. As Yia held her between his legs, she jumped up and down with her new skirt, causing the bells at the bottom to jingle. She laughed in delight and jumped up again and again.

Niam was watching TV. I asked her if I could show her a slideshow of my trip with Blong to Laos and Thailand. There, on the big TV screen, was the Chiangmai guesthouse next to the zoo where Blong and I stayed with my St. Olaf advisor and his wife who were leading the Term in Asia. *Niam* saw the Hmong Thai friends and the Hmong Thai villages we visited in Chiangmai. Then, there were pictures of Grandfather's grave, my uncle's family, our Moua relatives, and the Burmese refugee camp near my uncle's village. In Blong's uncles' village near Chiangrai in northern Thailand, unfamiliar faces of my mother-in-law's people greeted *Niam*. In Laos, she saw the morning market where vendors sold fresh pork, chicken, and fish. There was the night market with Hmong Lao vendors and young Buddhist monks in saffron sarongs at the old royal capital of Luang Prabang. In the sleepy town of Phonsavanh, she saw pictures of the Plain of Jars, a mysterious field of megalithic jars scattered in clusters of one to several to hundreds.

After four hundred pictures, *Niam* said, "Oh, you don't have any pictures of my people. You only have pictures of your people."

It was true that I had not visited my maternal uncle's daughter in Laos. I had forgotten to get my first cousin's address or phone number from my aunt and uncle. Besides that cousin, however, I did not know of other relatives in Laos or Thailand from *Niam*'s side of the family.

"*Niam*, let's go to Laos and Thailand. I was talking to Aunt, and she wants to go, too. She says her father is getting old, and she wants to go see him," I said.

"No, I don't want to go," said *Niam*.

"Come on. It'll be fun. We can go see all the old places we used to live. We can go see Uncle's daughter in Laos. Aunt can see her father."

"No. I don't want to go," she said. "I don't want to go with you."

There. She said it. *Niam* wanted to go to Laos and Thailand. She just did not want to go with me. Other moms would have played nice and said things such as, "Oh, I don't know if I can go," or "I'm too old," or "I don't have any money," but not *Niam*. She goes for the jugular.

Kai and *Nyab* came home at dinnertime. Although they had a kitchen with a dining room table, *Nyab* placed the food on the coffee table in front of the TV. I remembered that this was where *Niam* usually liked to eat her meals. There was steamed tilapia stuffed with herbs, leftover farm-fresh chicken, steamed white rice, hot pepper sauce, and a bowl of boiled greens. There was not enough room to sit around the coffee table. *Niam* sat on the footstool, which had room for two.

"*Niam*, I'll sit next to you," I said.

"Ah, I'm not your mother," said *Niam*.

I knew *Niam* didn't really mean that. Hmong mothers often said things like this to show how hurt they were. Still, I didn't know how to respond to her. I pretended I didn't hear her and scooted in next to her on the footstool. She moved closer to the edge.

Risk

"What are you afraid of?" asked one of my James P. Shannon Institute colleagues.

We were talking about risk. Our facilitator had broken the group of twenty-two into smaller groups of threes and fours.

"What is risk?" asked the facilitator. "Talk about a situation where you've taken a risk. Answer these questions: Who did what? Why is it a risk? What happened? Then come up with a definition for risk."

When it was my turn, I said, "When I got married, I didn't do a traditional Hmong wedding. My mother, older brother, and uncles were so upset that they didn't come to the church wedding. Since then my mom and I have not talked. It's been a year, a couple months, and how many days. My mother has a stand at the farmers' market, so I decided to go help her. I wasn't sure if she'd talk to me or ignore me or what. I got there, and she said, 'What are you doing here?'"

"What are you afraid of?" repeated my colleague.

"What am I afraid of?" I reiterated. "I'm . . . I'm afraid that if I don't do something now, if I wait until she's not mad at me, that it'd be too late. I wouldn't have a relationship with my mother. That's what I am afraid of."

What is risk? Risk is doing something even though you know there is the possibility of loss, danger, or injury. It is the courage to do something out of one's comfort zone. I could not say I was courageous. I was a kid who did not fully understand the implications or the consequences of asking *Niam* to not collect a bride price.

I was willing to risk loss, danger, and injury in order to rebuild my relationship with *Niam*.

The next time I visited Kai's house, *Niam* had not returned from church yet. On a previous visit, I noticed that my niece, who was almost a year old, did not have board books. I brought her several books.

"She doesn't know how to look at them yet, Mai," said Kai.

"Oh, these books are board books, so she won't be able to rip them," I explained. "They're just picture books that she can look at."

I sat down on the floor with my niece and flipped through *The Cheerios Book*.

"Okay, let's look at this one. What's this animal? Look, it's a monkey," I said.

My niece looked up at me and started slapping the books. We flipped through more books, looking at the colorful pictures on each page. My niece smiled and hit her chest.

"*Nyab*, why does she hit her chest?"

"Oh," she laughed. "*Niam* says it means she's happy."

A half hour into my visit, *Niam* came back from church.

"Hi, *Niam*," I greeted her.

Niam did not look at me or respond. She walked past me into her bedroom.

Maybe she didn't hear me? I told myself.

Nyab set the coffee table, and we sat down to eat lunch. Although *Niam* sat at the coffee table with us, she did not say anything to me through the whole meal. The rice I ate caught in my throat. I watched *Nyab* feed my niece rice and pieces of pheasant that she tore up with her fingers.

"Here, drink some water," she said to my niece, who was standing between her mother's legs.

I watched as my niece put her mouth gently up to the spoon of water and sucked it in.

Nyab gave her another spoonful of water, and she sucked it in again.

"How does she know how to do that?" I asked in amazement.

"I don't know," replied *Nyab*, smiling.

After dinner, I left. I did not say good-bye to *Niam*, who had retreated to her bedroom without saying a word to me. *Niam* had committed one

of the sins of being a *nyab* that she always warned me not to do: hide in
the bedroom.

Yia and I visited *Niam* to give her *The Seven Samurai*, Akira Kurosawa's
masterpiece about seven samurais hired to defend a village from bandits.
Though it was in Japanese with English subtitles, like the Bollywood
films or Korean dramas, *Niam* would have no trouble understanding the
story. She would appreciate the distinct qualities of each samurai along
with the slow buildup of the story. She would have laughed so hard that
she cried for the young samurai who did not know what to do when a
young woman threw herself on the ground and said, "Are you not a man?
What are you waiting for?" It was a classic movie that I was so sure *Niam*
would watch again and again.

"I don't watch this," said *Niam* when I handed her the DVD.

Yia and I exchanged blank glances.

*Did she mean she could not watch the DVD because they did not have a
DVD player yet?* I wondered.

"*Niam*, I'll bring my DVD player so you can watch it," said Yia.

Later on, in the car, I said, "She's not going to watch it."

"Why not?" asked Yia.

"Not right now. She's never home."

Now that *Niam* was farming, she usually slept at the garden in what
looked like an old chicken coop or maybe it was a shed where the farmer
had previously kept his pigs. The sagging building with peeling white
paint was now occupied by Hmong farmers. On the left side of the shed,
behind the mesh-wire fence, the farmers stored their boxes of tomatoes and
other vegetables. On the right side was an old couch and love seat that they
used as both bed and closet. Old blankets and clothes hung on the back of
the love seat and couch. Further inside the shed, the farmers cooked their
meals with a small fire, which also kept them warm. The smoke from the
fire permeated the couch, love seat, blankets, and clothes in the shed.

*I should have gotten her the short-wave radio from Hmong Minnesota
Radio*, I thought. That would have been a more useful gift. She could

listen to Hmong radio down at the farm while she was working or in the evenings when she was done with work.

"It is those on whom we rely most who will disappoint us most," said Pastor Vang at one of his Sunday sermons at First Hmong Baptist Church.

"In order to right the wrong, you must return to the source of the trauma and ask for forgiveness."

I knew I deserved all of *Niam*'s anger. I had deeply wounded her. That wound was a cave, deep and dark. I knew I had disappointed her. The wound and disappointment were like weeds in a garden, sucking up the sun and nutrients in the ground. After the church wedding, they sprouted and grew around *Niam*'s heart. As the days and months passed when *Niam* and I did not talk to each other, the weeds dug deeper into her heart to the point where she got used to the discomfort. Given this, one visit, one phone call, two visits, two phone calls were not going to cut it. I knew this was a test to see if I really wanted a relationship with *Niam*. It was the traditional Hmong refusal, which wasn't really a refusal but a face-saving tactic. In case the person asking was not sincere, you wouldn't embarrass yourself that you were too eager to accept the offer. In order to convince *Niam* I was sincere, I would have to do it a hundred times and get rejected a hundred times. Each time, however, I had to get up and keep going back.

If this is what it takes to convince Niam *that I want a relationship with her, then I'm gonna do it,* I told myself. I knew I would have to take this brutal beating, but I was not sure how much more I could take. And although *Niam* had not yelled at me yet, I was sure she wanted to. I was preparing myself for it. Sometimes I wished she would just yell at me and get it over with instead of letting me wonder when it would happen. Sometimes, after a hard visit or phone call, I threw my hands in the air and cursed *Niam* for being the stubborn stump of a woman that she was.

I knew this was a test of wills—mother against daughter. It was only a matter of time until one of us gave up or gave in, and it was not going to be me. I had time—youth—on my side. But I wondered what it was going to take to cut down the weeds around *Niam*'s heart so we could re-establish our relationship as mother and daughter. I feared that if we did not pluck out the weeds from our relationship, they would suffocate us.

Going to *Niam*'s house to see her, calling her, bringing her gifts had not worked. I needed a different strategy, one that she understood.

"I want to help *Niam* on the farm," I said. "You think I should do it?"

It was Thursday night, and I was at Kai's house, talking to him about what he remembered about our father. What I really wanted to know was, *Was it safe yet?*

"No, Mai, you probably shouldn't do that. She's still mad at you," said Kai.

I wondered when she was not going to be mad at me. It was the summer of 2005. "Where does *Niam* sell on Fridays?" I asked.

"I don't know," answered Kai.

"Last year, she sold at St. Luke's. Is she still selling there?"

St. Luke's was a big Catholic church on Lexington and Grand in St. Paul. It was one of the St. Paul Farmer's Market neighborhood sites.

"I don't know, Mai."

Kai and *Nyab* Kai had not been helping *Niam*. He was working full time; she was in cosmetology school. Between their jobs and shuttling my niece to and from her mother's house, they did not have time to make the hour drive to and from the farm. Kai was also afraid that if he helped her, *Niam* would farm even more land. She would start expecting him to help all the time. Then what would he do?

"Where is she on Saturdays?" I asked.

"She's downtown."

"How about Sunday? Is she still in Woodbury?"

"No. The tent is too heavy for her now. She can't set it up by herself."

Kai meant *Niam* was at the main farmers' market site in downtown St. Paul on Saturdays and Sundays. The site was covered, so *Niam* did not have to put up the white E-Z Up tent.

At 6:00 AM, I asked Blong to pray for me. Blong shook his head. I was being a little dramatic. I drove to St. Paul, stopping at the Burger King drive-thru near Metro State University to pick up two number fives: sausage and egg biscuits with hash browns, an orange juice, and a cup of coffee with cream and sugar.

When I arrived at the market, I walked around and looked for *Niam's* former "Free Steaks & Glass" van. I saw the front of the van but did not see *Niam*. I walked around to the back, where I knew she would be.

"Hi, *Niam*," I said.

Niam had backed up the van to the table. Both the back doors were open. She stood between the doors, hunched over, putting red potatoes in trays.

In Hmong, she said the equivalent of, "To what do I owe this pleasure?"

"I came to help you," I said, standing there, waiting for an invitation.

I did not think *Niam* would yell at me in such a public space, but I was not sure if she would accept my help. *Would she send me away?* I wondered.

"Oh, wow, I get a free meal today," said *Niam* sarcastically.

I put the two Burger King bags down by the van's wheels.

"What do you want me to do?" I asked, ignoring her comment about the free food.

"Put the yellow potatoes on the table," she said.

"Okay."

I was eager to help and got inside the van. *Niam's* Yukon Gold potatoes were in a huge green laundry basket. There were small and big ones mixed together. I separated the potatoes according to size. I set up four rows of four trays of Yukon Gold potatoes on the table.

"What do you want me to set up next?" I asked *Niam*, who had just finished her own four by four rows of red potatoes next to the Yukon Golds.

"Set up the cucumbers," she instructed. "Don't carry them out. They're too heavy."

The cucumbers were in cartons and buckets in the van. I pulled the heavy bucket to the edge of the van and sorted the cucumbers according to size. I set up four by four rows of cucumbers on the other side of the

Yukon Golds. Next, I set up four by four rows of snow peas. I could tell it was the last of the pickings. The pea pods were big in size. Some had brown spots on them from the lack of rain. Others were yellowing a little bit from the ninety-five-degree days. I brushed the dirt off of one, snapped off the ends, and took a bite. The sweet green taste reminded me that, although they were not pretty to look at, they were still good to eat. *Niam* also had hot yellow banana peppers, shallots, beets, and pumpkin leaves for sale. With two of us, we were able to sell the vegetables and refill the trays on the table as soon as they were emptied. The bundles of vegetables were one dollar each, and the trays were two dollars each or three trays for five dollars.

"Watch the table," said *Niam*. "I'm going to the restrooms."

I watched as *Niam* walked away from the table toward the restrooms. I noticed that her clothes hung loosely on her. She seemed smaller in size. And she was still limping. *Her right knee must be acting up again*, I thought. I was sure it was still swollen. Her thin hair was graying, but *Niam* refused to dye it black or perm it. Little wisps of the salt and pepper hair escaped *Niam*'s barrette and the thin purple scarf. Her face was covered with little brown sunspots. Her skin clung tightly to her bones.

At lunchtime, Kai brought *Niam* some rice, beef laab, and a can of coconut juice.

"Oh, you're here," he exclaimed when he saw me. "When did you get here?"

"6:30," I said.

"Where's *Niam*?" asked Kai.

"She took a bag of cucumbers to the guy who backed up the van for her this morning," I answered.

Niam was good about thanking people who helped her. Wherever she had her farm, she always made sure she brought vegetables to the owner.

"She couldn't do it?" asked Kai.

"I guess there were too many cars," I responded.

"Is she still mad at you?" asked Kai.

"I don't know. I came this morning, and it was fine. She hasn't said anything mean to me yet."

Kai laughed.

"Parents can suspend judgment when they need you," a friend once told me.

While I watched the table, *Niam* took two naps in the van. She also had time to eat lunch, use the restrooms a couple times, and walk around for an ice cream cone and spring rolls. I wondered if she had time to do any of these things when I was not there.

Although I had called the house several times, *Niam* was never home. She had been sleeping at the farm since her land was plowed in May. She did not come home unless she had to get more seeds or plastic bags or she needed a good shower. If you wanted to see her, you had to drive to the farm or the farmers' market site.

After work, I made the one-hour drive from north Minneapolis to *Niam*'s farm in Lonsdale, passing through towns named Webster and Little Chicago. The quarter-pounder, grilled chicken club sandwich, and thirty-two-ounce Sprite from McDonald's sat on the passenger's seat. I was sure *Niam* would have preferred rice, boiled chicken, and boiled greens. After a day in the sun, these simple Hmong foods would be more refreshing than any greasy hamburger. But I did not want to waste any more time, going home first to make the Hmong food.

I parked my Camry by the side of the road. The McDonald's bag in one hand and the Sprite in the other, I walked across the field toward *Niam*'s blue van. She had parked it in the shade of the trees on the other side.

Niam's farm was pregnant with sugar snap peas, standing up to my waist, carrying sweet pods. The tips of another plot of peas looked so tender I fantasized about stir-frying them with garlic and hoisin sauce. *Niam* had tomato plants full of green tomatoes already. She had two rows of shallot onions whose green leaves stood tall, proud of their youth. I could see myself pulling them up, peeling off the brown outer layers to reveal the white bulbs, and bundling them into handfuls. *Niam* had dill, screaming, "Pick me while I'm young! Pick me while I'm young!" She had tall, thin cilantro already "old" with white flowers. She should have been picking them. I saw the familiar white and yellow flowers of the potatoes next to the yellow flowers of the cucumber vines already carrying prickly young cucumbers. Her hot pepper plants were bonsais full of green fruits. The exposed bulbs of the sweet Spanish and red and yellow onions were bigger than my wrists. The pathetic onion plants in my backyard were the size of my pinky finger. In the middle of the two roads going in and out of the five-acre plot, *Niam* planted kohlrabi and beets. She wasted no space. *Niam* planted this sea of green all by herself. And this was just the one plot. She had another plot by the farmhouse full of zucchini, green and red lettuce, bell peppers, and eggplants.

"After all this time, you have now come?" asked *Niam*.

She smiled at me, I thought. Her face had that red leather skin of farmers who spent every day in the sun without sun block. Her once-black pants were now a charcoal gray, washed one too many times. They hung on her thin frame. Although it was sunny and hot, she had on a long-sleeved shirt to protect herself from the sun. Her salt and pepper hair lay wet under a wide-brim hat. The hat was tilted to the side with the string around her chin, holding it in place. She had masking tape wrapped around the thumbs and the first fingers of each hand. These were the fingers she used to pick vegetables. The long hours in the sun made *Niam*, who was probably in her late fifties, look like she was ten years older.

"Have you eaten yet?" I asked. "I brought you a hamburger."

I sat the bag and drink down on the paint-peeling metal table, some-one's former lawn furniture. *Niam* opened the van by its side door, climbed in, and threw out big plastic laundry baskets and white buckets from the back. She strung rubber bands around her wrists, readying herself to bundle vegetables into one dollar or two dollar bunches.

"What would you like me to pick?" I asked her.

"Pick twelve bundles of that Vietnamese vegetable, 'oakaley,'" said *Niam*, pointing toward the greens near the shallots.

She meant molokhia or Egyptian spinach. A vegetable native to Egypt, it was also popular in Middle Eastern and Mediterranean regions, Japan, and Southeast Asia. Like okra, it was slimy and added flavor and texture to soups and stews.

"Pick fifteen bundles of green onions. And then pick twelve bundles of *zaub txu ntuj*."

Zaub txu ntuj, or literally "vegetable rice sky," is called such by Hmong people because it has ricelike grains and grows high up to the sky. Commonly known as pigweed, it was used as fodder for pigs back in Laos. However, it is edible amaranth. Most people know amaranth for its seeds, which can be ground up and used. The young leaves, however, are eaten as vegetables. It is similar in taste to spinach but hardier.

"Do you have rubber bands?"

"No," I answered.

"Here," she said, handing me the sash that she had sewn with two deep pockets to hold rubber bands and change. "Tie this around your waist."

With that, she walked away toward the red and white onion fields. I tied the sash around my waist and stuffed two handfuls of rubber bands in the pockets. I strung twelve rubber bands around my wrists so I would know when I had picked twelve bunches of vegetables. I headed toward the shallot onions. *Niam* had just tilled the ground between each row of vegetables with her 6.5-horsepower tiller. It had made the ground soft and thus hard to walk on. Walking down the three long rows of shallot onions, I looked for the bunches with exposed thumb-sized bulbs. I pulled up the whole bunch, separated each one, shook off the dirt, and then bundled them with a rubber band.

Having picked the onions, molokhia, and amaranth, I was sweating like an ape who had run around all day. I sat on the side in the shade, sucking in the Sprite so hard the straw was flat. The hardest part about harvesting was squatting then standing up, only to squat some more, only to stand up again. My thigh muscles, unaccustomed to such activity, were hot with pain.

Niam came back to the shade, carrying an armful of big red and white onions. She dumped them on the ground and then sat down to peel off the outer brown layers. She chopped six inches off the green tops and then bundled four or five big onions together for two dollars.

"Have a drink," I said, handing her the cold Sprite. She took a sip and handed it back to me.

"*Niam*, why are you making so many bunches of onions?" I asked, staring at what looked like forty bunches, with more onions at *Niam*'s feet.

"I'm making some for Sunday, too," answered *Niam*.

I nodded. Since onions were hardy vegetables that did not wilt easily, it made sense to pick enough for two days.

After an evening of restful sleep, I woke up and lay still in bed. My shoulders and back throbbed with pain.

It was not as bad as when Blong's sisters came to help pick hot peppers. After picking two big buckets, they later told me that it took them a month to recover. Although I had laughed at them, I understood the pain of bending over, being on your knees, sitting on your bottom, and getting up to pick chile peppers the size of a pinky finger on plants that were not even knee high. Our bodies were used to sitting at desks in air-conditioned offices for eight or nine hours a day. They did not know how to adjust to manual labor. It was the equivalent of a couch potato who never exercised deciding he would jog the whole day without warming up. Most young Hmong people like me no longer farmed. Our idea of farming was going out once or twice in the summer to help our parents harvest cucumbers or hot peppers.

By the time I had gotten home from *Niam*'s farm, my pink shorts and white T-shirt were dirty. My feet and legs were grimy and itchy from walking through the fields. I now understood why, even on ninety-five-degree days, *Niam* wore long-sleeved shirts and long pants when she went to the garden. My face and arms, sticky with sun block, were coated with a thin layer of dirt. It now made sense why *Niam* did not wear the sun block I'd bought her. A magnet to dust and dirt, the sun block made for an excellent mud mask and exfoliant. My whole body, it seemed, was dirty. Even after soaking in the bathtub for fifteen minutes and then scrubbing every inch of my skin, my fingernails were stained black.

I did not mind the dirt and dust. I loved being out at the farm, far away from unbalanced budgets, grant writing, ringing telephones, unanswered e-mails, and meetings across town. Out in the field with the sun on my face and the wind whispering in my ears, I could have been a happy farmer in Laos. Each family had their plot of land on which they planted rice, corn, cucumbers, pumpkins, sugarcane, different varieties of potatoes, and other vegetables. The whole family had to work together to make sure they had enough rice to feed them all through the winter months. I told Blong I could not imagine having to plant, grow, and harvest my own rice. Here in America, we went to the Asian store and paid thirty-five to forty dollars for a hundred-pound bag of rice.

Most of the time I was at *Niam*'s garden, I was there by myself. I used to think that being on the farm with *Niam* would give us time to talk. I could interview her about the vegetables she grew in Laos. I could ask her about her life before she married my father. I did not realize there would be such distances between us, with *Niam* being on one acre and me on another acre in the five-acre plot. There were always so many vegetables to harvest that we each harvested different ones in different spots. We talked only when we brought the vegetables to the van or when we took breaks to drink water or eat a snack.

I liked being at the farm because, immediately, I could see the fruits of my labor. *I can do this*, I thought. This time, I picked fourteen bunches of purple onions, fourteen bunches of yellow Spanish onions, ten bunches of leeks, ten bunches of celery, one bucket of Thai chile peppers, and one bucket of shallots. It was more vegetables than *Niam* could have picked by herself. The leeks and celery were items I had not seen on *Niam*'s table last weekend when I helped her. Although they were ripe, she did not have time to harvest them. Instead, she focused on picking zucchini and cucumbers, items she knew would sell for sure. As I walked through the field, I saw ripe rutabaga, carrots, bitter balls, and basil untouched.

Although *Niam* could plant acres of vegetables, when everything was ripe, she could not harvest it all in time. *Niam*, by herself, did the same work of planting, weeding, harvesting, and selling at the farmers' market as other Hmong couples or families. The only problem was when she sold vegetables at the farmers' market, there was no one to plant, harvest, weed, or kill the bugs. And in order to have a steady stream of fresh vegetables to sell all summer, she needed to plant multiple times. She needed to weed and thin these vegetables so they could grow properly. If she spent time planting, weeding, or killing the bugs, she could not sell her vegetables at the farmers' market.

When I left *Niam* at 9:00 PM, she was still picking cucumbers. *Niam* had on her headlamp so she could see in the dark.

"*Niam*, that's enough for tomorrow. Don't pick too much or else they'll go to waste," I told her.

"Okay. But my bucket isn't full yet."

"I know, but it's getting dark, and you still have to wash all the vegetables."

"You go home. It's not good to drive when it's so dark."

"Okay, *Niam*. I'll see you tomorrow."

As I walked to the car, I thought about how *Niam* still had to wash the potatoes, beets, onions, leeks, celery, and cucumbers. I wondered how long it was going to take her. When was she going to get to sleep? I sat in the car with the air conditioner on full blast. I wanted to help, but my body felt like lead. I still had to make the one-hour drive back home.

After I had helped *Niam* several times at the farmers' market and at the farm and she had not yelled at me, I told Blong he should go and help, too. I figured this was the safest way to get through to *Niam*. Besides, he was not doing anything on Saturday and Sunday mornings. *Niam* could use more help, and I would have more fun with Blong there.

"Sure. Why not? Just get me up," said Blong.

On Saturdays, I got up at 6:00 AM to cook breakfast for Blong and me, and to make lunch for all of us. Although Blong thought it was unnecessary, I wanted us to eat in the mornings. I knew that when we got started, we would not have any time to eat until well after the market was closed. With *Niam* working late into the night and the market starting so early, I was sure she didn't have time to make food.

"You don't even have time to eat your own vegetables!" I complained to *Niam*.

When Blong and I arrived early enough, we helped *Niam* put up the white E-Z Up tent. Around the four legs, we strapped sandbags to hold the tent in place in case of strong winds.

"There was not a time when you came early," *Niam* would later correct me.

I laughed. "That's why I said, 'When we arrived early enough . . .'"

"By the time you got there, I'd already got the tent and set up the table. Then you just came to stand there. You were so late that you might as well not come," continued *Niam*.

Next, we set up the three tables into a U-shaped configuration. On the tables, we arranged the vegetables that could fit into the trays: potatoes, peppers, green beans and snow peas, tomatoes and shallots. Neat rows of red, green, yellow, and white colored the table. In front of the tables, upside-down buckets held two wooden planks. On the planks, we placed the bunches of beets, greens (pigweed, molokhia, amaranth), big onions, table onions, cilantro, and dill. All of this needed to be set up by 7:00 AM, when the first customers arrived.

While Blong talked to the customers and sold the vegetables, *Niam* and I refilled the trays. Blong and I were the ones who chitchatted with the customers and answered questions such as,

"Is this lettuce?" asked the customer, pointing to the mustard greens.

"What are these funny-looking things?" asked the customer, pointing to the bitter melons which looked like cone-shaped cucumbers with ridges.

"Are these hot?" asked the customer, pointing to the yellow habaneros.

"How do you eat this?" asked the customer, pointing to the kohlrabi.

We had substantive conversations about how to eat kohlrabi, cook beets, make dill pickles, and can tomatoes. People wanted to know where *Niam's* farm was and if we sprayed our vegetables. Blong and I enjoyed seeing and talking with the same customers week after week.

It was also our job to write and put up the signs for all the vegetables. The American customers tended to buy more vegetables when there were clear signs with the prices on them. They could just point to what they wanted and not worry about asking questions in English to Hmong farmers who spoke broken English. Blong and I corrected *Niam's* signs that said "Shallow onions" to "Shallot onions."

Blong was good at negotiating with the customers who wanted to buy in bulk or who wanted good deals from us. Unlike me, he did not mind the negotiations. We sold vegetables until twelve noon and then helped *Niam* pack up. This consisted of putting all the unsold vegetables back in the different buckets or boxes and stacking them neatly in the van.

"Did we sell anything? How come there's still a whole van full of vegetables?" said *Niam* sometimes.

When Blong and I were there, *Niam* got to do a lot of things. With a soft cloth, she wiped and polished her tomatoes, which she did not wash. Getting the tomatoes wet made them rot faster. Polishing meant she would be able to sell them the next several days. *Niam* also caught a nap in the van to make up for the few hours of sleep she got the night before. She used the restroom. She ate her food. She strolled down the aisle to see what the other farmers were selling and for how much. She bought kettle corn from the Laurent Brothers, who also lived in north Minneapolis. Sometimes, on Saturdays, she drove our Camry down to the farm to harvest more vegetables for Sunday. She especially wanted to pick her tomatoes if it looked like it was going to rain. Other times, she pulled up the weeds that had grown over the vegetables.

Blong and I helped *Niam* three summers in a row. Even after our daughter Erica was born and was able to walk, we took her with us to the farmers' market to help *Niam*. Sometimes Yia came and helped as well.

During the week, when Blong and I were working, *Niam* sold her vegetables by herself. She did not have time for what she called "idle" chitchat.

"You buy?" she asked the customers.

When they slowly said, "Um, yes, I'd like to get some tomatoes, please," she quickly replied, "Which one?"

She pulled off the white plastic T-bag, opened it, and waited for the customers to choose their trays.

"Buy three for five dollars—cheaper. Very good," she said when she wanted them to buy more.

Listening to *Niam*, I felt rushed and nervous for the customers. It was not that she did not understand the importance of small talk. It was just that she had to bag the vegetables, give out the change, refill the trays, and help the next customer all by herself.

Niam spoke the most essential part of a sentence and did not waste time on articles or pleasantries. She did not have time to bargain with the Southeast Asian or Eastern European customers who wanted three bundles of vegetables for $2.50 (a savings of fifty cents). She had little patience for customers who examined every bitter melon or cucumber in a tray. They switched the ones they did not like with others from a different tray and, in the process, messed up four rows. "This one not good. Switch!" complained these customers. They wanted *Niam* to give them a new one. When she did, they then wanted to take the "not so good" vegetable home with them.

Although helping *Niam* at the garden and the farmers' market was a lot of work, after awhile, it felt natural. *Niam* did not resist the help. In fact, she was friendly. Conversations seemed to float easily back and forth between *Niam*, Blong, and me. And with us helping *Niam*, my brothers came to help her as well. Through hard work, I regained my position as the peacemaker in the family.

Saying Nothing at All

I was seeing *Niam*, but I still missed her. I did not say anything to her. A therapist friend suggested I say, "I miss you," and leave it at that. It sounded easy enough, but I could not get myself to say it. The words, heavy as lead, were lodged in my throat. I could not spit them out.

I was sure *Niam* missed me, too, but she did not say anything, either. There was no "I miss you" or "What have you been up to?" or "How are you?" Nothing. *Typical*, I thought. Hmong people did not say, "I love you" or "I'm sorry," either. It was not that we did not have these feelings or that we did not have the Hmong words for them. It was just that we did not say them to each other. As with writing, Hmong people believed in "show, don't tell." They believed it was better to show someone you loved them by doing things for them. What was even better was doing what they wanted before they asked you to do it. That was how you showed your parents you loved them.

Niam has often said, "We parents love you by giving you a place to live, food to eat, and clothes to wear." They loved us when they went to work every day. Although their jobs as janitors or factory workers were not what they had envisioned for themselves, they took care of their families. When they told us to go to school, do our homework, and behave in class, they loved us. "Don't smoke," "Don't come home with full bellies," "Learn to cook and clean so your in-laws won't send you back home" was love. Farming acres of vegetables was love.

To *Niam*, words were empty promises easily blown away by the wind. When she was wrong, she did not say, "I'm sorry." Instead, she was super nice to you. She made you your favorite dish. If you were at the grocery store, she allowed you to get a treat. She smiled her sly smile in the hopes that you knew she was sorry. You did not discuss what happened, who said what to whom, or who was right or wrong. You behaved normally as if nothing happened, as if her words had not almost killed you. You pretended everything was just fine, like the sun rising in the morning. That was how it was with *Niam*.

In the four years that I had been married, *Niam* had never once been to my house. Not that Blong and I had invited her. If we did, would she have come? She never once asked what Blong does for a living. But I knew she knew. Plenty of our relatives and their kids have called Blong for legal advice. They all talked; they always talked. As we say in the Hmong community, "Gossip is faster than the telephone." *Niam* never once asked about my in-laws, but, again, I knew she knew. *Niam*'s older sister, my aunt, lived in Merced with my in-laws. My cousins knew Blong's uncle.

Niam did not even ask the questions that Aunt asked:

"Does he love you?"

"Yes."

"Is he patient?"

"No," I answered, laughing. "He loves me, but he is not patient."

Blong thought about things quickly and made decisions quickly. I, however, needed time to mull things over, let things sink in, talk to my friends about it, then decide. My deliberate decision-making often frustrated Blong.

"But once I make a decision, I'm good," I tried to reassure him. "It just takes me awhile to get there."

I was sure Kai and *Nyab* had told *Niam* of my pregnancy. But she did not ask about it. No "How are you feeling?" or "How far along are you?" or "Do you know if it's a boy or a girl?" I, her only daughter, was pregnant with her granddaughter, and yet she asked me no questions. I had a kidney transplant, and yet there was no "Are your doctors okay with you having a baby?" or "Are you still taking anti-rejection drugs? Is that okay for the baby?"

She said nothing about it, so I said nothing about it. It was as if I were not five months pregnant. It was as if I were still just her daughter, her unmarried daughter.

What else did we need to do to get *Niam* to acknowledge that I was married? What other Hmong ritual or tradition did Blong and I need to do to get her to start calling him by his proper title of *Vauv*?

Clearly, it was not enough that nine months after the church wedding, *Hlob* had gone to my house and finished the *rooj tshoob*. The bride price, which I had not wanted my family to collect, was paid. Fines to right the wrongs of doing the church wedding before the *rooj tshoob* were paid. Although it was true that Blong and I did not go to our own *rooj tshoob*, men from both sides of the families had taken care of the *rooj tshoob*.

Blong and I were married in the traditional Hmong way, finally. What else was there to do?

Blong and I had decided to name our firstborn, Erica, after Eric, my kidney donor. *Would* Niam *babysit Erica after all that has happened?* we wondered.

I was supposed to ask *Niam* if she would be willing to do it. We decided we would pay whoever watched our child. We did not want *Niam* to find out that we had paid someone else to watch our child without first asking her. We knew *Niam* was busy with the farm from May to late September and would not be able to do it then. We also knew she was already watching Kai's two kids, so it was understandable if she chose not to watch a third kid.

People told me that kids "fix" things—broken relationships, no relationships.

"Oh, when she looks at that baby, she won't be able to resist!" they said.

I was not so sure. People also said time heals things. Four years had not healed my broken relationship with *Niam*. It had, perhaps, numbed the pain, but I know *Niam*. She is an elephant; she does not forget.

After a couple months of not asking *Niam*, Blong said, "You're never going to ask her, are you?"

"I will!" I insisted. "Just let me do it on my time."

I knew Blong did not believe me. I did not believe myself. I did not want to ask *Niam* right away. I did not want her to think that was the only reason why I helped her at the farm and farmers' market. But I was not sure when I was going to ask her.

On a Sunday at the downtown St. Paul Farmer's Market when things were slow, I decided to ask *Niam*. Blong was home, but Kai had come to help out. Kai peeled off the dead brown skins from the big red onions. I, too, took advantage of the open space.

It's time. Whatever it is, you need to know, I told myself. *If she doesn't want to do it, you need time to find daycare.*

"*Niam*, when we have our child, would you be willing to watch her?" I asked.

"So, why can't your in-laws do it?" asked *Niam*, smiling slightly.

"Because they live in California," I reminded her.

"I can't do it during the summer," said *Niam*.

"That's okay."

"Maybe I will take them to the garden with me?" asked *Niam*.

She proceeded to tell me how back in Laos they used to take the little kids to the farm when they did not have anyone to watch them. The boys filled their time by making mud pies out of mounds of dirt and their own piss.

"Me, I saw every bird's nest," said *Niam*, who spent time roaming around the farm by herself.

Although *Niam* had not exactly said, *Yes, I will watch your kid*, it was as good of a "yes" as I could have expected. I could live with that for now. When I got home, I told Blong.

"That's it? That's not a 'yes,'" he said with a quizzical look on his face.

"It's a soft 'yes.'"

A New Beginning

A week after Erica's birth, *Niam*, Kai, *Nyab*, and my niece came to my house.

"Why didn't you wrap up your stomach?" asked *Niam* when she saw my gut hanging out. I could not help but wrap the robe tighter around myself to hide my gut.

"Back in Laos, we wrapped up our stomachs right after we gave birth," said *Niam*.

I had heard something to that effect, but I did not know how or when to do it.

"I was at the hospital," I explained. "The nurse came in and massaged my stomach so I could get rid of all the blood."

"It doesn't matter. You could've wrapped it up," insisted *Niam*.

Niam, like other Hmong women her age, believed that wrapping up your stomach tightly with a long sash would shrink it back to its pre-pregnancy size. I wished *Niam* had been at the hospital during and after Erica's birth, but I knew she was busy at the farmers' market.

"Now you'll know what it means to be mother and father," said *Niam* as she held Erica for the first time.

She meant Blong and I would finally understand the pain kids put their parents through. Blong, sitting next to me, laughed. I was nervous, but glad that *Niam* had come to visit. Glad that she was holding my daughter in her arms. *Niam* unwrapped Erica from her swaddle.

"Grandma, she's got your pinky toe," said Kai as he touched Erica's left foot. "That toe is definitely yours."

Niam laughed. I looked at Erica's left foot, and sure enough, her pinky toe was a small macaroni noodle just like *Niam*'s.

"I brought you some *tshuaj*," said *Niam*.

She took out a quart-sized Ziploc bag of what looked like straw-colored dried sprigs. "Take three or four of these and cook them with the chicken," she instructed. This was in addition to the fresh Hmong herbs used specifically with chicken.

I nodded and thanked her.

"Well, we better go," said Kai.

It was about 8:00 PM on a Sunday night. *Niam* was starting to nod off. I knew it had been a long day for her.

"Okay," I said. "Thanks for coming."

ALL THE HMONG WOMEN wanted me to be on the traditional postpartum diet of rice and boiled chicken for a month. They believed this bland meal would be gentle on my vulnerable body, thus healing it and preventing me from aches and pains in my old age.

"Thirty days is not too long for good health in old age," I told myself.

At the hospital, my family doctor had reminded me that Hmong women had given birth for centuries without medication. I was sure I could do without medication until I felt the contractions. I loved chicken, but I did not know if I could eat three meals of the same thing every day for thirty days. Steamed rice, boiled chicken, and broth flavored with salt and special Hmong herbs did not sound that exciting. Especially without hot pepper sauce (thinly sliced hot peppers with green onions, cilantro, lime juice, and fish sauce) to wash down the chicken. I did not even know if I could stand the smell of the special herbs for thirty days.

In Laos, where meat was scarce, not everyone got to eat it. It was a privilege to eat chicken, which was reserved for the postpartum woman. In America, with so many food choices, I wanted to be on the "chicken-plus" diet.

"You know, chicken plus fish, pasta, shrimp, ice cream," I told Blong after my family had left.

"There's no such thing," he said, raising his eyebrows.

He wrapped Erica up in her swaddle and placed her back in her basket on the floor, next to the couch where I was sitting.

"Okay, maybe not ice cream. I'm not going to go out and get myself a greasy hamburger and fries, like some other women. But how about fruits and vegetables? Those are good for you. Plus, your body needs a balanced diet, doesn't it?"

Blong shrugged and gave me a resigned look of, *How would I know? Why are you asking me?*

"I don't understand how it could just be rice and chicken for a whole month. Why can't you have fruits and vegetables, too?"

"Call *Pog*," suggested Blong. He meant Grandma, my mother-in-law. Now that we had Erica, it was appropriate for us to call my mother-in-law "Pog" so that Erica would know what to call her.

I nodded and looked at Kou Vang's *Soul Calling* painting on my living room wall. It was an original painting of three shamans playing their *qeej*, green with life. On the left side, you see the face of the most prominent shaman. With the *qeej* in his mouth and his hair flying across his face, you know he is in motion. The second shaman is in the middle, and he has just turned so you see his side profile. The last shaman has just squatted with his left foot in front and his *qeej* to the left of that foot. Swirls of golden shaman chants follow where the *qeej* leads. At the top, rich hues of red, purple, and flecks of gold show the intensity of the fight for souls.

After *Niam*, Kai, *Nyab*, and my niece left, I could not help but cry a little. Four years, and this was the first time they stepped foot into my house. Erica, by being born, was able to melt *Niam*'s heart in a way that

I could not. If I had believed a baby had this much power, I would've had a baby years ago.

"They're foolish young people," said my mother-in-law, whom I now called *Niam*—or *Pog*, in front of Erica. She, in turn, called me *Nyab*. "They don't know anything. Forgive them."

We were at Kai's house. I had not planned to take my mother-in-law with me to visit my mother, whom I now called *Niam Tais*. Nevertheless, I did not know how to sneak out of the house with Erica and her diaper bag without anyone asking where I was going.

I had needed a break from the visitors who had come to help me two weeks after I gave birth. I tried not to be overwhelmed with *Niam*, Blong's aunt, and Blong's brother, who escorted the ladies on the flight from California to Minnesota. Blong's cousin had also dropped off *Niam's* maternal aunt, *Niam Tais*, who lived in Milwaukee, five hours away. (Yes, I called my mother and Blong's great-aunt by the same name. Hmong relationships are complicated. I am sometimes at a loss for what to call people.) There was one newborn to six adults.

Erica was the second grandchild in the family after more than a decade. And since some people had suspected that I might not be able to conceive, her arrival was exciting.

Blong and I had a small TV with no cable and no Hmong movies or music for *Niam* and the aunties. There was not much to do all day long. Blong's brother, who was used to playing video games or watching movies on his flat-screen TV, sat in the dining room and counted the cars that drove by.

I understood it was a privilege to have three women come help with the baby so I could rest. But all of a sudden, my three-bedroom house felt like a one-bedroom cocoon with six adults. I wanted to retreat into my bedroom, but my "good Hmong girl" self would not let me.

"Niam, I didn't tell my mom that you all were coming with me," I said in the car on the way to St. Paul.

I did not know how to explain showing up at my mother's house with three uninvited guests. I had only meant to tell *Niam* that I was going to visit my mom, not take her along with me. Somehow, the telling turned into an invitation. And the one invitation turned into three. The aunties both squeezed into the back next to Erica's car seat.

"If she says anything to you, you can just say, 'Oh, I was on my way here and they asked me where I was going. When I told them, they insisted on coming with me,'" suggested *Niam*.

I was relieved we had a plan.

"Don't be mad when your mom yells at you," said *Niam*.

"Oh, I'm not mad," I said, focusing on the road.

"When you've done something wrong, they will yell at you, but let them," she continued.

I nodded. Then we were at Kai's house. I stood outside the blue rambler with Erica's diaper bag. *Niam* carried Erica in her car seat. The aunties helped each other up the stairs.

"Oh, *tuaj los*," said my mother when she saw my mother-in-law. She opened the door and welcomed us inside.

"*Niam Tais*, this is *Niam*," I said, introducing my two moms to each other.

"Come in, come in," said *Niam Tais*, ushering us into the house.

Although we had shown up unannounced, *Niam Tais* made us a meal in what seemed like minutes. Although Blong's aunts were toothless, both having left their dentures at my house, and my mom was not feeling well, we all sat at the table and ate. We then came into the living room and sat down.

"They're foolish young people," said my mother-in-law. "They don't know anything. Forgive them."

I have learned to say nothing in situations like this. Situations that were not for arguing. Situations where people talked about you as if you were not there. Unlike Blong, who is a bull, charging at the flash of the matador's red cape, I have learned that the tongue-lashings were cut in half if you did not add fuel to the fire. If you kept silent, neither agreeing nor disagreeing, neither confirming nor denying, your parents did not have anything or anyone with whom to argue.

"Oh, I don't think anything of it," answered *Niam Tais*.

No one believed her, but we were all making nice.

"If they believed I was an important mother, then they wouldn't have done that," continued *Niam Tais*.

I was not sure if she was talking about Blong's family and how they did not pay a bride price for me until nine months after the church wedding or if she was talking about how Blong and I did not go to the *rooj tshoob*. Knowing my mother, she probably meant both. It was clever how she was able to accuse both parties by using the all-encompassing Hmong word *lawv* or "they." And it was so quick and seemingly innocent that no one had a comeback.

"I am not anyone important," said *Niam Tais*.

Hmong elders were notorious for saying the exact opposite of what they meant to say. This was *Hmongspeak*. You were not supposed to toot your own horn and say, *Look at how important I am!*

"They're educated people," continued *Niam Tais*. "They know how to treat people."

Again, a slight so quick and seemingly innocent. And it was technically true. How could you dispute it?

"Please tell them what to do. Please give them advice," begged my mother-in-law.

"Oh, even if I did, they won't listen," said *Niam Tais*.

"They'll listen," answered *Niam*. "Why wouldn't they?"

"I am not valuable. My words are not important. They have no respect for me," insisted *Niam Tais*.

Later, my mother would remind me that Kai and I once called her a "Garbage Lady," after she took us to collect aluminum cans around our neighborhood in Frogtown to make extra cash.

I do not remember how my mother-in-law responded. I do not remember where my four-year-old niece and two-year-old nephew were. All three of us were characters in a Charlie Chaplin film. Someone had turned the mute button on us while my two mothers met for the first time since Blong and I married four years ago.

Blong's aunts sat on the couch next to my mother-in-law. Both were hard of hearing and had left their hearing aids at home. Neither heard much of the conversation. They clung on to each other, smiled, and watched TV. After about an hour, I herded everyone back into the car and drove home.

I was tired of holding my tongue, of not saying what I was thinking, of not knowing, of not having answers. Today, I had come to help *Niam* at the farmers' market with a purpose. Today was the day, I decided. I was going to ask *Niam* why she had not called Blong by his proper title of *Vauv* as she was supposed to. Blong had always called my mother *Niam*, as he was supposed to. *Niam*, however, called Blong by his first name, or she did not call him anything at all. She might as well have called him "Stranger," since that was how she treated him.

I waited until we were done selling for the day. We put back in the van all the tables and vegetables we had not sold. We swept up the vegetable scraps on the floor. The Hmong vendor selling raspberries next to us was gone.

"*Niam*, before we go, I have to ask you something," I said.

I knew this was the equivalent of a girl saying, "We need to talk" to a guy, which is always a bad start. My heart pounded in my ears. *Niam* stopped in her tracks.

"Blong and I have been married for six years now. We have a two-year-old. The *rooj tshoob* is done. A bride price has been paid. Why haven't you called Blong *Vauv*?"

I stood next to the van. *Niam* was facing me. There were still other Hmong vendors around, but they were far enough away not to hear our conversation.

"Well, his name is Blong, isn't it?" said *Niam* with a sly smile.

I smiled and shook my head. She was not wrong, but she was not getting away from this one, I decided. I waited.

"Okay. Since you've asked, I'll tell you," said *Niam*, her voice tight and serious now. "I'll tell you the truth so you know. The *rooj tshoob* is done, but I have not called him *Vauv* because you have not done the *mov rooj tshoob* for us."

I listened intently, wanting to make sure I understood every word.

"The *mov rooj tshoob* is important because it recognizes me as your mother. It gives people permission to call Blong your husband. They know what to call him—*Vauv* [Son-in-Law], *Yawm Yij* [Brother-in-Law]. People can call you to come and join their parties and gatherings."

I had no idea that the *mov rooj tshoob* was so significant, that it had that much meaning. That it was such a critical piece of the *rooj tshoob*. I did not know it was so important to *Niam*. For so many years, this was the missing piece?

"At the *rooj tshoob*, the Yang representatives said that you prevented them from coming to do it," continued *Niam*. "That you would call the police on them."

"No, *Niam*, that was not me. I never told them that."

"Your mother-in-law was so afraid you'd call the police on them. One of the Yang guys, you know, your cousin's aunt's ex-husband, he told your mother-in-law, 'Don't worry. If she calls the police on us, let the world hear that our daughter-in-law called the police on us for doing a *rooj tshoob* and paying a bride price for her. Let us get that reputation.'"

"You mean the little guy?"

"No, not that one. This is the one before that one."

Hmong parents always spoke about different extended family members as if they were your immediate family. When you did not know who they were, parents had little patience to connect the dots for you.

"*Niam*, I spoke to Blong's dad. I told him to go and do whatever he needed to do to save himself. I did not prevent them from coming. I never said I'd call the police on them."

"No, they said you would call the police on them."

"No, when *Hlob* was trying to convince us to come to the *rooj tshoob*, Blong had told him, '*Hlob*, if you're coming to my house to visit me, that's fine. But if you're coming to my house to force me to go to the *rooj tshoob*, I will call the police on you.'"

"So you guys did say it?" asked *Niam*.

"Not me!"

"I don't know; that's what they said."

"No, I never said it."

I understood that Blong had said something along those lines, but it was important for *Niam* to know that I did not say those things.

"Your Moua uncles had sent word to the Yang people how many times, but they ignored them. They said you'd filed a lawsuit to the White House so that all young Hmong people who got married wouldn't have to pay bride prices. They had to wait to see if it would pass. If it did, then they didn't have to come. Since it didn't pass, the lawsuit came to the Hmong 18 Clan Council. They read it and closed the case without merit. That's when the Yang people came to do the *rooj tshoob*."

"What?"

This was news to me.

"*Niam*, I know what they're talking about."

The Hmong Marriage Bills were legislation introduced by Minnesota Senator Mee Moua in 2002 and Minnesota Representative Cy Thao in 2003. The spirit of the bills was to allow the way the Hmong married to be legal marriages so we would not have to get married twice, once culturally and then legally. This was happening at the state, not at the federal level. In addition, the bills never specifically addressed the bride prices. Blong and I had followed the bill and had attended committee hearings. Blong had spoken out against certain measures in the bill.

"Blong and I had followed the Hmong Marriage Bill," I told *Niam*. "This was something that Mee Moua and Cy Thao were working on. I wish I was that smart and it was my idea so I could claim it. But it wasn't me who wrote it."

"I don't know what to think. That's what they said."

"I didn't do it. No, I did not do it," I repeated, shaking my head.

"Why did they say that? They said they know Hmong traditions. Your cousin's aunt's ex-husband said, 'Your daughter scolded you so much. She prevented us from coming. She wanted the *rooj tshoob* to be between you and her. We're only here because we rebelled against her.'"

"I've never said anything bad about you," I insisted.

"They also said that the Thaying guy in Wisconsin, he's in jail because of you, and if he's going to get out of jail then you need to go and free him."

In early 2009 in Milwaukee, Wisconsin, a Hmong woman, in the process of divorce, testified about how her husband, Thaying Lor, had kidnapped, raped, and culturally married her at the age of twelve. He was twenty-five at the time. The bailiff, who heard this, alerted law enforcement, and Thaying was charged with five counts of sexual assault. Out of respect for the culture (or was it fear?), the victim did not press charges.

"What?"

Again, news to me.

"Oh, my goodness. I had nothing to do with that. Nothing. First of all, if I could free him, I wouldn't. He deserves to be in jail for raping his wife when she was only twelve. Second, that happened six years after I got married: how could I be responsible for him being in jail?"

"I don't know. That's what they said."

I didn't know what was going on either, but it was clear people were still spreading rumors about me.

"*Niam*, I'm not that powerful. I couldn't have done all this. It's all lies. They're making up excuses to cover their asses for what they didn't do."

"They said a lot of other bad things about you." She paused. "It's okay. It's in the past now. We'll let it go," said *Niam*.

Why didn't she want to tell me? I wondered. *Does she finally believe that I had no part in the things the Yang people had accused me of? Were they such painful things that she doesn't want to remind herself of them?*

Part of me wanted to know. Having heard the things I've supposedly done, what else was I capable of? But I knew those bad things would stain my soul and I would not be able to get them out. I could see that *Niam* was trying to protect me.

"Well, we'll leave it at this," continued *Niam*. "If you don't do this meal, we will both continue to live our own miserable lives. Each of us brokenhearted in our own ways. It won't kill me."

"Okay," I agreed, exhausted from the exchange.

Niam drove off in her van to get more vegetables for Sunday's farmers' market. I stood in place, overwhelmed with the information. I was amazed that the *mov rooj tshoob* was it. It was true that not doing it had not killed us, but these years had been miserable. The misery had seeped into my cells. The worry, hurt, anger had wounded and aged me.

If the mov rooj tshoob *is that important to you, it can easily be done,* I thought.

In my head, I was already figuring out the space where we could have the *mov rooj tshoob* and what dishes we could make or cater. Never mind that Hmong people did not cater the *mov rooj tshoob* and the only choice for space was the girl's home. But I figured it was not that hard. In my mind, it was a done deal.

But why had I not understood how important the *mov rooj tshoob* was? Why had I not known how important it was for *Niam*?

It was ridiculous how I had not known. I'd had plenty of cousins marry in the traditional Hmong way. I'd helped cook and clean for the *noj rooj tshoob* afterward. I could see Hmong people shaking their heads at how stupid I was for not knowing this. I get it. I deserved it.

But then I thought about the many seemingly basic Hmong things young Hmong Americans such as me did not know or were not told about.

For example, when our parents said "the Yang Store," we did not know they meant Good Deal Oriental Food on Lowry Avenue in north Minneapolis (because Mr. Yang is the owner). Or that "the Xiong Store" is Bangkok Market & Video Rental (Mr. Xiong owns it). We went to the Hmong stores without bothering to ask about the owners. Did it really matter when all we wanted was papaya salad? We did not take the time to know the owners because we were shy. (The elders would say we didn't appreciate the importance of relating to other Hmong through the clan system.) We wanted our papaya salad and to be on our way. Mostly though, we did not want to look like fools who could not answer questions such as:

"Are you related to so and so?"

"Which of the Yang groups do you belong to? The five, seven, or nine?"

The numbers refer to the number of plates into which various cooked portions of meat can be divided for a religious ritual. That is, the person is trying to find out how closely connected you are.

When we came home and saw guests visiting our house, we had not realized that it was rude of the boys to not shake the men's hands and welcome them to the house, even if they've never met them before. We figured these were not our guests here to see us, so we walked on by to our rooms. As girls, we were not supposed to ask if the guests wanted water to drink. And even when the guests said "No" to our very rude question, we were supposed to bring them water anyway. We had forgotten that resistance and refusal were face-saving tactics, in case we weren't serious about bringing them water. As *Niam* says, "If you're asking me if I want it, then I don't. But if you're going to give it to me, I'll take it."

At family gatherings, sometimes we did not even know the names of our first or second cousins, especially the ones from our mother's side of the family. There seemed to be so many of them, and they were not our primary contacts. Only those related to our own fathers or husbands were.

Our female cousins married out, and we rarely saw them after that. Then the men in our families changed their names to older adult names after they married and had kids. And sometimes those new names were totally different from their original ones. How were we supposed to keep up? Where was the memo about the name changes? At these family gatherings, I secretly wanted name tags that said, "Mr. So-and-So, formerly known as X" or "Miss So-and-So, daughter of Mr. and Mrs. So-and-So." Or better yet, how about a downloadable family tree that included pictures with names of parents and their kids?

If we had trouble with the cousins on our mother's side, we certainly did not know how we were related to our "cousins," "uncles," or "grandparents" who were not really cousins, uncles, or grandparents but were somehow part of our extended family anyway. Sometimes we only saw these relatives once in a while at funerals or weddings. We did not know their names or the proper titles to call them. And we were too embarrassed to ask for fear we may forget yet again.

We participated in but did not fully understand the significance of animist rituals. For example, at traditional Hmong funerals, we are told that the *qeej* player can "speak" to the spirit of the deceased. He does this through the notes he plays on the *qeej*. How many young Hmong Americans actually understand the *qeej* player's song? Then, at some point in time, the immediate family members sit with incense in their hands in front of the drum and *qeej* player. They bow when the *qeej* player says certain things. How many young Hmong Americans understand why they are sitting there and when to bow? They sit there because their parents tell them to do it so they may receive blessings from the deceased. But what kind of blessings? Did they want those blessings?

I know it's rude to ask or question things, especially Hmong things, but it's my nature.

Back home, I was excited to share my news with Blong. I was a cat who just caught a mouse and wanted to share it with my friend. Blong was as surprised as I was by the accusation that I had started or spearheaded the Hmong Marriage Bill.

"Maybe they confused you with Mee Moua?" Blong suggested.

"No! I could believe it if these were white people, but these are Hmong people, and they don't confuse Mee Moua with Mai Neng Moua. They know our parents. They know our uncles."

"You did say they could do whatever they wanted to save themselves," Blong reminded me.

"Yeah, whatever ritual or cultural things they wanted. Not make up lies about me!"

"Remember that phone call with *Txiv* where he said, 'They could do things to you'? I asked him what he meant. He kept saying, 'Things. Things!' then finally he spelled it out: 'They could kill you.'"

Blong did not tell his dad that we were about to meet "they" of "They could kill you." My cousin's dad had passed away, and we were about to set foot into the funeral home.

"Yeah, I do remember that conversation," I said. "It was kind of crazy."

"Well, the Thaying thing is stupid," said Blong, moving on. "That was years later. The timing isn't even right."

"I know! Isn't it? What about the *mov rooj tshoob*?" I asked. "I thought we could rent out—"

"What are you talking about?"

"I could look to see what space is available."

"No. We've talked about this! You said you were done. You didn't want to do anything anymore." Blong glared at me. "Remember?"

I wanted to say, *What are you talking about?* but it was now coming back to me. We had talked about it a couple times. They were quick exchanges. Blong's uncles had explained it to him, and he had said something about how they had given money for the *mov rooj tshoob*.

"We don't need to do anything anymore, right?" Blong had asked.

He had not exactly spelled it out, but I had nodded and said, "Yes, we're done. We're not doing anything more."

"I didn't know what I was saying 'No' to! I didn't know that's what that was."

"What?"

"I didn't know that's what I was saying 'No' to," I repeated.

"I heard you," said Blong, shaking his head.

I could understand his frustration. I'm two years older than he is. I'm college educated. This was something I should have known. But the *rooj tshoob* was that heap of black satin cloth from which I was supposed to sew a Hmong shirt. I could see what it was supposed to be. But I had no pattern with specific steps to show me the way.

I had been a bridesmaid in a *rooj tshoob*. I had gone to several *rooj tshoob* in my extended family. Still, it was some mysterious ritual I never understood. Watching something and participating in a specific task did not seamlessly transfer information to me. I needed to understand the big picture, and then I needed to know the specific steps. I was that deprived kid who needed a whole Q&A session to ask the basic questions. My brain wanted to turn the ritual over, look at it from all sides, and see how it was put together. Once I understood it, I could be sold on it.

I needed someone to lay out the *mov rooj tshoob* for me. Someone to say, "This is what you're saying 'No' to and these are the consequences." Without that, I was too dumb to ask questions. Well, I would not even have known what questions to ask.

And even if I knew that the *mov rooj tshoob* was the missing piece, if I had wanted to do it, to whom would I have gone? Would I have told Blong, who would have told his dad, who would have told *Hlob*, who would have sent word to my Moua uncles here in Minnesota? I did not know.

"I thought the meal was the same process as the *rooj tshoob*. I mean, *Hlob* came up and did the *rooj tshoob* already, so what else was there to do?"

"There's the *mov rooj tshoob*! If and when we were happy, they'd do it. Didn't I tell you that?"

"*They* would do the *mov rooj tshoob*? I thought *we* had to do it. I mean, *Niam* made it sound like we would do the *mov rooj tshoob*."

I am a writer (and, as it turns out, a very literal Hmong American). Specific details matter to me. I am Hmong, but I was acting like the non-Hmong person asking if Hmong people still collect a bride price today.

"No, my family already paid for the *mov rooj tshoob*," said Blong. "It was agreed that your family would do it."

"Oh. I didn't know that."

"You knew that. I told you."

"Right," I said nodding.

The pieces of the puzzle were settling in place. Blong had told me something like that. I wanted to ask if he'd been waiting for me to say I was "happy," but I knew I had to quickly piece it together so he wouldn't be mad at me. I could hear the frustration in his high-pitched voice. It was incredible what I did not know. I knew he could not believe what he was hearing.

Why was I so stupid? I berated myself.

I had been wondering what was going to happen next. I had been waiting for Blong's relatives or his father to sit us down and talk to us about it. But like everything else that had happened with the *rooj tshoob*, Blong's uncles had talked to him about it, and then we had chitchatted about it. That was talking about it. That was it. I kept waiting for something bigger, more formal to take place.

"This is so basic. Why don't you know it?" asked Blong.

"It is not so basic! I don't know; maybe it is," I sighed. "I don't know why I don't know, okay? I just didn't know it. How do you think that makes me feel? To be blindsided by something so basic, according to you, that I should've known it?"

Maybe there were reasons for all this confusion. All I could think about was *poob plig*, soul-loss. Being sick with kidney failure meant I could not go on the Term in Asia my senior year in college. After the renal transplant when I was better, I could have gone abroad but did not. But going abroad never crossed my mind as if I could never revisit that decision again. It was almost ten years before I realized I could make that trip to Laos and Thailand.

And later, on our way to Chicago, Blong and I were on I-94, merging left onto I-894. We were having a casual conversation about something. I heard Blong's "Oh, shit." Then the sudden force of the airbags knocked my glasses into the back seat. My vision blurry, I told Blong I could not see clearly. When we caught our breaths, we stepped out of the steaming car. Green liquid flowed past our feet in crooked lines like veins. Somehow, we had skidded across four lanes of highway and crashed into the concrete median. We looked back and saw the lines of cars. I wondered how we had missed them. We walked away with minor injuries. We abandoned Blong's blue Honda Civic at the nearest junkyard.

After the accident, Blong would not drive for several months. Having to drive "all the time," I got angry at him. When he did drive, I was critical of his driving. "Slow down. You're going too fast," I told him. I never told him his driving made me anxious. I never told him I did not trust his driving.

Even now, years later, when a car drives by, I think it is coming too close. I instinctively slow down. I even start sweating a little. As I drive, dark objects on the left or right make me gasp with fear. My cells die little deaths at those frightful moments. My heart pumps a little harder. I think those dark objects might hit my car.

I told Blong that some of our souls had been left at that concrete median. Although Blong offered, I did not push for a shaman to *hu plig* for us. Maybe I should have listened to my instincts.

As with the car accident, my soul had been left at the church altar.

How did this *poob plig* from the *rooj tshoob* manifest itself in my life?

My therapist friend reminded me that family was more than blood. Like LGBQT folks who have had to create their own families, I, too, could create my own family. I believed her, and yet I could not allow myself to get close to my neighbors or coworkers. Even with close friends and cousins, I, the one who usually called or wrote, stopped calling and writing.

This wasn't me. I was the woman whose name is not "Whisper," who wrote a letter to the Asian American Renaissance to make sure they understood how angry I was that, in a showcase where other Asians performed music, dance, and theater, the only art from the Hmong were ripped-off interpretations of the Lao or Thai dances.

I was the woman livid at the Hmong guy who said, "Aren't you afraid that by the time you're done with college, you'd be too old, and no one will want to marry you?" And when the boys joked about how serious I was while the girls laughed nervously, I said, "I know it's a joke, but there's a part of you that believes it, too." And when a Hmong boy who had taken a modern dance class (and so I thought he was more progressive) said, "Here on campus, we're on the same level, but when we're back in the community, you need to know your place," I told him, "I expect more from you."

Now, even on issues I cared about, I told myself, "There are already others working on it." It was too much work to take a stand. Or perhaps the arrows had broken through my thin skin and I could not stand being yelled at again.

After all that had happened with the *rooj tshoob*, I never wanted to deal with or have anything to do with it again. Yes, every time Blong asked if I was done with it, I was. When he asked if I wanted to do anything more, I did not.

My spirits, in their efforts to save me from the trauma, had pushed the *mov rooj tshoob* back into a remote corner of my brain. Carefully buried under the labels "for later," "maybe important," "should be addressed soon," it was forgotten.

Was poob plig *explanation enough for why I had forgotten about the* mov rooj tshoob? I wondered. *Or was I just trying to cover my ass for my stupidity?*

I did not share my theory with Blong for fear he would get angrier. Or worse, he would agree that I was stupid.

"Well, I'm not doing anything anymore," said Blong.

He knew who he was. He was secure in his decisions. He said it with such finality, like a period at the end of a sentence. No nonsense. No gimmicks. Nothing more. Stop.

"Why? Why not?"

"Because we're done with it, remember?"

"No, no, no."

My plans for the *mov rooj tshoob* came crashing down on me. It was so easy in my mind.

"Why can't you do it? It's important for *Niam*. It's important for me."

"I haven't changed my mind about the bride price. Have you?"

"I haven't changed my mind, either, but what about what *Niam* said? How it was important for her and how we'd be miserable if we didn't do it. I don't want to be miserable the rest of my life."

"What? You think you do the *mov rooj tshoob* and then you and *Niam* will be happy?"

"Maybe. More than now."

Blong shook his head, rolled his eyes, and took a long breath. Then he said, "Look, doing the meal isn't going to fix what you don't have with your uncles."

Blong was probably right. I did not have much of a relationship with my uncles before the wedding, and the *mov rooj tshoob* would not make us one big happy family. What then was the good of the *mov rooj tshoob*? *Niam* had said it recognized her as the mother. It was the equivalent of the American reception that allowed family and friends to celebrate the union of the couple. No, that was not correct. That would be my incorrect young Hmong American interpretation of it. I took an important Hmong custom which I did not fully understand and simplified it incorrectly. As my cousin said, "American receptions are just the parties. They're not that important." The *mov rooj tshoob* was much more than the reception. It was the ceremony with the church of witnesses watching it.

"But why can't we just do this one piece of it?" I asked.

"Because we can't. It all goes together."

I had wanted a strong man, someone who could stand up for me and for himself. Someone who would choose me over his parents. Blong had chosen me over his parents. He stood his ground against my clan who questioned his manhood and his Hmongness when he listened to me. But here now was this strong man standing against me. I hated Blong when he was against me.

Do what I want! I wanted to scream. Instead I asked, "Why does it have to be all or nothing?"

"Because that's how it works! You can't just pick and choose only the parts you like and do that."

At this point, I felt like, why not? We stood our ground, but *Hlob* had already come and done the *rooj tshoob* anyway. They paid the bride price even though we had not wanted it. If the *mov rooj tshoob* was so important to *Niam*, why couldn't we do it for her? That would not be compromising, would it? At this point, I was reminded of my earlier conversation with Kai about the bride price.

"Why can't we compromise?" I had asked him.

"Because there is no compromise," Kai had said.

It was their way or no way.

Blong was a boulder in the middle of the path. To move him, I needed a bulldozer or divine intervention, neither of which I had.

"I don't know how we can move beyond this," I told Blong.

Here I was again in this familiar space between individual and community, between Blong and *Niam*. My desire to be true to myself was once again in conflict with the "good" girl that *Niam* and the Hmong community wanted me to be.

What am I going to do if he is unwilling to move on this? I wondered.

"You made it sound like 'We're going to therapy or I'm divorcing you,'" said Blong.

"No, I didn't."

"That's how it felt."

I shrugged. There was nothing to say to that.

"It came out of left field," Blong continued.

"No, it didn't. I've been talking to you for years. I've been telling you what I've been unhappy about. You haven't been listening."

Or perhaps, like the chitchats about the *rooj tshoob*, I had not said it in a way that he understood or could hear. I had belittled my need by making our "conversations" quick exchanges that did not seem that serious.

It had been six years since we had married. We had a two-year-old daughter. I was stressed about money, being the one who had the steady income with health insurance covering myself and Erica.

After he was done with his Equal Justice Fellowship at Legal Aid, Blong opened up his own law practice. He wanted to help hardworking everyday people who struggled to navigate the legal system. The ones who made "too much" to qualify for Legal Aid services and yet did not have enough money to hire a law firm to help them. He steered away from the big firms that would have meant twelve- or fourteen-hour days and no family time.

Blong did divorces, civil commitment defense, and criminal cases. He tried to specialize in wills and trusts, but Hmong people did not believe in wills or trusts. They believed that if you talked about your own death, it was a self-fulfilling prophecy that would cause you to die sooner. When you die, they believed, the relatives will take care of things. Blong had a couple cases where the parents wanted certain things in their wills, but the sons did not agree with them so they never wrote the wills. Instead, the Hmong elders made video recordings of their wishes, which were not legally binding, so the relatives were able to do whatever they wanted.

To save money, Blong converted our second floor into his office and worked from home. His solo practice was like fishing. Sometimes you got the big one, and other times you did not get anything. He had to get his own clients and do his own billing. I could see that he did not like the business of operating his own business. After Erica was born, he took care of her and practiced law at the same time. Sometimes he met with clients at home during her naps. This setup was easier when she was little and took regular naps during the day.

I was jealous that he was the one who stayed home with her. I felt like I was missing out. After a full day of work and then coming home to cook dinner, I did not have the energy to write. On weekends, when I could have written, I wanted to play with Erica.

Through several months of couples therapy, I learned that for Blong, his decision to not do the *mov rooj tshoob* was about integrity—doing what you say you will do. As I had told myself when I moved out against

Niam's wishes, *If you're going to do this, you better make it work. You better not come back home.* Crawling back home meant I'd failed and that I shouldn't have done it. It meant my family would not respect me.

For Blong, who also believed as I did—that a woman should not be bought and paid for—it must have seemed like I was flip-flopping. First I was against the bride price, now I was okay with it.

"Why can't you shift your view about it?" asked a friend.

Hmong Catholics such as Blong's family reframed *hu plig* and *khi tes* as prayers, blessings, or good wishes for the future instead of animist rituals that bound the spirit to the body. My friend wanted me to see the bride price as honoring our parents for having raised a good daughter.

I, too, wanted to shift my views about the bride price. I wanted to strip it of its cultural context and see it as a gift to *Niam*. But it's hard to do when I am told it gives my husband and his family rights to my labor, sexuality, and reproduction. With my limited knowledge of Hmong culture, I don't know if that interpretation is true. But no one has rights to my sexuality or my children.

It's difficult for me to feel differently about the bride price when money changes hands. When I am deemed less worthy or of lower status because my bride price was only $5,000 compared to my cousin's bride price of $20,000.

It is hard to do, in my case, when I am told that money was thrown down at the *rooj tshoob*, as for the California couple, like they were buying a sow. Or when I am told you pay a lesser bride price for a divorcée or widow because they are like used cars. When I am told that if you are a "good" *nyab*, the bride price would never be used against you. Well, *Niam* is a good *nyab*, and it was used against her.

And you still wonder why I have a problem with the bride price?

My friend Margie wrote about her father, a survivor of the Holocaust, while I wrote about the bride price, two "ghosts" that haunted us. Other fine writers and friends—Carolyn, Marcie, and Joan—wrote about being black, Native American, and Japanese American. We read our works in a series we called Ghost Stories: Five Women Writers Read Works on

Historical Trauma. These women helped me understand the historical trauma Hmong women faced over time. From being forced to marry men we did not date to feeling like we have been bought and paid for, many Hmong women have been the victims of the bride price.

"WHEN YOU SAID you were against the bride price, you didn't really know what you were against, did you?" asked Blong.

"No, I knew what I was against. I just didn't know the consequences."

"I did."

I gave Blong a look out of the corner of my eye.

"So if you knew the consequences, you might have been okay with them doing it?" asked Blong.

Had I realized that I was asking my clan, a whole people, to change their practice? Not really; my mind was on my nuclear family. If I had known that my whole clan would not come to the church wedding, that *Niam* and I would not talk for more than a year, that my uncles and older brother would not acknowledge my husband, that my relatives would disown me, that Blong's clan would make up lies about me, that years later I would still be dealing with it, why would I have wanted that?

"It was a good thing I didn't know," I said. "It should've happened to you. You would've made a better feminist."

Blong made a decision and never wavered from it. Despite the rocks people threw at him, he stood there and took it. I made a decision but questioned if it was the right one. As people threw rocks at me, I held up my shield of logic and explanations. When they told me how bad I was, I tried and tried to explain how I was really a good person who had done a lot for the Hmong community. I wanted them to like me; I wanted to be a good daughter and a good daughter-in-law.

I had not changed my mind about the bride price, but now that I had a daughter, it was not just about me anymore. I worried that my daughter was going to pay for my sins by being excluded from her cousins. That she, like me, will want and long for more family. I did not want her to live an isolated Hmong life as I had. I wanted her to be surrounded by family. Having a child helped me to understand that *Niam* still loved me. I understood because I knew how I felt about my child. I knew I could be mad at her for the seemingly stupid things she may do but that I could love her at the same time.

I called *Niam* to give her an update on membership at the farmers' market stall at Sears on Marion and I-94. She had heard from other Hmong farmers that this new market was busy and wanted to see if it was a site where she should sell her vegetables, too. I told her it was not that busy and they were not taking new vendors.

"Are you home?" I asked. "If you're home, I'll come over."

"It's slippery outside; don't come," she said.

It was the first snowfall, and it was not slippery, but *Niam* did what all Hmong parents did: worry about their grown kids.

"I'm at work. It's not too far," I said.

Since my office was in downtown St. Paul, it took me ten minutes to drive to Kai's house on the east side.

My mother and I sat in Kai's living room. She had put in some Thai movie dubbed in Hmong. Like the classical music that wafted out of loudspeakers in the downtowns of small-town USA, the big flat-screen TV buzzed in Hmong. Sitting on the little stool against the leather sofa, I looked out the window, which showed an almost panoramic view of the street. This was their second house after they had moved out of the Margaret Street house. It was a little after lunch, and there was no one in the street. The houses sat quietly, soaking in the warm sun on this cool winter day, waiting for their owners to get back home. *Niam* sat on the leather sofa kitty-corner from me.

I had taken half the day off to write. I told *Niam* I wanted to write a book about how Hmong women got married—how she got married, how I got married, how other Hmong women got married.

"*Niam*, how old were you when you got married?" I asked.

"Eighteen," said *Niam*.

"I remember you saying something about being an 'old maid.' Eighteen is not old."

"At eighteen, they said I was an old maid. Before the war, men wanted to marry the older girls, but during the war, they married the thirteen- or fourteen-year-olds."

By "the war," *Niam* meant the Secret War.

"What? There weren't any more eighteen-year-olds?"

"The eighteen-year-olds were already married."

"I heard that when *Txiv* came to marry you, there was already another man who had come to *tuaj nqis tsev hais*."

"Who told you that?"

"When I went to visit Uncle and we were talking about all the wedding problems with Blong and me, Uncle said that they had come to the house with the umbrella already."

Niam smiled as if she was a little embarrassed. "They didn't bring the umbrella yet."

This was different from what I had been told. For the Hmong, the umbrella draped with the striped black and white sash that Hmong women wrap around their turbans symbolizes the intention for marriage. It also represents the transformation of a girl to womanhood. (After the *rooj tshoob*, the sash is removed from the umbrella. Married Hmong women then do not include the striped back and white sash on their turbans when they wear their Hmong outfits.)

"Who was the guy who wanted to marry you?"

"He was a close relative, one of my mother's people."

"He wasn't your first cousin, was he?"

"He was. He had three wives already."

Three wives? I thought he had two, I said to myself. "You never dated him, did you?" I asked *Niam*.

"No. He had heard of me so he wanted to marry me."

I pondered the decision of a man to marry a woman based on her reputation. He knew her mother, his aunt. He knew her father, the *tasseng*. Her brothers were a colonel and lieutenant colonel in General Vang Pao's army.

His relatives had told him *Niam* was tall and big like my uncles. She could bear him many children. They saw that she was a hard worker who got up early in the morning to cook. She would make a good wife for him and a good *nyab* for his parents.

And his three wives? They would be upset at first, but they would get used to it like they had with the others. Having never dated *Niam*, he could not have been in love with her. But love could come later for both of them.

"He was from a different village," continued *Niam*. "He had flown in and was walking toward the village when we met at the river. I was coming back from the garden."

"Were you by yourself?"

"There was a bunch of us. On one side of the river was the military camp, and on the other side was our village. In the middle was the river. There were people at the river. We were at the river and were about to cross to our village when he saw me."

"What did he say to you?"

"He said, 'I want to marry you,' and grabbed my hand."

"Did he come by himself?"

"He came by himself."

"He didn't know you'd resist, did he?"

Niam smiled. "We fought. I kicked him and made him mess up his hair."

"Did your girlfriends help you?"

"No."

"Did people hear you guys fighting?"

"Yes, people came running and soon there was a line of people on the hill, watching. I escaped and ran home."

"What did he do? Did he just go home?"

"No, he came to my house to spend the night. But before he came to the house, he went and got some of his relatives. They all spent the night at my house. In the morning, they wanted to start the *rooj tshoob*."

"When did *Txiv* come and get you?"

"That night. He came with three-four other guys, and I snuck out right past those guys. They didn't even hear me."

So this is what caused the confusion. The two prospective husbands were at the house at the same time.

"In the morning, when your dad's people came to inform my family that they intended to marry me, the Xiong guy and his men were still rubbing the sleep from their eyes."

It must have been an almost comical scene. A group of men asleep in the house, waiting for the break of day to start the *rooj tshoob*, while messengers from a different clan came to the house to inform the prospective father-in-law that they wanted to marry his daughter.

"So the Vue people didn't know whose proposal to accept."

"What did they do?"

"They told the two groups to figure it out. They said, 'Whoever really wants to marry our daughter, come back with the proposal.'"

"What did *Txiv*'s messengers say when they came to your house?"

"They said that I had run off with him."

I knew that our clan leader had told my father to go get *Niam*. Having heard the story of how *Niam* had kicked her first cousin, he had brought reinforcements with him. They were ready for resistance, or, if they needed to, they were ready to kidnap her.

"What? That's not true. *Txiv* came with three other men. Why did they say that?"

"They thought that it would get them out of the problem of me having to marry the Xiong guy by saying I didn't want to marry him. That's why I ran off with your dad. But the Xiongs said, 'Hey, if you don't want to marry her, if it's just her wanting to marry you, we'll go and get her. We'll marry her.'"

"So your dad and I had to pay off that guy by giving him one silver bar."

"Who came with *Txiv*?"

"There was three of them. Your uncle in Merced. Your cousin's dad. Another guy."

"I remember you saying something about *Txiv* not dating you. Is that true?"

"We didn't date like you young people today with a boyfriend and girlfriend but talked like friends."

"I heard that you didn't go to Grandfather's house, that you went and hid out in the jungle."

"Oh, we went to Grandfather's house. They then told us to go and hide in the jungle because they thought the Xiong guy and his people would come after me."

"Would they really come after you?"

"Sure, if they really wanted to marry you and they thought you were theirs. Hmong people, if you accept a gift from them, even if it was a small gift, they'll use that against you. They'll come and say, 'Oh, she likes us. She accepted the gift from us.' And when you say, 'I don't like him,' the old people will say, 'But you accepted their gift. You must have liked them.'"

"That's stupid. So you just can't accept anything from a guy."

"Hmong people, a man touches your hand and you are his."

I shook my head at how ridiculous it was for a Hmong man to "make" a woman his. It was scary that a girl could be trapped so easily. What was this? The caveman days where a man could just knock the woman over the head, drag her off by her feet to make her his, where might made things right?

Although I did not think this kind of stuff still happened today, I knew Blong had a legal case dealing with this exact issue. A Hmong woman had hired Blong to represent her because this old Hmong man was suing her for not marrying him after she had accepted a gift from him. After the judge dismissed the case against her, the Hmong woman told Blong, "Men like him are rocks that I trip over when I walk. There are plenty of them on the ground."

"Where did you hide? Where did you sleep?" I asked *Niam*.

"Your two aunts, your dad, and I went and put up a tarp and slept under that."

"How long were you there?"

"Just a night; after your grandfather paid off the Xiong guy, they came and got us."

"How much was the bride price for you?"

"Six silver bars."

That was not what I had remembered. Where did I get the figure of four silver bars? I had no idea. "But that wasn't a lot, right?"

"It was what the people, the country paid at the time."

In other words, it was not highly unusual. From the stories I had heard, it had seemed like my father and grandparents paid so much for *Niam*.

The next day, I still had questions for *Niam*. I stopped by Ha Tien on University Avenue to pick up fried shrimp with heads on, fried blue crabs, and boiled pig stomach, large intestines, and tongue. I poured the take-out onto plates and set them on the table. Ha Tien was like a lot of the other mom and pop shops that sold rice, canned goods, and fresh vegetables. The difference was that Ha Tien had a deli inside. On the storefront window was a painted roast pig and duck. True to its word, the deli sold roast pig and roast duck among a slew of fried and boiled delicacies. There was also warm tapioca dessert, tricolor bars, and hot pepper sauce.

Niam heated up the deer stew she had made earlier in the morning. We sat at the dining room table, across from the large flat-screen TV so we could watch a video of Hmong men fishing and hunting in the jungles of Laos somewhere.

"Oh, ladies and gentlemen, look at the fish they've caught," said the voice on the video. "Wow! They've really caught a lot of fish here."

"He says 'a lot of fish,' but I only see two or three in the net," I commented to *Niam*.

On the video, two men threw nets into a small stream. Both wore short shorts. I thought the announcer said this was the Mekong River, but the river looked small. The camera showed a bounty of fish on large banana leaves, then it panned to a guy scaling the fish. He separated the guts into one pile and threw the fish into another pile. He slit the fish open and flattened it so it could be smoked over an open fire. Then finally the men were eating.

"Is it good?" asked the announcer.

"It's really good," answered one of the men.

The camera panned over the bowl of fish stew, the smoked dried fish, and a black pile of what *Niam* said was the fish guts from earlier. None of the men had plates in their hands, just spoons. With the exception of the fish stew, the other "dishes" were in little piles on banana leaves. Each man took what he wanted from the different piles.

"It looks good," said *Niam*. "But we can't eat like that anymore."

I did not know this life. But videos such as this must remind the elders of a former life that some still long for but could never again have. *Niam* licked her fingers, which were coated with the sticky sauce of the fried crab. The crab, like the fried shrimp, was delicious but too much work, I thought. I dipped a piece of the boiled large intestines into hot pepper sauce. I finished lunch by cleansing my palate with *Niam*'s boiled pumpkins flavored with a little bit of sugar. This was pumpkin from the summer that she had brought home and stored in the basement. After lunch, I sat on the leather sofa that faced the large window that looked out into the street.

"*Niam*, the Xiong guy that wanted to marry you, was he a soldier like my uncles?" I asked.

"Yes. He was in charge of a *keb*."

I did not know what a *keb* was. I was not even sure if that was a Hmong word or a Lao word.

"Was that a group of soldiers?" I asked.

Niam nodded in agreement. She went back to the dining room table to finish eating the crab. My second niece was asleep on her Dora sofa that had been pulled out like a hide-a-bed. I saw a bottle in her mouth and removed it and set it by the sofa.

"Years later, I met two of his wives and they told me . . ."

"You mean the Xiong guy's wives?"

"Yes. They told him, 'Well, you thought you were such a good guy that when you went there, she would just follow you home. She didn't even want you.' He got so mad that he beat them up. I told them, 'He was already upset. You should've just laughed at him in the corner by yourselves.'"

I wondered why the Xiong guy would think that *Niam* would just follow him home when she had never met or seen him.

"Some girls, the guy's just a little leader but they think that's good and they will marry him," explained *Niam*. "Back in my day, we did not date like you girls do now. We talked to every guy."

I had heard this before from *Niam*. I suspected that while most of the girls might not have had one serious boyfriend, a few must have. In a small village setting, I imagined that it was like the small towns where everyone knew everyone else's business, so a girl had to be careful to whom she was seen talking. And if a man could claim you as his by just touching your hands or giving you a gift, you couldn't touch or accept anything from him. Having been to the Hmong villages in Thailand, I understood that by going to a girl's wall at night, you could talk in relative privacy. And it was mysterious and romantic—a sweet voice or a love song on the mouth harp through the walls.

Niam has said girls in her time were modest. They cared with whom they were seen. They could not just go and hang out with boys. They could not even be in the same space near each other. I remembered that *Niam* had told me that boys and girls could not pee in the same spot because if they did, the girl would get pregnant. To the literal Hmong American me, this did not make any sense then. Now I understood *Niam* was trying to explain why I needed to stay away from boys in a way I would understand as a little girl.

If I had known *Niam* considered it rude to hang out with boys, would I still have hung out with them? She must have told me. I know she told me boys and girls could not be friends. I did not grow up with these standards. My Sunday school teacher, Nancy, at the Christian and Missionary Alliance Church in Pittsburgh, told me I could be anything I wanted to be when I grew up. And I believed her. I did not know from whom I learned it, but I grew up thinking boys and girls could be friends. It could not have been from any of my aunts.

"Of the guys you talked to, was there one that you wanted to marry?"

"No. There wasn't, but there were guys who wanted to marry me."

"Did you want to marry any of them?"

"No. Back then, you didn't choose your husband. They chose you."

She meant the parents chose their *nyab*. *Niam*'s comment reminded me of when I tossed balls with the boys at the Hmong New Year. The girls stood in a single line on one side of the room and the boys stood in a line on the other side. Back and forth, we tossed the ball to the person we liked. I never liked standing in these lines because, like the bindings of the Hmong costume, I felt constrained. I had to stand in place while the boys who were not tossing balls got to walk around, look at all the girls, and take their pick of who they liked. I wanted to see who else was standing there. I, too, wanted to pick who I liked.

"So, were there people that *tuaj nqis tsev hais* you?"

"No. Back then, if you knew the guy, they'd come to your house and you'd take off with them. Or if you didn't know the guy, they'd kidnap you. *Tuaj nqis tsev hais* was only for those situations where the girl didn't want to marry the guy at all."

"Oh, that's different from what happens today."

"It is different."

"But I thought that Hmong parents wanted their daughters to marry by *tuaj nqis tsev hais*. That that was the best way for a woman to marry."

In fact, I remember *Niam* specifically telling me to not run off with a guy.

"That's to get face."

Niam told me the story of my cousin's wife. "They came to get her, and she didn't want to marry them. She had her own boyfriend. She told them, 'One, live. Two, die.'"

What *Niam* meant was that she had two choices: live or die. She lived, and they now had a household of kids.

"You can't die, you can't run away, so you learn to live with it," continued *Niam*.

I raised my eyebrows at the options, which were no options. What choice did a woman have?

"If you didn't want to marry a man, could you say no?"

"Yes. You never say 'yes.' You have to argue with them."

"But what do you say?"

"You say you don't want to marry them. You say he's too old for you. You don't see a future for the two of you. You don't want a life with him. And if you win, then you don't get to marry him. But if you lose, then you marry them."

The possibilities of a woman winning this argument did not seem high, especially if she was young. How was she supposed to win verbal judo with some old guy who brought six silver bars to bribe her parents? How was she supposed to win when no one had prepared her to argue these things? The process seemed archaic and scary to me. As a young girl in *Niam*'s time in Laos, I imagined that you just did not know who you were going to marry or when. Even if you had a serious boyfriend, there was no guarantee that you would get to marry him. Some guy that you have never seen or talked to could just come and kidnap you to be his wife.

"*Niam*, you were eighteen when you married *Txiv*. How old was he?"

"Probably five or ten years older."

"Ten years older? He was really old!"

This reminded me of the Hmong women who responded "fifty or sixty" when I asked them how old they were. There was a huge difference between fifty and sixty, but for Hmong people, age was relative. Traditionally, Hmong people did not celebrate their birthdays each year. There were more important markers of life that we celebrated.

"How come he wasn't married yet?" I asked.

"He was poor. He didn't have the money for the bride price."

"But he had finished school by then, right?"

"School? There wasn't school. There was just learning your ABCs."

"But he knew how to read and write in Lao, right?"

"Yes, he knew how read and write in Lao."

"Did *Txiv* date my aunt?"

I could not remember who had told me, but I thought my dad had dated my aunt in Merced.

"No, your aunt was already married. In fact, she was a widow. Her husband was a soldier, and he had been killed. She had her two boys already."

I was using the excuse of my writing to talk to *Niam* about things we had never talked about. I did not know why we had not talked about these things. Maybe it was because I had never asked her. Maybe it was because I was not ready to listen.

When our second child, Samantha, was born in 2009, Blong and I made a decision that he would work outside the house. He applied to several places. For some jobs, since he was a lawyer, people worried that he was too educated and wouldn't stick around. For other jobs, since he wasn't in his mid-fifties with thirty years of experience, he was not qualified enough.

"How could I be both at the same time?" wondered Blong.

His self-esteem took a hit.

"It's not that you're not qualified," I explained. "When it comes down to the final candidates, it's about fit. Fit with the organization, fit with the team."

It didn't help. In fact, I made it sound like he didn't fit in anywhere. Finally, he applied to the Minneapolis Civil Rights Department and was accepted as a complaint investigations officer.

At this time, we decided we needed daycare. We asked *Niam* if she'd be willing to look after the girls. True to her word, she watched them until she started her garden in May. Then Yia took over responsibility for the girls. When he could no longer do it, we asked my aunt if she could do it. Sam learned to walk at my aunt's house. Once my aunt couldn't do it anymore, I asked my cousin's wife to watch the girls.

We decided to take our kids to my family members even though there had not been a lot of communication between them and us. We knew they would watch over our kids as if they were their own. Even if they were still mad at us, we knew they'd love our kids.

"It'd be great if the kids could learn to speak Hmong," I told Blong.

Although Blong and I were fluent in Hmong, we spoke mostly English to each other. Besides, after one Hmong lady in Laos told me I spoke Hmong like a Chinese lady learning Hmong, I was not so confident in my Hmong-speaking skills.

"Or at least be in a place where Hmong is spoken on a more regular basis," agreed Blong.

In the course of three years, *Niam*, my cousin and his wife, and my aunt and uncle got to know Blong better. By this time, we'd seen plenty of drug deals and prostitution on our street. We'd had our back door kicked in and been burglarized twice. In addition, I was almost robbed in broad daylight outside my back door. With two kids under the age of six, I told Blong I did not feel safe in my home and neighborhood in north Minneapolis. My heart raced when I heard the gunshots and tire screeches. At first, I ran to the windows to see what was going on and called the police. Later on, I slid further down on the couches in hiding.

"Look, I'm five feet tall and a hundred pounds. I know there are plenty of people who are bigger, taller, and stronger than me," I reasoned.

One time when Blong had gone to visit his brother in Madison, Wisconsin, I sat in our bedroom with my back against the wall. I called a cousin who is a nurse and described my symptoms to her.

"My heart's racing. I'm sweating. I have to take deep breaths to calm down."

"Where's Blong?" she asked.

"Oh, he's out of town. He went to visit his brother in Madison and will be back in a couple days."

"Okay," she said.

"Is something wrong with my heart?" I asked.

"No, nothing's wrong with your heart. You're having an anxiety attack."

Blong and I had to make a decision: move out to St. Paul or the suburbs or stay and make the neighborhood better. We decided to stay. In 2012, the incumbent Hennepin County commissioner in District 2 announced that he was resigning. Blong decided to run. It was the first time any Hmong person in Minneapolis had run for an elected office.

"I want to run for county commissioner," he consulted with me.

"What's that?" I asked him.

"They take care of policy issues at the county level," he explained.

"Okay, what are those?"

He told me about the responsibilities of county commissioners. I nodded, but I didn't even know my own county commissioner. *Did I vote for him?* I wondered. When Blong told me that one of the people running was a sixteen-year veteran of the state legislature, my heart dropped.

"Oh, honey. Why can't you just run for something like school board? You know who she is, right? She's got sixteen years of experience. A lot of people know her. Nobody knows you."

"She might win, but we're going to make them work hard for it," responded Blong.

Blong ran a good grassroots campaign with a team of young Hmong staff and volunteers. His lawn signs, blue with gold lettering, were all over District 2. "They're like the bat signal calling you," I told Blong. "You can spot them a mile away."

Blong contacted two Hmong artists who wrote, sang, and made a video called, "All This and More." Then a blogger from Comedy Central wrote a blurb about "All This and More." He compared it to something the Black Eyed Peas might have written. More local media started paying attention.

Blong got almost 40 percent of the votes, which was impressive for a first-timer. In any other election he might have won. He lost to the sixteen-year veteran of the state legislature, who was the DFL-endorsed candidate. (DFL is Democratic-Farmer-Labor, Minnesota's chapter of the Democratic Party.)

In June 2012, my family decided to do the *mov rooj tshoob* for us.

"If we do it, will you come?" asked *Niam* over the phone.

"Yes, we'll come," I told her.

Blong and I thought the *mov rooj tshoob* was happening because we had taken our kids to our family members to watch, showing them that we needed them. That, perhaps, they'd realized Blong wasn't as bad as people made him out to be. That since both sides had reconciled or since Blong and I had "earned" it, it was time to do the *mov rooj tshoob*.

However, when I talked to *Niam* about it, she told me a different story.

"I didn't want the Yang people to accuse me of keeping the money for myself," said *Niam*.

She was afraid that if she didn't do the *mov rooj tshoob*, the Yang clan would accuse her of being greedy. She called my uncles, and they set a date. Unfortunately, when that date came, my cousin got married and they had to do a *rooj tshoob* for her. The next time they wanted to do it, my uncle died and they had to do a funeral for him. Finally, the third time, *Niam* said, "It's got to work this time or we're done. Whoever can come will come."

"Just keep your mouth shut. Don't say anything no matter what they say. Just grin and bear it. Let them do their thing and be done with it," I told Blong.

We were in the car on I-94 eastbound to Kai's blue rambler in St. Paul. I knew Blong wouldn't like what I said, but he nodded.

"The less you say, the better," I continued.

Blong again nodded. I knew he was doing this for me.

Typically, the bride, groom, and their entourage arrive together. We showed up at 8:00 AM as instructed by Blong's uncle. Apparently, they'd shown up earlier. When we got to the house, the food preparation was almost done. I saw a handful of aunties and uncles outside and smiled at them. Since the First Hmong Baptist Church had their annual picnic on this day, I didn't see many of them. But that was okay. I wanted to get things done quickly.

Blong and I made our way down to the basement, where they'd set up chairs around two long tables. There were men already seated at the table, including my first cousin on my mom's side, representing my uncle. Blong took his seat at the table. I stood back from the table with my four non-Hmong friends and the women, including *Niam*. I tried to interpret for my non-Hmong friends as best I could, but I, too, didn't know what was going on.

I remember bits and pieces of what was said. My uncle opened the *mov rooj tshoob* with, "You were like animals that had left their pens, animals that were vulnerable to tiger attacks. But now you have recognized your master and you have returned home." Later on, this uncle continued, "Your other wedding did not count. This is the one that matters." At some point, my cousin counseled Blong to be humble and for me to seek out good Yang wives from whom I could learn.

When it came time for speeches, *Niam* did not want to say anything. She, too, wanted this to be over quickly. Then my male cousins, who had always been nice to us, came over with glasses of beer to recognize Blong as their *Yawm Yij* or Brother-in-Law. The older uncles wouldn't let them overdo it, so Blong got only two or three glasses. Then we must've had lunch, but I didn't really remember the food.

As we left, Kai handed over the handwritten list of all the gifts that had been given by my family and friends as part of my dowry. *Niam* gave the big green suitcase full of my Hmong clothes. Nine years after our legal marriage, we were officially married in the eyes of the Hmong community.

LATER, *Niam* TOLD ME that Blong's uncles informed my Moua family that Blong and I were such bad kids, they couldn't tell us what to do. That is, we were unwilling to come earlier and would only come to eat.

"*Niam*, that is not true!" I said. "I told you we would come. We came when Blong's uncles told us to come. If they had said to show up at 6:00 AM, we would've been there at 6:00."

I WAS ANGRY THAT we were still being painted as rebellious kids even when we were compliant.

"IT'S LIKE THE RUMORS they spread about you, *Niam*, about how bad you were, how you didn't love my grandparents when they didn't even know what happened," I said.

"They're like little dogs who bark at you behind your back. But then when you turn around to confront them, they look around innocently, saying, 'Who, me? I didn't say anything,'" said *Niam*.

I laughed at the image of Hmong people as Chihuahuas, barking at me.

"At least have the guts to say things to my face," I said.

In 2013, the Minneapolis city council member for Ward 5 ran for mayor along with thirty-four other candidates. Blong threw his name in the hat for city council along with three other candidates, all first-timers. From lessons learned the previous year, Blong ran a smarter campaign by doing things such as designing and printing all six literature pieces at once. He flew to California, and his parents hosted a fundraiser for him. Individually, many Hmong donated to his campaign. An uncle invited us to a *hu plig* for his son and urged people to work for Blong's election. However, neither the Yang nor the Moua clans came out in force to help Blong.

I CALLED *Niam*.

"*Niam*, which Moua uncle should I call to help us?" I asked.

"Don't call. They're not going to help you," said *Niam*.

"Why? Everything's done, the *rooj tshoob*, the bride price, the *mov rooj tshoob*. What more is there to do?"

"When you got married the way you did, you said you didn't need them anymore."

"It's been ten years. How much longer is it going to take for all of you to forgive me?"

"I can't say, but you did what you did."

"How long do you need? Another ten years? A hundred years?"

Niam didn't say anything. Blong was about to drive, and the girls were in the back seat. Erica was five years old and Sam was three. They thought I was yelling at them. They started to cry. Blong looked at me. "Hang up the phone!" he mouthed.

"Yes, I didn't listen to you. I did what I wanted. I can't change the past. What do you want me to do?"

"Pray to God. Even if they don't help you, if it's your destiny, you'll win."

And with that, the battery on my cell phone died. The girls were still crying. Tears rolled down my cheeks as I shook my head.

"Why do you keep trying?" asked Blong. "You know they're not going to help you."

"But we did everything already. I don't understand," was all I could muster.

Blong shook his head. I knew it was painful for him to watch me try time and again and get rejected. And yet, I was always hopeful that something would work out. I kept thinking if I found the right person to speak on our behalf, if I found the right words, things would work out differently. But I didn't know how to navigate this traditional Hmong world.

I e-mailed Uncle Naw-Karl.

"You and Blong have not done anything wrong by not following Hmong traditional marriage patterns," encouraged Uncle. "The majority of Hmong people are just followers and can never understand the process and price leaders have to pay."

I didn't feel like a leader, maintaining my original action as Uncle had suggested.

"When Hmong people do something for you, you owe them for life. Avoid such thing," counseled Uncle.

Unlike me, Uncle was secure in his own actions. When I asked him why he hadn't shown up at my cousin's church wedding, he stated that he didn't want to live a lie.

"Hmong people always say 'Hmong must love Hmong,' but it's not true," said Uncle.

He was right. Most of my extended family members considered this uncle too individualistic, someone who wanted to do his own thing. They didn't approve of his actions or words. He certainly did not feel the "Hmong must love Hmong" from his own extended family members.

"DON'T WORRY," said Blong. "If we win, it just makes our story even better."

"I hope so," I sighed.

"GO QUIETLY," counseled Pastor Vang.

That is, live a quiet life. Hmong people believe that if you're living a good life, people won't hear about it. They only hear about it when there's trouble.

"Live your life well," continued Pastor Vang. "They are watching you."

I KNEW THAT SOME in the community were waiting for us to fail. They wanted to be able to say, "Nay, nay, you didn't listen to us. You don't think you need us? This is what happens when you're on your own."

I hoped to God Blong was right.

NORTH MINNEAPOLIS had a Hmong population of about ten thousand, split between Wards 4 and 5. We had to secure the Hmong votes. In addition to the registered voters, we knew there was a whole bunch of eligible Hmong who had not registered to vote. We had young staffers go door to door to figure out where the Hmong voters lived. While the other campaigns focused on the "traditional" voters, Blong courted the Asian, Latino, and East African voters in the ward.

Blong won. He became the first Hmong person to hold elected office in Minneapolis. Along with the first Somali and the first Latina, Blong was one of seven new city council members, making this council the city's most diverse ever.

The *mov rooj tshoob* is done.

Blong and I have two anniversaries—the legal one in August 2003 and the Hmong one in June 2012. My uncle says the one that counts is the Hmong one. The anniversary we celebrate is the one at the church where we wore our Hmong clothes.

I am a writer, spinning tales of what it means to be Hmong in America. We Hmong are at the center of my stories. We are complex characters. We are the heroines, heroes, and perpetrators who don't need to be translated so others may understand us.

I had told myself when I moved out against *Niam*'s wishes, *If you're going to do this, you better make it work. You better not come back home.* There are many ways to be Hmong. My way is one way.

Epilogue

Blong and I drove three hours to a small town in Minnesota to meet with a Yang clan leader. I had heard this man speak on several occasions. He was knowledgeable about Hmong funerals. He had been a *mej koob* in many *rooj tshoob*. He had helped to resolve many cultural issues. His wife was even a shaman. I asked to meet with him to learn from him.

"Your *rooj tshoob* had issues, but it's done now. It's not the fault of any one person. Not you, not Blong," said this leader.

"Oh, I don't know," I said, laughing. I didn't know how sincere he was in saying this. "It might have been our fault."

The leader, Blong, and I laughed.

"It's the lack of knowledge from our leaders," stated this leader. "They don't have a good understanding of culture, not just Hmong culture, but any culture. Right now, if you believe in the church, then everything must go through the leader in that church. That way, when he speaks, you understand him. These leaders have given the wrong message. How is it wrong?"

I sat up in my seat. I was surprised to hear a leader say this about his colleagues.

"When you are a leader and you force your culture upon another person, that creates misunderstandings. That was the life in the past. Right now, about 60 to 70 percent of the elders are still in this stage. But I'm going to change that."

I was about to ask how he was planning to change it when he said, "For example, my own brother lives in a different city and joins that leader. He loves them and does everything for them. The day he dies or gets in trouble, however, that leader is going to come back to me and say, 'He's your brother, what do you say? What do you want to do?' In the past, he wouldn't have done anything because he didn't want to offend me. This way of leading in the past is too narrow. Even I don't like it. I want to change this so that if my brother belongs to this group, if he loves them and they love him, no matter what happens, they should go ahead and take care of it. Then they can call me. I'll come and see what else needs to be done. If there's nothing, I thank them, and I'm happy. This is the life we need to lead from now on."

I nodded and quickly glanced at Blong, who was also nodding. The leader's wife came into the room and brought each of us a drink.

"Thank you," Blong and I said.

"I've even changed how I do the *rooj tshoob*. I don't need messengers, the two elders responsible for the *rooj tshoob*, and *mej koob*. It is the two young people getting married so why are we parents discussing old problems that we created that have nothing to do with them? I don't think we should follow that way anymore," continued the leader. "So, if you're a young man, and you want to marry your girlfriend, you need to face your future in-laws. Don't kidnap a girl like in the past. You face her parents and you say, 'I want to marry your daughter.' The dad then has an opportunity to say, 'I am happy that you want to marry my daughter. You may take her with you.' Then you go and plan your wedding."

"But what you're saying sounds very American," I said.

"So, you do that here in your town?" jumped in Blong.

"Yes. We have. We do."

"Really?" I asked. "Down here, you've changed it in that way already?"

Blong and I couldn't believe what we were hearing from a leader well versed in many aspects of traditional Hmong culture.

"Yes, us Yangs and a few other clans, not every clan, but a few," confirmed the leader.

"They're willing to do it?" I asked.

"Yes."

"So, the young people . . . ," I stammered, shaking my head. My brain was moving too fast, and my mouth couldn't keep up. "If a guy wants to marry his girlfriend, he just goes and talks to her parents?" I asked.

"Yes, talk to them and bring her home."

"But Hmong people are strict," interjected Blong. "If I show up without my leaders, my future in-laws have no respect for me."

"Yes, that is true. But we need to change. I've changed. I haven't forced anyone else to change."

"When you, when your sons have done this in the past, how receptive has the other side been?" I wanted know.

"Well, you talk to them and warn them. If they're okay with it, that's good. If they're not, we don't force anyone. We'll do as they like," he said. "But when it's your daughter that's getting married, you make the decision and you do it. This is how we move our lives forward."

"So, say the Hmong from St. Paul, you tell them to come talk to you, and if you're okay with it, then they can just take her?" asked Blong.

"Yes. If my daughter is okay with it, then I'm okay with it. It's her decision. It's her life. I give her that power. I give her that decision to make. It's their wedding, so they need to prepare for it."

"But if you change it like that, then who pays for the *rooj tshoob*? Is there a bride price?" I asked.

"It's your daughter, so, as parents, you help with the expenses. We don't talk about a bride price anymore. We talk about a gift you want to give to the in-laws as a token of appreciation so that you become connected."

"So, when did you start this?" asked Blong.

Unfortunately for us, the leader began changing the *rooj tshoob* in this way after Blong and I married.

"That's too bad," continued Blong, shaking his head.

"Thank you for telling me about this. I haven't seen too many leaders do this," I said.

"Hmong traditions, if you wait until everyone is on the same page about everything, that day will never come. The young people are already changing. The way to not have headaches is to stay ahead of the game. We need to change."

Acknowledgments

Ua tsaug (thank you) to my husband, Blong Yang, who was strong when I was weak, who always supported me.

Ua tsaug Niam for letting me tell our story and for listening when I read it to you. Forgive me for the parts that hurt you. Thank you to my brothers, Kai and Yia, who always loved me.

Thank you to my family and friends who supported Blong and me over the years: Esther Dawolo, Tabassum Farhat, Shirley Herreid, Pastor T. Cher Moua, Dr. Rev. Naw-Karl Mua, Frank and Carol Sitcler, Pastor Tong Zoo Vang, Eric and Douangta Vang-Sitcler, Yer and Xai Moua-Xiong.

Thank you to the poor souls who read and provided valuable feedback on the many, many versions of the manuscript. From the smallest details to the big ideas, you pushed for clarity and challenged me to dig deeper. You made my story even better: Valerie and Dennis Dahlman, Mohammad Gaba, Terry Groetken, Shoonie Hartwig, Jim Heynen, Gary Yia Lee, May Choua (Anne) Lo, Muhubo Malin, Joy Marsh Stephens, Pos Moua, Bruce and Barbara Nordstrom-Loeb, Donna Trump, Ma Vang, Khamseng Vue, and Mi Yang.

Thank you to Blong's family who supported Blong and me in so many ways and loved us despite our faults: Amy, Angela, Nou, Bee, Soua, Aunt Choua, and my mother-in-law, Cha Mee.

Thank you to my editor, Ann Regan, who believed in the importance of my individual voice.

Thank you to Txong Pao Lee, Uncle Nhia Her Moua, Uncle Pa Blia Moua, Uncle Houa Moua, Yang Cheng Vang, LeePao Xiong, and Tong Ger Yang, who shared their cultural knowledge with me.

Thank you to my Loft Mentor Series mentor and cohort (Barrie Jean Borich, Rachael Hanel, Rebecca Kanner, and Margie Newman), whose published works inspired me (made me jealous, really).

Thank you to the Bush Foundation, the Jerome Foundation, and the Minnesota State Arts Board for supporting emerging artists such as me.

For More Information

Bertrais, Yves. *The Traditional Marriage Among the White Hmong of Thailand and Laos.* Chiangmai, Thailand: Hmong Center, 1978.

Cooper, Robert George. *The Hmong: A Guide to Traditional Life.* People's Democratic Republic: Lao-Insight Books, 2008.

Donnelly, Nancy. *Changing Lives of Refugee Hmong Women.* Seattle: University of Washington Press, 1994.

Faderman, Lillian. *I Begin My Life All Over: The Hmong and the American Immigrant Experience.* Boston: Beacon Press, 1998.

Gerdner, Linda. *Demystifying Hmong Shamanism: Practice and Use by Hmong Americans Across the Lifespan.* Golden, CO: Bauu Press, 2015.

———. *Hmong Story Cloths: Preserving Historical and Cultural Treasures.* Atglen, PA: Schiffer Publishing, Ltd., 2015.

John Michael Kohler Arts Center. *Hmong Art: Tradition and Change.* Sheboygan, WI: The Center, 1986.

Lee, Gary Yia. *Culture and Customs of the Hmong.* Santa Barbara, CA: Greenwood, 2010.

Leepalao, Touger. *Hmong Funeral Procedures: Txheej Txheem Kab Kev Pam Tuag.* St. Paul, MN: Hmong Cultural Center, 2013.

———. *Hmong Wedding Procedures: Tshoob Kos.* St. Paul, MN: Hmong Cultural Center, 2013.

Moua, Chai Charles. *Roars of Traditional Leaders: Mong (Miao) American Cultural Practices in a Conventional Society.* Lanham, MD: University Press of America, 2012.

Mouavangsou, Choua. *Traditional Hmong Marriage Ceremony Values.* Lima, OH: Wyndham Hall Press, 2010.

Mua, Naw Karl. *Hmong Marriage in America: The Paradigm Shift for a Healthy Generation*. Thailand: N.p., 2002.

Symonds, Patricia. *Calling in the Soul: Gender and the Cycle of Life in a Hmong Village*. Seattle: University of Washington Press, 2004.

Thao, Paja. *I Am a Shaman: A Hmong Life Story with Ethnographic Commentary*. Minneapolis: Southeast Asian Refugee Studies Project, Center for Urban and Regional Affairs, University of Minnesota, 1989.